Mit den beiden ***Semester checks*** und dem dazugehörigen Lösungsschlüssel am Ende des Buches können Sie sich selbständig eine **Rückmeldung** zur Erreichung der **Lernziele** einholen.

Die Seiten ***Literature along the way*** möchten Ihnen Lust auf die Beschäftigung mit klassischer und moderner englischsprachiger Literatur machen.

Grammar revisited wiederholt und erklärt die wichtigsten Grammatik-Themen.

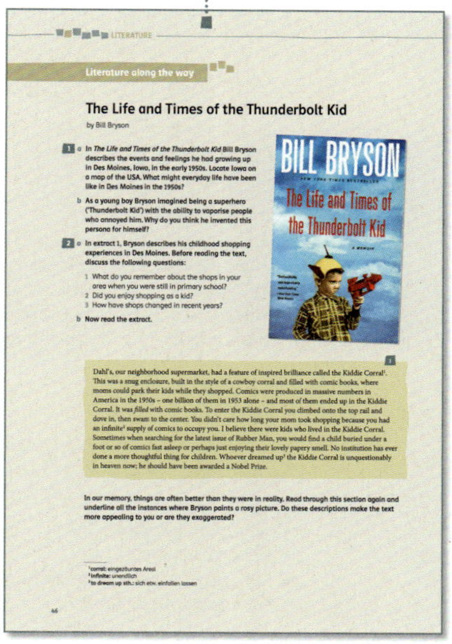

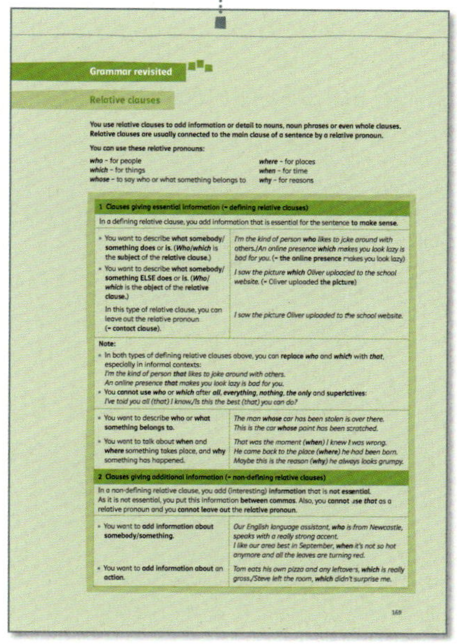

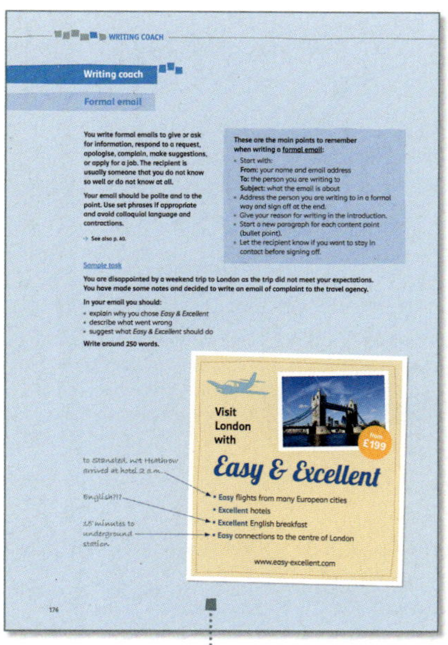

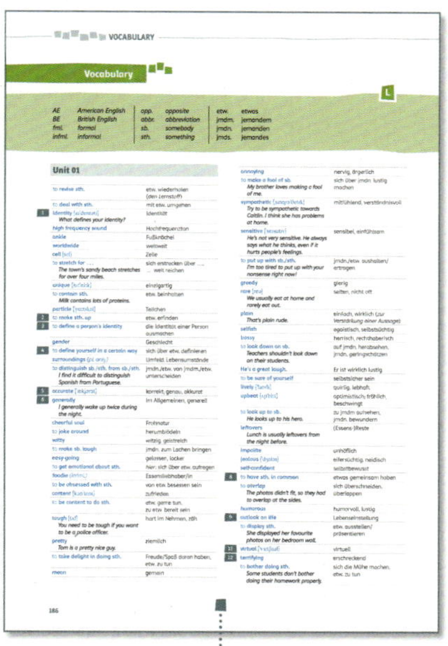

Der ***Writing coach*** macht Sie mit den Besonderheiten verschiedener **Textsorten** vertraut. Authentische Schreibaufträge und Modelltexte zeigen Ihnen exemplarisch, worauf es bei der Bearbeitung ankommt.

Das ***Vocabulary*** im Anhang enthält den Lernwortschatz in der Reihenfolge, wie er in den Units vorkommt. Wörter, deren Aussprache sich vielleicht nicht gleich erschließt, sind durch Angaben zur Lautschrift ergänzt.

Hinweis zu **SRP-ähnlichen *Listening*-Aufgaben**: Um eine flexible Handhabung im Unterricht (oder auch zu Hause) zu ermöglichen, besteht der Audio-Track immer aus einer einmaligen Aufnahme des Hörtextes mit nur einer kurzen, thematischen Einleitung. Der Track kann jedoch beliebig oft abgespielt werden, um auf individuelle Bedürfnisse einzugehen.

Symbole

Registrieren Sie sich mit dem Nutzerschlüssel (hintere Umschlagseite innen rechts unten) auf *Mein öbv*.

c8j5ie — Online-Code, der zu den Audio- und Video-Dateien im Internet führt. Geben Sie den Code einfach in das Suchfeld auf www.oebv.at ein.

03 — Verweis auf die CD Ihrer Lehrkraft

radio FM4 — Hierbei handelt es sich um einen original FM4-Beitrag.

BBC 01 — Verweis auf die DVD Ihrer Lehrkraft mit original BBC-Beiträgen

p. 12 — Verweis auf weiterführende Übungen im Practice Pack

Kennzeichnung von Aufgaben, die Sie mit den Formaten der standardisierten Reifeprüfung vertraut machen

Hinweis auf eine sprachliche Besonderheit

Contents

Semester 03

Listening	Writing	Speaking	Way more
▪ How to behave online (4W) ▪ A conversation about family and friends	▪ A meme ▪ An acrostic ▪ An informal email about nasty postings ▪ A blog comment about life at 16	▪ What defines you? ▪ Presenting a meme and a selfie ▪ Finding out what you have in common with … ▪ How times have changed	▪ **Strategies:** The function word 'to comment on sth.'; Function words revisited; Learning a language
BBC ▪ Some students discussing their art homework assignment ▪ … and viewing: Interactive new media art (BBC) (MC) ▪ A presentation about lyrics in pop music (4W)	▪ A paragraph about a museum ▪ A formal email giving feedback on the Air and Space Museum ▪ A blog comment on Ed Sheeran's *Shape of You*	▪ Describing art ▪ Paired activity: What kind of art club? ▪ Individual long turn: Street art ▪ Presenting 'the perfect museum' ▪ Presenting your favourite music/bands	▪ **Strategies:** Refresh your memory: Paired activity & Individual long turn & Formal email; Reading – Multiple matching (MM)
radio FM4 BBC ▪ Shopping conversations ▪ An unusual shop (FM4) (MM) ▪ … and viewing: A classic sales technique (BBC) (4W)	▪ Different situations – different texts ▪ A formal email complaining about a phone case ▪ A poster promoting a product ▪ An article about an ad	▪ What's your shopping behaviour? ▪ Shopping conversations ▪ Your favourite shop ▪ Describing pictures showing shopping scenes ▪ Ads and buying habits ▪ Presenting a Super Bowl ad	▪ **By the way:** At the mall ▪ **Strategies:** Email of complaint; Article; The function word 'to specify sth.'; Language in use – Open gap fill (OGF)
▪ A conversation about plans for New Year's Eve (4W) ▪ A lecture on the importance of traditions ▪ A radio phone-in show on traditional stories	▪ An article about a popular Austrian custom ▪ A PEEL paragraph on reading stories to kids ▪ What do you think about gender stereotypes in fairy tales? ▪ A new ending for a fairy tale	▪ Describing pictures showing traditions ▪ Paired activity: How would you like to spend New Year's Eve? ▪ Inventing a custom ▪ Individual long turn: Reading stories to kids	▪ **Strategies:** Main idea and supporting details; *Advise* versus *persuade* – what's the difference?
radio FM4 ▪ Nature sounds ▪ Some people talking about what they enjoy doing in nature (MM) ▪ Environmental problems caused by eating meat (FM4)	▪ Haiku poems ▪ A blog post about an environmental problem ▪ A fact sheet about an animal rescue centre ▪ A blog comment about eating meat	▪ Describing environments ▪ Individual long turn: Beautiful places ▪ Environmental issues ▪ Discussing cartoons ▪ Presenting ads for/against eating meat	▪ **Strategies:** The function words 'to outline sth.' and 'to point out sth.' ▪ **By the way:** Primary forests
radio FM4 ▪ Different varieties of English ▪ An interview about criticism of how the Oscars are awarded (FM4) (4W)	▪ A PEEL paragraph about learning English ▪ An article about English as a world language ▪ A film review	▪ English in our daily lives ▪ The British Empire ▪ Loanwords ▪ Individual long turn: Films at home or at the cinema? ▪ Paired activity: A film project	▪ **Strategies:** The importance of situational context; How to write a film review

Contents

Semester 04

Listening	Writing	Speaking	Way more
▪ A conversation about a social project at school ▪ An interview with a blind judge from a US Supreme Court (FM4) (MC)	▪ An inner monologue about a sign ▪ PEEL, PEEL, PEEL! ▪ A diary entry from the perspective of Bob, the cat ▪ An article presenting a book/film dealing with outsiders	▪ Talking about disability and homelessness ▪ Talking about *A Street Cat Named Bob* ▪ Paired activity: How to raise money for a project	▪ **Strategies:** Inner monologues; Paragraphs – the PEEL strategy revisited; *Convince, persuade, advise, recommend* and *suggest*

Listening BBC	Writing	Speaking	Way more
▪ News stories ▪ … and viewing: The changing face of reading (BBC) (4W)	▪ Memes ▪ A news report ▪ Writing reports	▪ The role of news media ▪ Describing charts ▪ A survey of social media use ▪ Your favourite book ▪ Paired activity: Choosing books for your class	▪ **Strategies:** Writing a report; Taking into account other people's views

Listening	Writing	Speaking	
▪ Should cities and their mayors get more power? (FM4) (4W) ▪ Different people talking about their experiences with volunteering (MM)	▪ A blog comment about young people and voting ▪ A PEEL paragraph about giving cities and their mayors more power ▪ Continuing *Lord of the Flies* ▪ A report	▪ Young people and politics ▪ Would you like to have the subject 'politics' at school? ▪ If you were the mayor, … ▪ Individual long turn: Good leaders ▪ Charities and volunteering	

Listening BBC	Writing	Speaking	Way more
▪ People who need medical help ▪ … and viewing: A documentary about vehicles (BBC) (MM) ▪ How AI can help in medicine	▪ Describing health problems ▪ A report about the future of cars ▪ Reviewing a sci-fi book/film ▪ A PEEL paragraph about an invention or a disease	▪ A simulation: What to do after an accident? ▪ Inventions ▪ Paired activity: Safe ways of travelling ▪ AI in medicine	▪ **Strategies:** How to 'explain the results' ▪ **By the way:** Take your medicine

Listening	Writing	Speaking	
▪ Some language assistants about what they found surprising in Austria (MM) ▪ *The Sound of Music*	▪ An email about cultural practices in Austria ▪ An article on intercultural understanding in school ▪ An inner monologue about a distressing situation	▪ Cultural practices ▪ Stereotypes about Austria ▪ A tour of your area ▪ Living together – learning from each other ▪ Describing pictures	

Listening	Writing	Speaking	Way more
▪ Five people talking about what globalisation means to them (MM) ▪ Tony Lloyd and Cuba (FM4) ▪ Fair trade coffee (4W) ▪ How to pick coffee	▪ A blog comment about globalisation ▪ Story: The immigration officer's point of view ▪ Why fair trade coffee? ▪ Explaining a production process	▪ Events that shrank the world ▪ Cuba ▪ Border crossing stories ▪ Individual long turn: Exotic food/Fast food places	▪ **Strategies:** Talking about advantages

Unit 01
Way to grow!

c8j5ie

In this unit you will:
- talk about who you are
- report on what other people have said
- discover the risks of selfies
- discuss teen issues
- revise how to deal with writing tasks
- improve your social media habits

READING + SPEAKING

1 a Read the statements below. They all have something to do with growing up and personal identity. What aspects do they deal with? Write headings for 2 to 6.

b Work in pairs and decide which statements you think are true and which ones are made up. (One is false in each group.)

1 Body

A Babies have over 90 bones more than adults.
B Teenagers hear high frequency sounds that adults can't hear.
C Your ears stop growing when you reach the age of 18.

2 ___________

A Rap singer JAY-Z was named Jayden Zebra when he was born.
B Pop star Prince officially changed his name to a symbol.
C Actress Anne Hathaway has the same name as Shakespeare's wife.

3 ___________

A The average eight-year-old native speaker of English already knows 10,000 words.
B Cows can have regional accents.
C The most common letter used in English is 'i'.

4 ___________

A Lady Gaga has a poem in German by Rilke tattooed on her arm.
B Emma Watson ('Hermione') has a tattoo of Harry Potter on her ankle.
C Elaine Davidson, the world's most pierced woman, has over 9,000 piercings.

5 ___________

A Less than 50% of Americans have a passport.
B Worldwide, around one million passports are lost or stolen each year.
C The only person who doesn't need to carry a passport travelling abroad is Queen Elizabeth II.

6 ___________

A If you uncoiled[1] all the DNA in your cells, it would stretch for 16 million kilometres.
B Like fingerprints, everyone has a unique tongue print.
C Human hair contains tiny particles of gold.

1 C is false (they never stop growing); **2** A is false (he was born Shawn Corey Carter); **3** C is false (the most common letter in English is 'e'; **4** B is false; **5** B is false (actually around 3 million are stolen each year); **6** A is false (it's 16 billion km!)

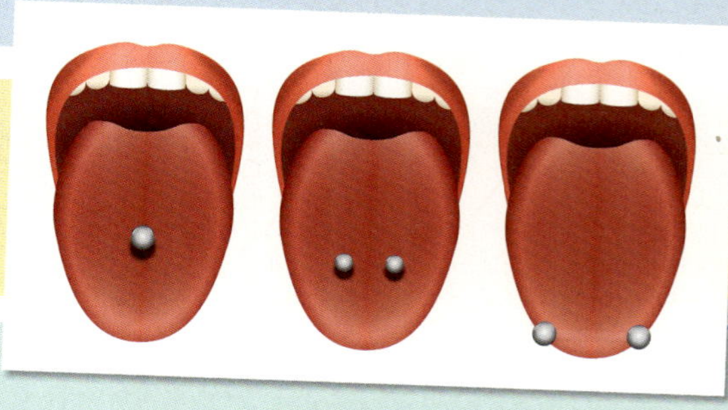

[1] **to uncoil sth.:** etw. ausbreiten/abwickeln

Who am I?

SPEAKING 2 **Make up statements about yourself (your hobbies, family, likes and dislikes, your summer holidays, etc.). Let your classmates guess which ones are true and which ones are lies.**
Example: *I can play the trumpet, I am terrified of spiders, and I once won a burger-eating competition.*

LANGUAGE 3 **Defining your identity**
Read through the words on the right. They are all categories of what can define a person's identity. Make sure you know what the words mean.

L appearance ▪ beliefs ▪ culture ▪ (eating) habits ▪ gender ▪ interests ▪ nationality ▪ social groups ▪ style

SPEAKING 4 a **Now discuss with a partner:**

1 What could you say about yourself regarding each of these categories?
(For example, what gender are you? What are you interested in? Where do you come from?)
2 How can these categories help you to describe who you are?
3 Are there any categories missing? What would you add?

b **Work alone. Try to come up with a ranking of these categories, considering which are the most important to you. (For example, are you a woman/man first? Is your school career the most important thing people should know about you? What would you say first if someone asked you where you come from? Which aspects of your life make you unique?)**

c **Compare your ranking in class. Does anyone define themselves in a similar way to you? Why might someone else define themselves differently? How could your surroundings change the way you see yourself?**

I see myself as (a) … (person).
The most important thing in my life right now is …
Most people would describe me as …
One thing that distinguishes me from others is …
One aspect I share with many people in this room is …

SPEAKING + WRITING 5 a **Look at the meme below and talk in pairs:**

1 What does this meme say about being a secondary school student?
2 Are the pictures an accurate description of your life?
3 Which pictures would you change to better fit your idea of being a student?

b **Create your own meme and present it to your classmates. Your meme should include one aspect of your life, but show it from two different perspectives. Include headings, such as "What my teacher thinks I do" or "What I think I do".**

READING 6 a Read the statements below describing a person from three different perspectives. Are they positive or negative about the person? Underline words and phrases in the text that tell you.

Tom's description of himself

Hi, I'm Tom. I'm generally a cheerful soul, and I'm the kind of person that likes to joke around with others. I have a very good sense of humour and always try to see the funny side of any situation. If my friends get into trouble or have a problem, I usually try to be witty and make them laugh. I'm easy-going and don't believe in getting too emotional about things. I'm a real foodie and am obsessed with pizza! I'd be content to eat pizza every day of the week if I could. I'm quite tough and don't worry too much about what others think of me.

Rachel

I've known Tom for five years, and I think he's pretty arrogant. Whenever something goes wrong, he takes great delight in making stupid jokes, which I think is really mean and annoying. He makes a fool of any friend who's having trouble. I think he should be more sympathetic and sensitive towards other people. I really don't know why Harry puts up with him! Also, he's extremely greedy and rarely shares his food. He'll eat his own pizza and half of someone else's too, which is just plain rude and selfish. I don't like people who are bossy and look down on others.

Harry

I really enjoy hanging out with Tom – he's a great laugh! I'm pretty quiet and shy myself, so it's fun to be with someone who's so sure of himself. Tom's always lively and energetic, making jokes even when things are difficult. He stays upbeat and cheerful when I'm having a problem with something. He's just so positive, and I really look up to him because of that. Tom lives for pizza and even eats my leftovers when I can't finish my meal. I know Rachel thinks he's impolite, but I think she's just jealous because he's so self-confident!

b How would different people describe you? How would it be different to how you'd describe yourself? Discuss your ideas with a partner.

LANGUAGE 7 a Describing personality

p. 6

Start a table of positive and negative adjectives you can use to describe what someone is like. Add all suitable words from the texts above. Finding opposites will add even more words to your list.

L

Positive	Negative
polite	impolite

b Compare your table with a partner. Look up the meaning of all the words you can't guess.

SPEAKING 8 a Find a partner you don't talk to very often. Tell him or her five positive things that you have noticed about them. For example, "I think it's great that you're hardly ever late for class" or "What I like about you is that you always help out other people when they don't understand something in class".

b Spend around five minutes discussing a range of everyday topics, such as your likes and dislikes as well as your personality. Then copy the Venn diagram below into your notebook. Write at least five things where you differ in the main part of each circle and at least five things you have in common with your partner in the overlapping part of the circles. Try to use some of the new adjectives from exercise 7.

LANGUAGE IN USE 9 Read the instructions for writing an acrostic. Some words are missing. Choose the correct word (A–N) for each gap (1–11). There are two extra words that you should not use. Write your answers in the boxes provided. The first one (0) has been done for you.

How to write an acrostic

Now you know a little more about your partner, make a list of **(0)** _____ that you think describe him or her accurately and **(1)** _____ . Include words that describe their personality, outlook on life and some of their hobbies, interests and **(2)** _____ . Come up with around 10 to 15 words.

Using these words, you are now going to create a special poem about your partner called an 'acrostic'. First, write the letters of your partner's name down the page of your book so that each letter is on a new **(3)** _____ . Once you have done this, think of short **(4)** _____ starting with each letter of their name that describe your partner. Choose words from the list you have made. Make sure you use a **(5)** _____ of interesting adjectives, and try to **(6)** _____ your sentences upbeat. You want to make your partner feel good about **(7)** _____ ! Try to limit each sentence to around 10 words, and make each one about a **(8)** _____ topic.

If you're a real acrostic **(9)** _____ , you could try to make the lines rhyme. To keep things interesting, if your partner has a short first name, then use their family name too. When you and your classmates are **(10)** _____ that your acrostics are good descriptions of each other, **(11)** _____ them on the classroom walls. Read some examples aloud.

~~A~~	adjectives	D	display	G	keep	J	range	M	themselves
B	confident	E	expert	H	line	K	sentences	N	yourselves
C	different	F	interesting	I	positively	L	skills		

0	1	2	3	4	5	6	7	8	9	10	11
A											

WRITING 10 Now follow the instructions to write an acrostic yourself.

Our virtual selves

READING 11 **Selfies are a big trend around the world and across all age groups. Look at the picture and discuss in pairs:**

1 Where might you find a picture like this?
2 What does this selfie show? What doesn't it show?
3 How do the people in the picture want to be seen? Are they successful in what they are trying to show?
4 Would you take a picture like this?
5 Why do people take selfies in general?

12 a Read the article on why we take selfies.
Some parts are missing. Choose the correct part (A–N) for each gap (1–11). There are two extra parts that you should not use. Write your answers in the boxes provided. The first one (0) has been done for you.

p. 4

Why we really take selfies: the 'terrifying' reasons explained

Radhika Sanghani asked psychologists why we really bother taking selfies. The answers are worrying.

Everyone takes selfies. It's a part of our modern culture that we all participate in (0) ______ . Most of the time we do it so we can post them onto social media, show everyone what we look like at our best and (1) ______ . Selfies don't seem to be affected by the standard social norms and barriers of ageism and coolism. Teens are obsessed, parents think it's funny to get involved in the trend and celebrities were simply made for them. They seem to fit everyone to the point where selfies take up all our social media newsfeeds, but (2) ______ ?

A recent study, led by Petya Eckler, of the University of Strathclyde, says it isn't. After speaking to several hundred female students, the team found that spending time on Facebook looking at selfies is (3) ______ . Constantly looking at carefully edited photos is bound to have an impact on whoever's browsing them, and it is not that surprising that it makes women (4) ______ .

But what the scientists in this study haven't answered is why we're taking selfies. We generally do it without thinking, but when we stop and ask ourselves why we're actually doing it – what will we find? If I ask myself why I occasionally take selfies, I'd say it's because it's (5) ______ with friends, or to show my friends what I'm doing. But that's not really true. If I ask myself really honestly, I'd say it's part of showing everyone 'Brand Radhika'. This is what I look like and this is how I spend my time (obviously I'll have chosen (6) ______).

Dr Terri Apter, psychology lecturer at Cambridge University, says taking selfies is all about people trying to figure out who they are and (7) ______ . "We all like the idea of being in control of our image and getting attention, being noticed, being part of the culture," says Dr Apter. When I speak to my most prolific[2] selfie-snapping friends, they all agree that (8) ______ of their image. "It's much easier to edit and control a selfie than a picture taken by someone else," a friend tells me. "You can make it look better." But the element of trying to "look better" isn't just plain vanity – it's about being noticed and accepted in society. We might take several selfies to pick the perfect one, but we don't just leave it there; we post it on Facebook, Twitter, Instagram, and the rest of it.

Dr Apter explains, "We're social beings. We want to engage with other people." But she then goes on to talk about the negative side: "There's also a sense that if we're not seen, then we're invisible. That (9) ______ ."

[2] **prolific:** produktiv, viel hervorbringend

It brings with it a new danger: poor judgement. We've heard about teenagers posting selfies in their underwear or even nude. They might not regret it at the time, but **(10)** ______ . Dr Apter thinks it's all much worse for younger people. "They're at a stage at which they're trying to define themselves," she explains. "They're trying out different personalities. They feel they have had an opportunity to say, 'This is who I am,' then they feel they have messed up. Then they feel ashamed."

Honestly, it makes me glad I'm no longer a teen, but I do remember that feeling of embarrassment and just how painful it can be when you've posted a picture that you regret. Teens today have it even worse – they can't escape selfies, and they feel they need 'likes', 'retweets' and 'favourites' on their pictures to **(11)** ______ . "It's their feedback," Dr Apter explains. "The only way you can count how interesting you are is by how many people like it – how many have retweeted or favourited it."

A	is that such a good thing	H	it's about being in control
B	the coolest thing I've done all week	I	projecting this to other people
C	can be depressing and frustrating	J	without any real thought
D	worry more about their own body image	K	selfies are never a good idea
E	how we spend our time	L	they certainly do later
F	feel that they are interesting	M	linked to negative feelings about body image
G	a fun way to capture a moment	N	no one will know

0	1	2	3	4	5	6	7	8	9	10	11
J											

b **Read the last paragraph of the article again. Do you agree with what it says about teenagers and how their self-image depends on other people's reactions to their selfies?**

SPEAKING 13 **Take a '*way2go!* selfie' with your English book! Who can find the most interesting place to pose with their book? Present your pictures and pick a winner. (But don't put yourself or others in danger when taking the selfie!)**

LANGUAGE 14 a Relative clauses

p. 6

Relative clauses can be used to give more information about persons and things. They are usually connected to the main clause of a sentence by a relative pronoun. Read the sentences in the table and circle the correct relative pronouns.

→ See *Grammar revisited, Relative clauses*, p. 169.

L

Giving essential information (→ you *can't* understand the sentence without this information)

1 An online presence whose / which makes you look lazy is bad for you.
2 I saw the picture that / who Oliver uploaded to the school homepage.
3 The artist whose / that music blog Hannah's been following will come to Cambridge next week.
4 Hannah's never been to the café in which / whose the concert is taking place.
5 This is the street where / which the gig will take place.
6 It started to rain the moment where / when Hannah stepped out of the café.
7 I don't know the reason why / when Tom is always telling rude jokes.

Giving additional information (→ you *can* understand the sentence without this information)

8 Our English language assistant, that / who comes from Newcastle, speaks with a very strong accent.
9 Tom eats his own pizza and any leftovers, which / that is really gross.
10 The author of the book, which / who you can download for free, lives in South Africa.
11 Cindy's car, why / whose alarm kept us up all night, is being repaired now.

b Read the sentences again. What could be the rule for when to use a comma and when not?

15 Complete the sentences with the correct relative pronouns and add a comma where necessary.

1 Everyone came to the sports event except for Mark ____________ was ill on the day.
2 He stepped on some Lego bricks ____________ his sister had left in his room.
3 It was snowing really hard when I left home. That's the reason ____________ I'm late.
4 Are you a person ____________ online presence is always up to date?
5 Tom makes a fool of any friend ____________ has problems. That's why Rachel doesn't like him.
6 You need to choose the people ____________ you interact with online carefully.
7 Tom likes making stupid jokes ____________ I think is really mean.
8 Hannah is going to visit her cousin Adam ____________ is studying in California. This is a picture of the hostel ____________ she will stay.
9 Do you remember the time ____________ we spent whole weekends building Lego sets?

16 When the relative pronoun is the object of the relative clause, you can leave it out. This only works when giving essential information. This is often called 'contact clause'.

p. 7

Look at the example below, then decide if you can leave out the relative pronouns in sentences 1–8.

Emma Watson is the actress who played Hermione in the Harry Potter *films.*
NOT: ~~*Emma Watson is the actress played Hermione in the* Harry Potter *films.*~~

Circle *is a film which she made in 2017.*
OR: Circle *is a film she made in 2017.*

1 The snapshots which I took yesterday are actually quite good.
2 The lesson that we had this morning was really interesting.
3 I feel sorry for people who always take selfies.
4 A guy who Mark knows has just made it into the national team for cross-country running.
5 Pat did this gardening project with Mr Bloom, who she had worked with before.
6 Have you got a laptop that I can borrow?
7 Have you thought of anything that fits our plan for the sports day?
8 Is that all that you have to say about this?

LISTENING

01

p. 8

17 a Many experts recommend actively creating a 'positive online identity' for yourself on social networks. What could they mean by this? Talk in pairs.

b You are going to listen to an interview with a youth counsellor on how to behave online. First you will have 45 seconds to study the task below, then you will hear the recording twice. While listening, complete the sentences (1–6) using a maximum of four words. Write your answers in the spaces provided. The first one (0) has been done for you.

After the second listening, you will have 45 seconds to check your answers.

0	Dr Phillips has tried to learn as much as possible about ____ .	*online communication*
1	Dr Phillips says it's unrealistic to ask people to ____ .	
2	It's important not to come across as ____ .	
3	Good behaviour is very important online because ____ .	
4	Your online identity should show how you ____ .	
5	You should post about an activity like ____ .	
6	When others post something positive, you should ____ .	

18 Do you agree with the advice you've heard? What are positive things you could post?

WRITING

p. 9

19 Read part of the email that Tom from Cambridge sent you.

> … and Rachel took these ugly pictures of me and posted them so that everybody could see them. They all laughed and posted nasty comments. I was so angry at her. She did say she was sorry in the end, but the damage had already been done …

S Strategies box

When you **comment on sth.**, you react to it by **expressing** your **opinion** or attitude towards it. This might also involve voicing criticism if this is what you think.

You have decided to reply to his email. In your email you should:

- say what you think about people who post nasty things
- suggest what Tom could do about the situation
- comment on the importance of a positive online identity

Write around 250 words.

Happy 16?

READING + SPEAKING 20 a Below you will find a list of activities that people from your parents' generation remember doing when they were teenagers. Work with a partner and read through the list. Try to guess the meaning of words you don't know.

1 Talking to your friend's parents on the phone before getting to talk to your friend.
2 Being on time for a date because you can't text them to say you'll be late.
3 Finding a payphone and spare change to call your parents to ask them to pick you up.
4 Taping your favourite song from the radio (and the DJ talking on the last 20 seconds of it).
5 Memorising directions if you want to go somewhere you've never been before.
6 Programming the video recorder to record your favourite show.
7 Finding spare batteries for your discman.
8 Writing letters to your friends by hand.
9 Formally introducing a potential boyfriend to your parents before a first date.
10 Being sent out of the classroom for feeding your Tamagotchi.
11 Doing maths without a calculator because they are banned.
12 Walking home from school and playing outside without any adults around.
13 Writing thank-you notes to people who have given you a present.

b What do you do in similar situations today? Write sentences and compare them in class.

c Which of the activities from the past are you glad teenagers no longer do? Agree on three.

21 Here's a list of issues that the same people think will always be problematic for teenagers, no matter when. Do you agree? Find reasons why these things are (still) a problem.

a feeling good about your changing body
b coping with bullying in any form
c finding a boyfriend/girlfriend
d scheduling enough time for work and for hanging out with friends
e living up to your parents' expectations
f being accepted for who you are
g being recognised and respected by your peers
h finding good role models
i living up to the images of teenagers that the media make popular
j your ideas: ______________________

____

LISTENING 22 a Listen to Hannah and Lizzie talking about their family and friends. Which of the topics in 21 do they talk about? Tick them off.

02

b Now listen again. Take notes on the details of the issues mentioned.

c What advice would you give Emily?

WRITING 23 Some people say your teenage years are the best years of your life. Considering all the aspects of teenage life you have discussed in this unit, do you think this is true? Make lists of what you like/dislike about being a teenager and compare with a partner.

STRATEGIES 24 **Refresh your memory: Function words**

Match the functions words to the definitions below. Some of them are quite similar in meaning. There is one extra function word that does not fit any of the definitions.

S

1 ~~to give your opinion~~ c	4 to explain	7 to recommend
2 to comment	5 to inform	8 to suggest
3 to describe	6 to present	9 to summarise

a You give people ideas about **what they could do** in a particular situation or **what they could think about**.

b You introduce something (an idea, a project, etc.), and you say **what makes it special and interesting** for the reader.

c ~~You say **what you think about something**. You express your attitude towards something.~~

d You say **what something is like**. You can give facts and details to make it clear and specific.

e You make something **clear and easy to understand**. You give **examples** and offer **good reasons**.

f You present something as **desirable and attractive**. You say **why** a certain choice is **the best one**.

g You express your **opinion** or **reaction** to something. You want to **criticise** something.

h You give **objective facts** about something.

WRITING 25 a **Read the blog post and write around three sentences for each of the bullet points below.**

Capricorn

Happy 16?

My mum and dad always say that being 16 is the happiest time in one's life, but I'm not sure if that's true. They have no clue what life's really like for 16-year-olds …

reply

- **give examples** of problems 16-year-olds might have
- **explain** why something might be a problem for 16-year-olds
- **describe** what life for a 16-year-old should be like
- **comment** on the opinion of the writer's parents
- **suggest** what a 16-year-old girl/boy could do about a problem
- **recommend** a person who could help 16-year-olds with a problem

b **Now write a blog comment on Capricorn's post using some of the ideas you collected in 23. Write around 200 words.**

p. 9

→ See *Writing coach, Blog*, p. 182.

LANGUAGE 26 a Topic vocabulary: Describing personality and attitude

p. 7

Unscramble the words in the box and use them to complete the word map. Then add more words from this unit and find as many opposites as you can.

cerehulf ▪ bysos ▪ eyas-gngio ▪ gyered ▪ jlaesou ▪ mnae ▪ qtiue ▪ snestivie

L

describing personality

☺
- brave
- charming
- ______
- curious
- ______
- lively
- patient
- ______
- ______
- sympathetic

☹
- annoying
- ______
- childish
- clumsy
- cruel
- ______
- ______
- ______
- rude
- selfish

b To help you remember so many different adjectives, you could try putting them into different groups. Here are some suggestions. Pick two and add as many words as you can, then compare.

- meaning similar to German words: *childish, charming, …*
- looking similar to German words, but with different meaning: e.g. *brave, sensible, sympathetic, …*
- describing emotions: *emotional, cheerful, jealous, …*

27 Complete the word map with the missing prepositions. Look up and add translations.

L

describing your attitude towards people and things

to take
- delight (12) ______ doing sth.
- charge (11) ______ sth.

to be
- content (1) ______ do sth.
- obsessed (2) ______ sb./sth.
- curious (3) ______ sth.
- kind (4) ______ sb.
- considerate of sb's feelings

to look
- out (5) ______ sb./sth.
- up (6) ______ sb.
- down (7) ______ sb.

- to put up (8) ______ sb./sth.
- to get along (9) ______ sb.
- to make a fool (10) ______ sb.

STRATEGIES **28** a **Learning a language**

There are lots of things you can do to improve your English. Here are some things you could try:

S

1 **Maximise your learning in class.**
You are here anyway, so why not make the most of it? Speak only English in class, take your work seriously and aim to learn something new every lesson.

2 **Study at home regularly, not just before a test.**
From now until your *Matura* exam, you will have to learn around 20 new words per week. This isn't a lot of work if you study and revise regularly, but you can't do it if you start the night before a test. Learning a language is more like a marathon than a sprint – slow and steady wins the race[1]!

3 **Use English for enjoyment.**
By now your English is good enough to use to do the things you enjoy. Use it to talk or write to friends and relatives around the world. Watch TV, videos or read books and comics you like in English.

b **Which of these things do you already do? What could you do more?**

Looking back: Learning goals of Unit 01

			✓✓	✓	!!
READING	▸▸▸ B1+	I can understand a straightforward description or article on the topic of personal identity. **(ex. 6a, 12a)**			
LISTENING	▸▸▸ B1+	I can understand straightforward factual information in clear speech on the topic of personal identity. **(ex. 17b, 22a/b)**			
WRITING	▸▸▸ B1+	I can write a poem, email or blog comment to communicate news, opinions and ideas on the topic of personal identity. **(ex. 10, 19, 25b)**			
SPEAKING	▸▸▸ B1	I can enter unprepared into conversation on the topic of personal identity to exchange information. **(ex. 4a/c, 8, 20b/c, 21)**			
	▸▸▸ B1	I can express opinions and feelings and respond to them. **(ex. 4a/c, 8, 20b/c, 21)**			
LANGUAGE	▸▸▸	I can use relative clauses to give information.			
	▸▸▸	I can use a sufficient range of vocabulary to express myself on the topic of personal identity.			

The three adjectives I would use to describe myself are ...

The best and worst things about being 16 are ...

[1] **slow and steady wins the race:** gut Ding braucht Weile

Unit 02
You call this art?

5i4ab6

In this unit you will:
- discover different kinds of art
- learn to express yourself
- improve your exam speaking skills
- give feedback on a museum visit
- see people jumping on a museum exhibit
- talk about your favourite music

SPEAKING **1** **a** **Look at the pieces of art below. In pairs, describe the pictures and then make up a title for each of them.**

b **Share your ideas with the rest of the class. Which titles were the best ones?**

A

B

painting
drawing
architecture
photograph
urinal/toilet

ancient/modern
concrete/abstract
colourful/plain
inspiring/dull
well-known/unknown
relaxing/disturbing

C

D

2 **a** **Which of the pieces of art above would you put up as a poster in your room? Give reasons for your answers.**

Examples: *I like the photograph of … because it's different./It would brighten up my room./ This poster would give me nightmares! It's disturbing./I'd put this up to annoy my parents.*

b **Do you have a poster you really like? Describe it and explain why you like it so much.**

3 **Read the thought bubble in picture B again. What else could the woman be thinking? Write down her thoughts using no more than ten words, then read them aloud.**

What is art?

LANGUAGE 4

p. 11

Talking about art

Look at the expressions below. Check the ones you don't know in a dictionary, then combine them in meaningful phrases. You can use an expression more than once.

Examples: *visual arts museum, creative street art, famous masterpiece …*

L abstract ▪ art gallery ▪ artist ▪ artistic ▪ artwork ▪ beautiful ▪ brilliant ▪ colour ▪ composition ▪ contemporary arts ▪ creative ▪ dance ▪ design ▪ expensive ▪ experience ▪ famous ▪ fine arts ▪ images ▪ imagination ▪ masterpiece ▪ museum ▪ music ▪ recording ▪ performing arts ▪ poetry ▪ sculpture ▪ statue ▪ street art ▪ style ▪ talented ▪ visual arts

LANGUAGE IN USE 5

Read the text about art. Some words are missing. Choose the correct word (A–O) for each gap (1–12). There are two extra words that you should not use. Write your answers in the boxes provided. The first one (0) has been done for you.

What is art?

Art is the human creative skill and imagination that creates something beautiful or meaningful, or expresses important ideas or feelings. Art has many forms, such as the visual arts (for example, **(0)** ______ or sculpture), music, dance and literature.

The visual arts include a wide range of **(1)** ______ disciplines, traditionally subdivided into the fine arts – drawing, painting, sculpture – and contemporary **(2)** ______ , which includes more modern developments, such as collage, film/video and photography, computer graphics, graffiti or land art.

Music and dance are part of the performing arts. Music works through the **(3)** ______ of various musical instruments or the human voice, dance through the movement of the human body. Music can be organised compositions, such as in classical **(4)** ______ , it can be based on improvisations, such as jazz, or can merge **(5)** ______ music with more modern forms of musical expression (world music). What is considered music may differ from culture to **(6)** ______ , yet everywhere it plays a key role in religious and other rituals such as marriage.

Literature is the term used to describe **(7)** ______ and sometimes spoken material and refers to works of the creative imagination, including poetry, **(8)** ______ , fiction, non-fiction, journalism, and in some instances, song. Works of **(9)** ______ , at their best, provide us with a vision of **(10)** ______ civilisation and give insight into and context to all the world's societies.

All art is a **(11)** ______ of what it means to be human. We do it for the joy of doing, for others to see, **(12)** ______ , experience and interpret. Thus, it can convey the full spectrum of human experience. Perhaps that is why it is so important.

A	artistic	F	symbol	K	sight
B	arts	G	hear	L	sound
C	creativity	H	literature	M	traditional
D	culture	I	music	N	human
E	drama	J	painting	O	written

0	1	2	3	4	5	6	7	8	9	10	11	12
J												

LISTENING 6 03 p. 12

a Do you agree with how the article in 5 defines art? What is art to you?

b Listen to the kids from Whitehall discussing their art homework assignment and tick the words in 4 that you hear.

c Compare your results with a partner. If they're not the same, ask your teacher to play the conversation again.

d Which of the topics would you like to write about?

> **!**
>
> ***classical:*** *(adj.)* describing an art form which belongs to a long, formal tradition, e.g. classical music/ballet
>
> ***a classic:*** a typical or famous example or work of art

LANGUAGE 7

a **Talking about art (continued)**
Work with a partner and choose five words from the list in 4. Write definitions of these words and create their word families. Check which verbs or nouns you can use with them.

b Share your lists to create a class pool of words that you can use to talk about the visual arts.

LANGUAGE 8 03 p. 12

Structuring informal discussions
Listen to the discussion on art in 6 again and make a list of all the 'filler words' (e.g. *well*, *I mean*, *you know*). Underline the words/phrases you hear more than once. Can you think of reasons why the speakers are using them?

STRATEGIES 9

Refresh your memory: Paired activity
Complete the advice for doing paired activities with words from the box below. There are two words you won't need.

come ▪ convince ▪ describe ▪ disagree ▪ discuss ▪ express ▪ follow ▪ interrupt ▪ observe ▪ suggest ▪ take ▪ understand

1 Read and ______________ the situational context.

2 ______________ turns speaking.

3 Let your partner know you ______________ what he/she says.

4 Agree or ______________ with your partner.

5 ______________ your partner politely to express your view if necessary.

6 Try to ______________ your partner with good arguments.

7 Make sure your partner can ______________ your arguments.

8 Invite your partner to ______________ his/her opinion.

9 ______________ all the aspects/ideas/issues given in the bullet points.

10 Try to ______________ to an agreement at the end.

SPEAKING 10 p. 10

Your English language assistant would like to organise an English-speaking afternoon club focusing on art. He/She wants to find out what kind of art you are interested in and has suggested a few ideas. Discuss the ideas on the right with a partner and agree on two that you would like to do.

Ideas for the English club:

- films/TV shows
- reading/creative writing
- music/dance
- painting/photography
- acting/drama

STRATEGIES **11**

Refresh your memory: Individual long turn

Study task 12 carefully. Then read the information below to help refresh your memory of what to consider when doing an individual long turn. Finally, give it a try!

S

1 You have about **8 to 10 minutes to prepare**. After that you will have to **talk for about 4 minutes**, which means you will have a bit over a minute for each bullet point. While preparing, **never** write down **complete sentences**. Remember, your talk should be like a presentation and not a reading performance.

2 Bullet point ***compare the pictures***: Imagine you are describing the pictures to someone who cannot see them:
- What is the main idea portrayed in the pictures? What do they have in common? How are they different from each other?
- What do the people in the pictures look like? What are they doing? What about the objects in the pictures? What can you see in the background/foreground? What colour, shape, etc. are the objects? What can you tell about the time of year or day? The weather?
- What is your impression of the pictures? What atmosphere do they convey?
- Do you prefer one picture to the other? Give reasons for your choice.

3 Bullet points ***present***, ***describe***, ***explain***, ***suggest***, ***comment***, ***recommend***, etc.:
- Brainstorm ideas and draw mind maps. Find advantages and disadvantages and give reasons for them. Try to give examples and evidence. Draw from your own experience if possible.

SPEAKING **12** **a** **Practise an individual long turn with a partner. Student A, prepare and compare pictures A; student B, compare pictures B. Then discuss the bullet points below together.**

A

B

- Give your opinion on street art.
- Explain what you would paint if you were a street artist.

b **Which of the bullet points was the easiest or the hardest to talk about?**

13 **Bring two pictures of your choice to class and compare them with a partner.**

A visit to the museum

READING 14 a **Have you ever been to a museum? Where did you go? What did you see? What did or didn't you like about it? Discuss in pairs.**

b **First study the *Strategies box* below, then read the texts about five different museums. Choose the correct texts (A–E) for each question (1–10). You can use a text more than once. Write your answers in the boxes provided. The first one (0) has been done for you.**

S **Strategies box**

Reading – Multiple matching (MM)

There are several different kinds of multiple matching tasks. This one is similar to the speaker matching listening tasks you are familiar with already.

- It can help to read the whole text first to get a general idea of the topic.
- Read each paragraph carefully and find options that fit.
- The options will not use the same words as the text.
- Finally, go through the options one by one to check and make sure you have written one letter for each number.
- Some options fit more than one paragraph, so they have two numbers.

America's finest

Visit an exhibition in Washington DC

Take a walk along the National Mall[1] in Washington DC and you will pass no less than 14 museums and galleries belonging to the Smithsonian Institution. There are thousands of exhibits on display and entry is free. Booking is not necessary, but there are likely to be many guests during main holiday times. Here are some of the highlights:

A **The American History Museum**
Devoted to the cultural, social, historical and political development of the United States, the **exhibitions** in this museum show the American experience from colonial times to the present. The American History Museum's **collection** contains more than three million **historical objects** from the ancient to the modern. At this **venue** you can see Alexander Graham Bell's first telephones, an early Monopoly board game and one of Michael Dell's first computers. The museum is open daily from 10 a.m. to 5.30 p.m.

B **The Natural History Museum**
The world's most well-known natural history museum gives visitors an understanding of the natural world and our place in it. You can **browse the museum's displays** of everything from insects to dinosaurs and **explore life on Earth** through the exhibitions and activities. In the Ocean Systems exhibition, a large rotating 360-degree globe **display** is presented which explains many of the complex aspects of the ocean, including what the ocean produces, how it changes and how it interacts with the atmosphere. The aim is to promote our understanding of how to protect and maintain our oceans. It's open every day from 10 a.m. to 5.30 p.m.

1

[1] **the National Mall:** *riesige, von Denkmälern, Regierungsgebäuden und Museen umgebene Grünfläche im Zentrum von Washington DC*

C The Hirshhorn Museum and Sculpture Garden

The Hirshhorn displays international modern and **contemporary art** in an outstanding circular building. Its architecture has won awards, and it features a collection of pieces by modern masters and new artists. The Sunken Sculpture Garden outside contains the Wish Tree, a white Japanese flowering tree which was given to the museum by artist Yoko Ono. Visitors may write their wishes on paper and add them to the tree's branches themselves. You can **take a tour** of the museum's highlights every day at 12.30 p.m. – just meet one of the friendly guides at the information desk in the lobby. This is a must if you yourself are artistic! The museum is open from 10 a.m. to 5.30 p.m. daily.

D The Air and Space Museum

If pictures and art are not your style, launch into the history of flight by surrounding yourself with icons of air and space travel. This **museum** contains hundreds of aircraft, spacecraft, missiles, rockets and other flight-related **artefact**s. It has a **planetarium** and an IMAX theater for out-of-this-world escapes where viewers can **take a 3D journey into space** on a five-story-high screen. You can take a ride in a flight simulator, see the spacesuits worn by the Apollo astronauts on the Moon and even hold a Moon rock. You can visit any day of the week from 10 a.m. until 5.30 p.m.

E The American Art Museum

If you're into photography and traditional crafts, then you'll enjoy the American Art Museum. It captures the dreams, character and imagination of the American people throughout three centuries. The museum is housed in one of the oldest **public building**s constructed in early Washington. Here you will find photography, portraits, modern folk art, African-American art, Latino art, and impressionist **painting**s, amongst others. In the museum's collection are **piece**s that draw on tradition – such as quilts – as well as **artwork**s that reveal a more personal vision. The museum is open each day from 11.30 a.m. to 7 p.m.

2

According to the descriptions, which museum is ideal if you ...

want to see art from different ethnic groups in America?	0	
are interested in seeing a moving model of planet Earth?	1	
would like to look at exhibits both indoors and outdoors?	2	
would like to be able to touch exhibits in a museum?	3	4
want to visit the most famous museum of its kind?	5	
are interested in how the early settlers in America felt?	6	
would like someone to show you around an exhibition?	7	
want to see how everyday technology has changed?	8	
would enjoy visiting a museum where the building itself is special?	9	10

0	1	2	3	4	5	6	7	8	9	10
E										

LANGUAGE 15 **Talking about museums and exhibitions**

Copy the following three categories into your notebook: places, things, activities.
Then sort the expressions highlighted in green in the text in 14 into the correct group.

p. 15

SPEAKING 16 Prepare a one-minute statement to give to the class: Which of the museums above would you most like to visit? Explain your choice.

WRITING 17 Look up museums in your area on the internet. Research some information about the most interesting one and write a paragraph about it that is like the ones you've read above.

STRATEGIES 18 **Refresh your memory: Formal emails**

Remember how to write emails which are more formal. Decide if the statements below are true or false, then compare your answers with a partner and the class.

S

	True	False
1 You shouldn't use short forms.	☐	☐
2 You should give a reason for writing.	☐	☐
3 You address the person you're writing to with *Hello* or *Hi*.	☐	☐
4 You always use an exclamation mark (*!*) after addressing the person you're writing to.	☐	☐
5 You write what your email is about as 'subject'.	☐	☐
6 You sign off with *Take care!*	☐	☐
7 You always use informal language if the person you're writing is younger than 30.	☐	☐
8 You write *I look forward to hearing from you* if you want to stay in contact.	☐	☐

WRITING 19 You have visited the Air and Space Museum and decided to write an email with feedback to the manager. Discuss the leaflet and the notes you have made with a partner before writing your email.

Visit the Air and Space Museum

10 a.m. until 5.30 p.m.
Closed Mondays.

Things to see and do:

- flight simulator ← *fantastic! fun!*
- planetarium ← *interesting! good atmosphere!*
- IMAX Cinema ← *tickets not included! films from the 1980s, popcorn on seats*
  3D – 5-story screen
  4 different films

Contact: john.overfield@spacemus.com

In your email you should:

- explain what you liked about the museum
- comment on your experience in the IMAX Cinema
- suggest ideas to make the museum more attractive for young people

Write around 250 words.

→ See *Writing coach, Formal email*, p. 176.

LISTENING + VIEWING

BBC 01

20 **Can you create art with technology? Think of reasons why/why not and discuss the idea with a partner.**

21 **a** **You are going to watch a report about an interactive new media artist. Write down three things that you think this person will use to make art interactive.**

b **Watch the report without sound first and take notes on the following questions:**

1 Which of your guesses were correct?
2 What else does the artist use?
3 What are the people in the video doing?

p. 13

c **You are going to watch the video with sound now. First, study the task below. Then, while watching, choose the correct answer (A, B, C or D) for each question (1–5). Put a cross (☒) in the correct box. The first one (0) has been done for you.**

After watching, take some time to check your answers.

0 Using technology

- A is only for video games. ☐
- B has always been part of art. ☒
- C can be expensive and difficult to set up. ☐
- D is different from using paint. ☐

1 Jen Lewin's project

- A will travel all around the US. ☐
- B lights up dark rooms. ☐
- C uses both old and new technology. ☐
- D reflects light off metal pieces. ☐

2 The museum director says Jen Lewin

- A involves people who visit her project. ☐
- B is very popular. ☐
- C uses people's voices in her art. ☐
- D makes images that look like paintings. ☐

3 Jen Lewin's installations

- A are all made of light bulbs. ☐
- B are located in a swimming pool. ☐
- C show you different landscapes. ☐
- D make you play with them. ☐

4 Jen's installations

- A are only popular with young people. ☐
- B connect people on the internet. ☐
- C move very fast. ☐
- D pick up the idea of social media. ☐

5 Jen tries to bring people together to

- A visit museums. ☐
- B create art as a group. ☐
- C be more critical of art. ☐
- D create new architecture. ☐

22 **Watch the video again. How does seeing the video help you to understand what you hear? Discuss your answers in class.**

SPEAKING

23 **If you were the curator of your personal museum, what would it be like? Prepare a short presentation on your idea of 'the perfect museum'.**

1 What objects would you put on display?
2 What would the building and its rooms look like?
3 How would you make the museum interesting for visitors?

That's my kind of music

SPEAKING 24 **What's your favourite music? Work with a partner and talk about the music/songs that you listen to. What do you like about this style of music? Can you agree on something you both like?**

LANGUAGE 25 a Talking about music genres

There are many different types of popular music. Match the genres to the features below.

classical music ▪ electronic music ▪ hip-hop ▪ jazz ▪ metal ▪ pop ▪ rock

L

Music genre	Features
	words spoken, not sung, heavy use of rhythm and rhyming words
	popular music, easy listening, frequently played on mainstream radio
	wide range of styles, importance of improvisation, band often includes a saxophone
	music written according to standard European forms or structures by people such as Beethoven or Mendelssohn
	synthetic music, computer instead of traditional instruments, often fast club or dance music
	popular music with a strong beat, usually with electric guitars
	louder and more aggressive than rock, fast, distorted[2] guitars

b **What genres of popular music are missing in the table? Add their features, find examples and share with your class.**

26 **Choose the correct words to complete the blog post.**

p. 13

green2k7

What a song!

I've just seen the most recent **(1)** melody / release by Ed Sheeran on YouTube. It's called *Shape of You* and it has got millions and millions of **(2)** views / tracks already.

I can't stop listening to it, I just love the way he sings and how meaningful the **(3)** lyrics / instruments are. I can really relate to the story he tells, it reminds me of some situations in my own life … What's more, the song has such a good **(4)** performance / rhythm and the tune is so **(5)** catchy / talented as well. Can you tell I've fallen in love with the song? I just might have to buy his latest **(6)** orchestra / album and listen to more of his songs. Maybe he's going to play at a **(7)** festival / studio somewhere around here?

Check out the music **(8)** industry / video on YouTube and leave a comment on what you think about it!

reply

[2] **distorted:** verzerrt

WRITING 27 **You have decided to comment on the blog post about *Shape of You*.**

In your blog comment you should:

- say what you think about *Shape of You*
- present your favourite singer or band
- recommend a music video with them

Write around 250 words.

→ See *Writing coach, Blog*, p. 182.

LISTENING 28 04 p. 14

a **Listen to Mark giving a presentation about lyrics in popular music.**

1 What does Mark do at the beginning of his talk?
2 What does he do at the end?
3 How does he use songs as examples?

b **Listen to the presentation again and answer the questions in note form. Compare your answers in class.**

1 How is your brain working when you listen to a song AND to its lyrics?

____

2 Why does Mark not talk about song lyrics he doesn't like?

____

3 Why does he like the song *All Four Seasons*?

____

4 Why doesn't he like most pop songs?

____

5 What does he think about more modern groups? Why?

____

6 Why does Mark think that Bob Dylan deserves the Nobel Prize?

____

7 Why does he think that Dylan's *Shelter from the Storm* still speaks to people?

____

c **Discuss the following questions with a partner:**

1 Do you agree with Mark's opinion on lyrics in pop music? Why?/Why not?
2 What does Mark do well? What could he improve next time?

SPEAKING 29 **Work with a partner. Prepare a presentation about (one of) your favourite band(s). Here are some things you could do in your presentation:**

- introduce the singer or band members
- play your favourite song
- explain the lyrics
- say what you like best about it

Try to structure your presentation as clearly as the one you've listened to.

LANGUAGE IN USE 30 a Read the article about how we decide which music we like. In most lines (1–15) there is a word that should not be there. Write these words in the spaces provided. 2–4 lines are correct. Make a ✓ in the space if the line is correct. There are two examples (0, 00) at the beginning.

What determines people's taste in music?

Whether someone loves Beethoven, death metal or Scottish bagpipe	✓	(0)
music, the brain's response is the similar same: dopamine[3] activity,	similar	(00)
which is connected with happy pleasure. However, there are factors	______	(1)
that influence preference make for a genre of music. The most	______	(2)
obvious is where and when you grew on up. We tend to listen to what	______	(3)
our peer group likes, and studies show that what you listen	______	(4)
to in adolescence tends up to be the genre that you stick with the	______	(5)
rest of your life. Another also factor is whether you've had formal	______	(6)
musical training. People know with musical knowledge tend to prefer the	______	(7)
music that they trained real to play, allowing them to listen to more	______	(8)
complex musical styles. Personality also plays a role. People scoring	______	(9)
highly on what's called 'openness to experience' are done more	______	(10)
likely to try new styles of music be which aren't in the charts	______	(11)
and aren't what their friends are with listening to. The bottom line is,	______	(12)
nobody has a good way to predict preferences. Who does figures it out	______	(13)
will get really rich, but I don't expect it to happen soon as the factors	______	(14)
mentioned and how they much interact are extremely complicated.	______	(15)

b Discuss the reasons for liking music with a partner. How do they compare with your experience?

LANGUAGE 31 Topic vocabulary: Music and museums

p. 14

Copy the following word map into your notebook, then use it to organise your music vocabulary.

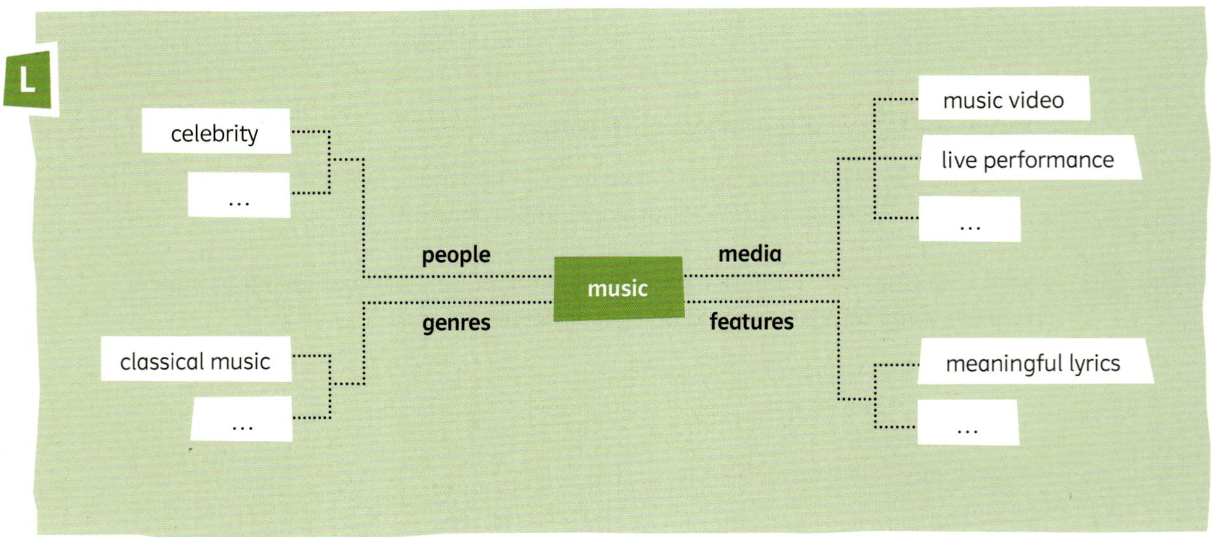

[3] **dopamine:** Dopamin (ein „Glückshormon")

b **Label the branches of the word map. Make sure you understand what all the expressions mean, then add more from this unit or your own ideas.**

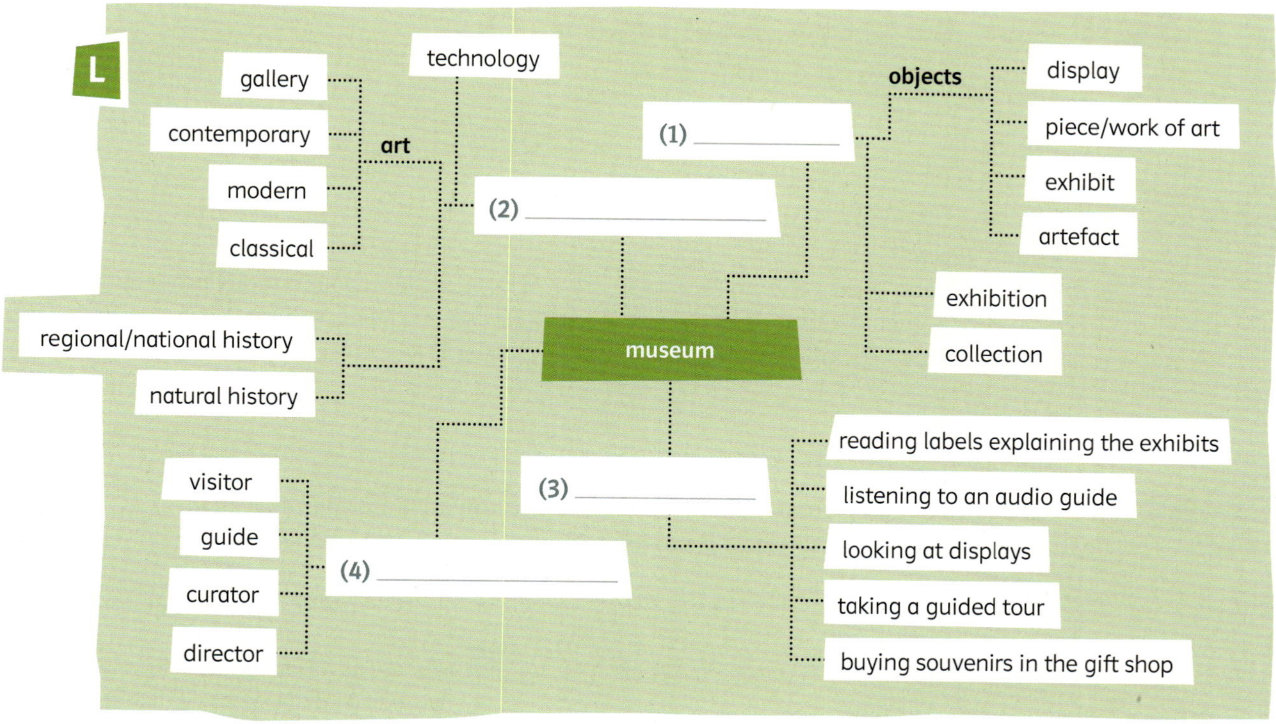

Looking back: Learning goals of Unit 02

			✓✓	✓	!!
READING	▸▸▸ B1+	I can find relevant information in a straightforward description on the topic of art. **(ex. 14b)**			
LISTENING	▸▸▸ B1+	I can understand straightforward factual information in clear speech on the topic of art. **(ex. 21c, 28b)**			
WRITING	▸▸▸ B1+	I can write a formal email to communicate news, opinions and ideas on the topic of art. **(ex. 19)**			
	▸▸▸ B1+	I can write a straightforward detailed description on the topic of art. **(ex. 17, 19, 27)**			
SPEAKING	▸▸▸ B1	I can enter unprepared into conversation on the topic of art to exchange information. **(ex. 1, 10, 22, 24)**			
	▸▸▸ B1	I can give a straightforward connected description on the topic of art reasonably fluently. **(ex. 12, 13, 23, 29)**			
LANGUAGE	▸▸▸	I can use a range of phrases to structure informal discourse.			
	▸▸▸	I can use a sufficient range of vocabulary to express myself on the topic of art.			

My personal definition of 'art' is . . .

A museum I really want to go to is . . .

Unit 03
See it. Want it. Buy it.

t6dy3i

In this unit you will:

- discuss shopping habits and preferences
- report what someone else has said or done
- find out if the Secret Service is following you
- complain about a faulty product
- learn how advertisers make you spend money
- write your first article

READING + SPEAKING

1 a Are you a natural born shopper or do you start to panic every time you see a shop? Take our quiz to find out. Circle your answers, then check with the key below.

1 *How often do you go shopping?*
A Whenever I can.
B Whenever I need to.
C Whenever I'm forced to.

2 *How do you prepare to go shopping?*
A I get dressed up and head for the ATM.
B I write a detailed list of what I need and where I can find it.
C I take a couple of aspirins.

3 *Who do you go shopping with?*
A A whole gang of friends.
B One or two friends at the most.
C No one.

4 *Where do you like to go shopping?*
A In a big shopping centre with lots of different products.
B Close to where my flat is. I can get all the necessities there.
C Online, where I don't get claustrophobic because of the crowds of people.

5 *How do you usually pay for your shopping?*
A By credit card (my mum's or dad's).
B Online.
C In cash.

6 *How do you shop?*
A I like to take a lot of time looking at everything and chatting to shop assistants.
B I like to get what I need as quickly and cheaply as I can.
C With a deep breath and my fingers crossed.

7 *For you a shopping trip is …*
A recreation: the best way to spend the day.
B a necessary evil: OK, every now and then.
C horror: even worse than homework.

8 *What makes you want to buy something?*
A When I see it on social media/a blog.
B When I need something.
C Nothing.

Mostly As
You are more than a natural born shopper, you're a 'shopaholic'. It's safe to say that shopping is your hobby and you couldn't be happier than when you're spending money.

Mostly Bs
You're a very practical shopper. You know what you need and how to get it without wasting too much time.

Mostly Cs
You are a 'shopaphobic'. You fear shopping more than anything else and will probably do anything to avoid entering a shop.

b Discuss your answers with a partner.

1 Do you agree with the description?
2 How do you feel about your own behaviour? Are you OK with it or would you like to change something?
3 How would your life be different if you were in one of the other categories?

"What would you like?"

LANGUAGE + SPEAKING 2 a Shopping phrases

Look at the word clusters below. All the words have been taken from shopping conversations. The first cluster shows words a shop assistant might use when talking to you, the second one shows things you might say in return. Work with a partner and see how many 'shopping phrases' you can find in each cluster. You can use all the words more than once. You will have to add the things that you want to buy.

Shop assistant

help ▪ the ▪ much ▪ changing rooms ▪ size ▪ to ▪ what ▪ are ▪ like ▪ can ▪ I ▪ do ▪ them ▪ cash desk ▪ for ▪ sorry ▪ you ▪ it ▪ it's ▪ being ▪ certainly ▪ who's ▪ served ▪ there ▪ next ▪ I'm ▪ we ▪ on ▪ could ▪ sale ▪ very ▪ don't ▪ have ▪ this ▪ in ▪ stock ▪ would ▪ try ▪ on ▪ yes ▪ they're ▪ thank ▪ pay ▪ at ▪ over

Customer

do ▪ a ▪ for ▪ you ▪ much ▪ it ▪ accept ▪ are ▪ thank ▪ looking ▪ some ▪ any ▪ credit ▪ I'm ▪ just ▪ pay ▪ card/s ▪ browsing ▪ have ▪ looking ▪ around ▪ how ▪ is ▪ they ▪ got ▪ that ▪ in ▪ take ▪ size ▪ I'll ▪ them ▪ can ▪ I ▪ by ▪ try ▪ one ▪ them ▪ on

b **Use as many of the phrases as possible to create shopping conversations and then act them out with a partner. How many shopping exchanges can you string together?**

LISTENING 3 05

Listen to four different conversations and take notes on the following questions:

1 What do the people (want to) buy?
2 What's the problem?
3 What happens next?

LANGUAGE 4 Reported speech

pp. 17/18

When you report something other people have said later, the meaning should stay the same. For this reason, certain things have to change, for example pronouns and expressions of time and place. Look at the examples below, match direct to reported speech and underline the changes.

L

Statements	
1 "I can't give you a discount." 2 "I'll get Lizzie's present next week." 3 "I need my kit tomorrow."	a Mark said he needed his kit the next day. b She said she couldn't give me a discount. c Steve said he would get Lizzie's present the following week.

5 **When you report questions, the word order changes back to that of a statement. Underline what changes apart from the word order in the examples below.**

L

Questions	
1 "Did you get Lizzie's present last week?" 2 "Can you mend this by tomorrow?"	a Steve's mother asked him whether he had got Lizzie's present the previous week. b Mark asked if they could mend his kit by the next day.

6 **To report orders, requests and advice you use the structure: subject – reporting verb – person – *(not) to* – verb.**

p. 19

L

Orders, requests and advice	
1 "Why don't you try Hebendam's in town?" 2 "Don't be scared!"	a She told me to try Hebendam's in town. b She told me not to be scared.

→ See *Grammar revisited, Reported speech*, p. 170.

Report the orders, requests and advice using the reporting verbs in brackets. There is more than one correct answer – depending on the perspective you choose.

1 "Don't climb the fence!" (warned)
2 "I think you should go to sleep now." (advised)
3 "Please don't bring any food to the school library." (asked)
4 "Can you come shopping with me?" (asked)
5 "Please pay at the cash desk." (asked)
6 "Stop it!" (told)
7 "Get up!" (ordered)

7 **Read the reported conversations and circle the correct forms.**

1 Rose asked Steve whether he had got / did get the mug for Lizzie's birthday. Steve replied that he had gone / went into town the Friday before / last, but that the shop assistant tells / had told him that they didn't have / don't have them any longer and advised him that try / to try Hebendam's. But then, Steve said, it had started / start to rain …

2 Dan told Hannah that he had bought / bought some lime green cableyoyos for Mark's birthday. Hannah asked what Mark had said / did say, and Dan replied that Mark said / had said that he really likes / liked the cableyoyos, but that he himself isn't / wasn't so sure. Hannah asked whether the shop didn't have / hadn't had them in any other colour, but Dan said that the shop assistant had told / told him that the darker colours were sold out / had been sold out.

3 Lizzie congratulated Mark on coming second in his competition the previous / last weekend and asked whether he is / was satisfied. Mark replied that he had been / was and told her that before the competition, he tore / had torn his silk kit. He said that he asked / had asked a department store to help / that helped him and they mended / had mended it for him tomorrow / the next day.

8 **If you report something which is still true, you don't have to change the tense. You can also keep the same expressions of time and place if they are still correct.**

Look at the examples and choose the correct description of the situation. Explain why you think the description is correct.

1 Tom said that he really loves it here in Bristol.

- [x] The speaker is in Bristol.
- [ ] The speaker isn't in Bristol.

Since the speaker uses 'here' – just like Tom did – he/she must be in Bristol now as well. Also, it's still true that Tom loves the place.

2 She said that she wants to go there tomorrow.

- [ ] She said this yesterday.
- [ ] She said this today.

3 He said that he really likes you.

- [ ] It is still true.
- [ ] It is no longer true.

4 She said we have to hand in the report on Tuesday.

- [ ] Tuesday was yesterday.
- [ ] Tuesday is in three days.

5 Emily said that she doesn't get any pocket money.

- [ ] Now she gets some pocket money.
- [ ] She still doesn't get any.

06

9 **When Steve tried to buy the Mr Fox mug at Hebendam's the next day, he got involved in a shoplifting incident. The store detective now asks all the people who are still in the store what they were doing right before it happened. Listen to what they say, take notes on the most important points and then summarise their statements in reported speech. Listen again if necessary.**

The following expressions might be useful:

Ms Johnson, the shop assistant, insisted that … She told the detective that … She wondered …
Steve explained that …
Mr Mop, the cleaner, claimed that … He asked the detective to …
Steve's granny noted that … She pointed out that …
Mr Williams, a customer, said that … He complained that … He asked the store detective to …
Ms Cunningham, another customer, suspected that … She highlighted that …

WRITING 10 **Choose one of the situations below and do the writing for it.**

1
Steve writes a 'Happy Birthday' card to Lizzie explaining why he didn't get her a present. (But in a funny way, he likes his sister ☺.)

2
Ms Cunningham writes an email to Hebendam's complaining that they arrested the wrong person for shoplifting because she suspects one of the 'young people' did it.

3
Mark writes a 'Thank You' note to Hebendam's for mending his silk competition kit.

4
Mark writes a text message to Dan asking whether he still has the receipt for the cableyoyos because he would actually prefer a different colour.

LANGUAGE IN USE

11 a **Study the *Strategies box*, then read the text about buying habits of US teenagers. Some words are missing. Complete the text by writing one word for each gap (1–11) in the spaces provided. The first one (0) has been done for you.**

S

Strategies box

Language in use – Open gap fill (OGF)

Open gap tasks often test your knowledge of word collocation – knowing which words are usually used together. What helps with this most is increasing your range of vocabulary through reading and studying. There are also some more practical things you can keep in mind when doing this kind of task:

- Every gap must be filled with exactly one word. Contractions such as *don't* or *I'm* count as one word.
- For many gaps, there is more than one possible answer. Write down only one!
- If you can't think of a word right away, start by thinking about what kind of word (noun, verb, preposition, etc.) the sentence needs.
- Make sure you use the right form of the word. For example, a noun can be singular or plural, a verb might need a suffix like *-s* or *-ed*.

What teenagers are buying

Teenagers buy a lot of different things, according to a new study. "Teenagers are spending (0) ______ on fashion, beauty products, digital media, food, video games and entertainment," lists Tamara Jeely, the analyst responsible for the study. The study surveyed 6,500 US teens who were an average age of 16.5 years old, in a total of 46 US states.

"More and more teens appear to be taking employment; 39 percent of teens said they hold a part-time (1) ______ . This is quite a big increase (2) ______ to last year."

Overall, the survey found that teens (3) ______ 38 percent of their money on fashion. "Clothing, accessories, footwear and fashionable sportswear are very (4) ______ . In addition to this, girls will spend about 10 percent of their income (that's pocket (5) ______ added to what they might earn) on beauty (6) ______ ," Ms Jeely explains.

When it comes to teenage males, they are spending the most on food (20 percent), clothing (15 percent) and then video games (13 percent). "According (7) ______ our data, the average teenage male is expected to spend $214 on video games this year, (8) ______ is quite a large sum," Ms Jeely states.

Restaurant (9) ______ make up 22 percent of total overall spending for teens. "When teens dine out, they tend to choose limited-service (10) ______ , like Starbucks or McDonald's, rather than the full-service dining experience that comes at a higher (11) ______ . The average check for a teenage meal is somewhere between $4 and $17."

0	money	4		8	
1		5		9	
2		6		10	
3		7		11	

b **Go through the article again. What do these figures relate to? 16.5, 39, 38, 10, 15, 22.**

Shopping experiences

SPEAKING 12 a Spend a few minutes thinking about your favourite shop.

1 What does it sell? 2 What does it look like? 3 What makes it special?

**b Now describe the shop to a partner without saying its name.
Can your partner guess which shop you are describing? Take turns.**

LISTENING 13 a You are going to listen to an FM4 feature about an unusual shop. First look at the topics below and tick the ones you think are going to come up. Then listen and write down a few words about the topics mentioned.

radio FM4

07

1 ☐ where the shop is:

2 ☐ name of the shop:

3 ☐ what you can buy there:

4 ☐ how expensive it is:

5 ☐ who owns the shop:

6 ☐ what the owner is like:

7 ☐ how to google the shop:

b You are going to listen to the feature again. First, study the task below, then, while listening, match the beginnings of the sentences (1–5) with the sentence endings (A–H). There are two extra sentence endings that you should not use. Write your answers in the spaces provided. The first one (0) has been done for you.

After listening, take some time to check your answers.

0	The shop is located in _____ .	E
1	Among other things, the store sells _____ .	
2	The journalist was surprised by _____ .	
3	He thinks typical customers might be _____ .	
4	The shop works with police forces to stop _____ .	
5	"Buy skulls" leads to _____ .	

A	finding the shop online	E	a suburban area of Toronto
B	the personality of the owner	F	parts of dead animals
C	animals from all over the world	G	people who illegally shoot wild animals
D	buying human skulls	H	scientists buying items for work

14 Would you like to visit this shop? What would you buy? Discuss your ideas with a partner.

B

By the way: At the mall

If you're visiting the USA, you're bound to spend some time shopping, so there are a few things you should know.

First of all, if you fancy a walk to the shops, be aware that this isn't common in America. Most people shop in large malls or superstores, such as Walmart, and will drive to reach these. In fact, in some cities, the opportunities for shopping 'downtown' in the city centre are limited.

If you're looking for a bargain, bear in mind that in Austria you pay the price you see on the label, but in the USA this is not necessarily the case. Depending on the state you're shopping in, you could pay up to 10% more than you'd expected when you get to the checkout because of the VAT[1], so always check before you buy!

On the positive side, shoppers in America generally expect good customer service, so you should find friendly and helpful shop assistants. If you need to return an item, you can usually do so easily – no questions asked. Assistants will often address you more informally than you may be used to, calling you 'darling' or 'honey', and they might stick around whilst you're shopping to give you advice or recommendations. You will often see shop assistants with headsets which make them look like the Secret Service. Using these they can request items from the warehouse[2] for you if you need a different size or colour.

If you're grocery shopping, you might feel overwhelmed by the huge range of products on offer. There can be whole aisles just with yoghurts and desserts, for example. And don't be surprised if the shop assistant automatically starts packing your bags for you at the checkout. This is all part of the service for many retailers and some even employ people known as 'baggers' especially for this function.

If you find yourself suffering from the insomnia[3] that jet lag can bring, don't despair. Some places are open 24 hours a day, 7 days a week, so you can always go and browse or buy, even on Sundays. You really can shop till you drop!

Which of these facts were most surprising for you? Talk in class.

LANGUAGE 15 Talking about pictures

Which expressions would you use to 'compare', 'speculate', 'describe' or 'give your opinion'?

L

1 ____________	2 ____________
In the background/foreground …; At the top …; In the middle …; On the left …; Behind …; Above …; In the bottom left corner …; Next to …	As far as I know, …; I'd say …; I'd like to point out that …; What I mean is …; My personal view is that …; I might be wrong, but …; It seems to me that …
3 ____________	**4 ____________**
In both pictures …; Both pictures show …; Neither of them …; The main difference between the pictures is …; In the picture on the left …, whereas the other one …; While the first picture shows …, the other picture doesn't …; In contrast to the first picture …	I suppose it's …; I expect/I imagine it's …; He/she/it must be …; He/she/it can't be …; I'm not sure, but they could be …; It's not very clear, but probably …; I can't make it out, but perhaps …; He/she/it seems to be …

[1] **VAT:** (*abbr. for*) **value added tax:** Umsatzsteuer
[2] **warehouse:** (Waren-)Lager
[3] **insomnia:** Schlaflosigkeit

SPEAKING 16 **Work in pairs. Student A, compare pictures A; student B, talk about B.**

1 What shopping situations do they show?
2 What do they have in common?
3 What is different?

A

B

READING · SPEAKING 17 **Read about two new ways of shopping, then discuss the questions below in small groups. Use the language from the right column of the table in exercise 15.**

No need to check out!

Amazon opened its first checkout-free grocery store to the public early in 2018. The shop uses cameras and sensors to track what shoppers take from the shelves and what they put back. Cash registers and checkout lines are no longer needed: customers get their bill after leaving because the store has their credit card on file.

Mirror, mirror …

Could interactive mirrors be the future of shopping? We're talking about the 'smarter', interactive mirrors in shops that can actually simulate how various outfits or products look on you. They modernise the whole buying process by making recommendations based on your personal data and finally sending a drone to deliver the shopping to your home, so you don't have to carry any bags.

1 What might be attractive about shopping in these places?
2 What problems could occur if you enter the shop with small children?
3 What other problems can you think of?
4 Which shop would you prefer? Why?
5 What other innovations in retail can you think of?

STRATEGIES 18 **a** **Writing an email of complaint**

Have you ever been dissatisfied with a product you have bought? What happened and what did you do about the problem? Take some notes, then talk to a partner for about a minute.

b **This is how you can write an email of complaint if you have a problem with something you have bought. Highlight the things which are new to you.**

S

- **Subject/Re:** Provide a brief description of your complaint (e.g. *Complaint regarding malfunctioning watch*).
- **Salutation:** *Dear Sir or Madam,* – if you don't know the name of the contact person.
- **Reasons for writing:** Say why you are complaining.
  I wish to complain about …, which I purchased (location/date) …
- **Main body:**
  - Be as clear and specific as possible. What exactly are you complaining about?
  - Why are you complaining about something? Justify your complaint. Provide details for the recipient to understand the problem. Be precise.
  - Explain what you expect to happen, what should be done about your complaint. Do you expect an apology, a replacement or a refund?
- Use **formal** and **polite language**, especially if you are asking for compensation.
- **Closing:** *I look forward to your quick reply* including signature.

19 **Study the set phrases a–m below.**

1 Would you use them as an opening (O) or closing (CL) statement?
2 Do you think they are rather mild or determined ? (Sometimes both may be correct.)

a I hope this matter can be dealt with promptly. CL
b I insist on a full refund.
c I am writing to express my total dissatisfaction with …
d I regret that I must write to express my disappointment about …
e I hope you will take my comments into consideration.
f I look forward to your quick reply. Should you require any further information, please contact me at …
g I am writing to draw your attention to …
h I look forward to receiving an apology.
i I hope you can give me a refund.
j I can be reached by phone at … at any time or by email at …
k I am writing to express my frustration at …
l I would like to have this problem solved quickly. If I do not hear from you within 10 days, I will have to contact …
m I feel completely misled and therefore …

WRITING 20

p. 20

***CaseComp*, an online shop, is advertising fabulous cases for all kinds of mobiles at reasonable prices. You ordered one, but the case you got is not what you expected. You have decided to write an email to the manager (*Dear Sir or Madam*) of *CaseComp*, based on the notes you have made.**

In your email you should:

- explain why you ordered a case from *CaseComp*
- describe the problem
- suggest what *CaseComp* should do

Write around 200 words.

→ See *Writing coach, Formal email*, p. 176.

Notes
more expensive than advertised,
dull colour,
quality?
broke when put on phone!

The power of advertising

SPEAKING 21 **How much do you think ads affect you and your buying habits? Discuss with a partner.**
Examples: *I look out for special offers before I buy anything. That way I can save money.*
If a food product looks really healthy in an ad, I might consider buying it.

LANGUAGE 22 Talking about advertising
p. 19

Copy the table below into your notebook. Then read the article and add the words highlighted in green to the correct categories.

L

People	Where you see ads	Kinds of ads	Parts of ads	What ads do
advertiser	tray	print ad	logo	promote

Ads as far as the eye can see!

Add this to the endangered list: blank spaces. Advertisers seem to fill every last one of them, with logos and slogans everywhere you look. In the USA, supermarket eggs have been stamped with the names of television shows, take-away food cartons promote airlines, even the trays used in airport security lines have been used for advertisements. A person living in a city sees up to 5,000 ads a day, and about half of the people in a survey said they think marketing and advertising today is out of control.

Marketers used to try their hardest to reach people at home, when they were watching TV or reading newspapers or magazines by using print ads. But consumers' viewing and reading habits are so different now that many advertisers say the best way to reach them is to try to catch their eye at every turn. "We never know where the consumer is going to be at any point in time, so we have to find a way to be everywhere," says one advertising executive.

Some people have had enough. It seems that simply having pictures and writing (professionals call these 'images' and 'copy') are no longer sufficient in ads. After some billboards started giving off the smell of chocolate chip cookies at San Francisco bus stops, many people complained, and the city told the company to turn off the smell. The feeling that ads are everywhere may also be due to the increasing use of name-brand items in TV shows and movies, a trend known as product placement. Just watch a James Bond movie with branded cars, watches and suits being featured.

Companies are finding new ways to offer free services to people who agree to view their ads, particularly on the internet or on cell phone apps. Old-fashioned billboards are being converted to video screens. These allow advertisers to change messages frequently from remote computers. Some of these screens provide news and information as well as ads and may even be interactive: An interactive ad for Adidas appeared in New York City. Passers-by said they liked the sign, which looked like a still picture of a sneaker until someone walked past it, triggering a motion sensor that sent a spray of miniature sneakers flying.

The important thing is to be aware of when you are being targeted by advertisers, whether it is on YouTube, social media, blogs or through traditional print ads, and make wise choices as a consumer.

SPEAKING 23 **Discuss the different kinds of ads with a partner. Which ones do you find most or least annoying? Agree on an order of most to least annoying kinds of ads.**

LANGUAGE 24

Word families: Advertising

Copy this table, add words from the article and complete as many categories as you can. Then compare your results in class.

L

Noun (abstract idea)	Noun (person doing it)	Verb	Adjective
advertising	advertiser	advertise	advertising/-ed

LISTENING + VIEWING 25

How can you make people want something? Collect ideas.

Examples: *Photoshopping pictures to make the product appear especially beautiful, famous people using the product …*

26 a

BBC 02

You are going to watch the first part of a documentary about a classic sales technique. First, make sure you understand all of the phrases below. Then, while watching, write down words that are said in connection with these phrases.

After watching twice, use the phrases and your notes to retell what you've heard.

create anxiety ▪ magic solution ▪ storytelling ▪ damsel in distress[4] ▪ defeat the villain ▪ the hero ▪ magic pill ▪ in danger

b

BBC 03

You are going to watch the next part of the documentary now. First you will have 45 seconds to study the task below, then you will watch the video clip twice. While watching, answer the questions (1–6) using a maximum of four words. Write your answers in the spaces provided. The first one (0) has been done for you.

After watching for the second time, you will have 45 seconds to check your answers.

0	In what year did Stanley Resor become the boss of an ad company?	1916
1	In Resor's opinion, which feeling should advertisers create to promote a product?	
2	What can the product Listerine help you with?	
3	What's the consequence of the woman's problem in the campaign?	
4	What's the name of the kind of ad campaign they use?	
5	How long did the campaign last?	
6	How much had the company earned after seven years of ads?	

SPEAKING 27

Work in pairs and:

- summarise what you've learned about the Listerine ad campaign.
- give examples of ad campaigns you know that work the same way.
- explain whether you think it is ethical[5] for a company to market its product this way.

WRITING 28

Design a poster to promote a product of your choice (real or imagined) that works like the Listerine ads. What problem could your product solve?

[4] **damsel in distress:** *in einer Geschichte:* (meist weibliche) Person, die gerettet werden muss
[5] **ethical:** moralisch richtig

READING 29

p. 16

Read the article about advertising at the American Super Bowl[6]. First decide whether the statements (1–6) are true (T) or false (F) and put a cross (☒) in the correct box. Then identify the sentence in the text which supports your decision. Write the first four words of this sentence in the space provided. There may be more than one correct answer; write down only one. The first one (0) has been done for you.

Here's why companies spend millions on Super Bowl ads

Careers can be defined by a Super Bowl performance – not just for players, but also for the actors in the game's much-anticipated commercials. Companies spend so much on Super Bowl ads chasing the same hope: that after the game, people will be talking about them. Consider the case of Jesse Heiman, whose face is more familiar than his name. Nerdy and decidedly plump, he has appeared in scores of movies and TV shows as an extra. But Heiman's fame soared during a Super Bowl when he was featured in a Go Daddy ad kissing supermodel Bar Refaeli, supporting the company's 'Where smart meets sexy' campaign.

The modern phenomenon of the Super Bowl ad begins in 1984 when Apple aired a 60-second spot titled '1984' that was more short movie than traditional ad. It recreated the atmosphere of George Orwell's book, with the promise "You'll see why 1984 won't be like 1984." "The industry was moving to a very fast, 15-second kind of world," says one advertising executive. "That ad was the start of the storytelling genre."

The appeal of the long advertisement rose even as those Super Bowl seconds became ever more expensive. For the 2016 Super Bowl, a 30-second spot cost a record $5 million. Networks can charge advertisers so much because the Super Bowl provides a television program that is watched by a large audience at the same time. Professor of marketing Tim Calkins says, "The Super Bowl can be a great investment. If you want to reach a large portion of the US population quickly, there is nothing quite like the Super Bowl."

It is why these ads try so hard to stand out. "Win the hearts and minds of America. This is what a Super Bowl ad needs to do," says advertising executive Gretchen Walsh. The success of Super Bowl ads can also be measured in the laughs it gets. Typical TV ads deploy humor about 20% of the time, but for the Super Bowl it's more than 50%. Either way, their goal is sheer awareness. The worst thing that happens to an ad is if no one likes it or hates it. Neutral is death.

	Statements	T	F	First four words
0	Super Bowl ads can affect actors' jobs.	☒	☐	*Careers can be defined*
1	Jesse Heiman's name was well known before his Super Bowl ad.	☐	☐	
2	Apple's 1984 ad was shorter than average ads.	☐	☐	
3	The Apple ad was based on a famous novel.	☐	☐	
4	Super Bowl ads are expensive because they are so long.	☐	☐	
5	Around half of the Super Bowl ads are funny.	☐	☐	
6	The biggest disaster is if everyone dislikes your Super Bowl ad.	☐	☐	

SPEAKING 30

Watch some Super Bowl ads on the internet. Present the one you like best in class. Explain what product it advertises and what makes the ad special.

[6] **Super Bowl:** Finalspiel der US-amerikanischen Footballmeisterschaft

STRATEGIES 31

p. 21

Writing an article

Imagine you want to be a successful journalist who wants to inform, persuade or entertain readers of a magazine or website with a good article. Find out which basic rules you should follow by matching the aspects below.

S

1 Consider your readership.
2 Give your article a catchy title.
3 Write a powerful introduction.
4 Link the paragraphs.
5 Address the readers directly.
6 Express your opinion.
7 Use colourful and descriptive language.
8 End your article in a powerful way.

a It should pull the reader in. It can be/contain a (provocative) question.
b Give examples and stories to support it. Draw from your experience.
c It should make clear what the article is about. It should be catchy to grab the reader's attention right from the beginning.
d Who is going to read your article? Where is it to be published?
e They should feel that they are involved.
f Your readers shouldn't have the feeling that they have wasted their time reading.
g Your readers should never lose interest in your article.
h Include strong adjectives.

READING + WRITING 32

Read the article below.
Which of the criteria above does it meet?
How does it achieve this?

≡ Advertising News | Articles | Videos | Podcasts

The 'Break Up' ad – just loving it!

How do they do it? Doesn't Coca-Cola always have such catchy ads? I'm forever waiting to see what they come up with next.

The best one is the 'Break Up' ad, which tells the story of a young couple who meet in a record store and fall in love over a bottle of Coke. The ad fast forwards[7] through their romantic moments and there's always an ice-cold Coke in there somewhere. They fight and break up, but in the end, he offers her his Coke. She's going to wipe the top of the bottle with her shirt but decides not to – then he knows the romance is back on!

You know what makes the ad so powerful? It's fast-paced and has this song called *Made for You*. So romantic, so compelling! And I just love the imagery – a bottle of Coke smashes when their relationship breaks, and a water drop slides down the bottle like a tear down a face. I'm telling you, it's just out of this world. And, of course, the characters are impossibly good-looking.

I imagine that this ad speaks to a young audience. They'll enjoy the fast-moving action and identify with the situations. It aims to make young people feel emotional as they share the rollercoaster of feelings experienced by the couple. Coca-Cola always picks memorable songs which help the audience to remember the ad, and this one is no different.

So, why don't you give yourself a romantic moment and check it out? You won't regret it.

[7] **to fast forward:** vorspulen

WRITING 33

The school magazine of your English partner school has started a series of articles on successful advertisements. You have decided to send them an article about an ad you like.

In your article you should:

- describe the advertisement
- explain what makes it special
- specify the target group

Write around 250 words. Give your article a title.

→ See *Writing coach, Article*, p. 178, before you start!

> **S Strategies box**
> When you **specify** something, you **explain** or **describe** something clearly and **in detail**.

LANGUAGE 34 a Topic vocabulary: Shopping and advertising

p. 19

Make a word map using the information below. Then compare your maps in pairs and ask your teacher for a model.

Categories:

- advertising techniques
- parts of advertisements
- people in advertising
- where you see ads

Expressions:

advertising executive ▪ billboard ▪ copy ▪ endorsement ▪ logo ▪ marketing executive ▪ mobile apps ▪ print ad ▪ target audience

b With a partner, go through the unit and collect expressions connected with 'shopping'. Use them to make your own word map. Discuss which categories would be useful, then create the word map and present it in class.

Looking back: Learning goals of Unit 03

			✓✓	✓	!!
READING	▸▸▸ B1+	I can understand a description of events, feelings and wishes. **(ex. 29, 32)**			
LISTENING	▸▸▸ B1+	I can understand straightforward factual information in clear speech on the topic of shopping and advertising. **(ex. 3, 13a/b, 26a/b)**			
WRITING	▸▸▸ B1+	I can write a formal email of complaint to communicate news, opinions and ideas. **(ex. 20)**			
	▸▸▸ B1+	I can write a straightforward detailed article on the topic of shopping and advertising. **(ex. 33)**			
SPEAKING	▸▸▸ B1	I can give a straightforward connected description on the topic of shopping and advertising reasonably fluently. **(ex. 12b, 16, 18a, 27, 30)**			
LANGUAGE	▸▸▸	I can use reported speech structures to retell what someone has said.			
	▸▸▸	I can use a sufficient range of vocabulary to express myself on the topic of shopping and advertising.			

A skill I'm now more confident about is . . .

One interesting 'trick' advertisers use is . . .

Literature along the way

The Life and Times of the Thunderbolt Kid

by Bill Bryson

1 a In *The Life and Times of the Thunderbolt Kid* Bill Bryson describes the events and feelings he had growing up in Des Moines, Iowa, in the early 1950s. Locate Iowa on a map of the USA. What might everyday life have been like in Des Moines in the 1950s?

b As a young boy Bryson imagined being a superhero ('Thunderbolt Kid') with the ability to vaporise people who annoyed him. Why do you think he invented this persona for himself?

2 a In extract 1, Bryson describes his childhood shopping experiences in Des Moines. Before reading the text, discuss the following questions:

1 What do you remember about the shops in your area when you were still in primary school?
2 Did you enjoy shopping as a kid?
3 How have shops changed in recent years?

b Now read the extract.

1

Dahl's, our neighborhood supermarket, had a feature of inspired brilliance called the Kiddie Corral[1]. This was a snug enclosure, built in the style of a cowboy corral and filled with comic books, where moms could park their kids while they shopped. Comics were produced in massive numbers in America in the 1950s – one billion of them in 1953 alone – and most of them ended up in the Kiddie Corral. It was *filled* with comic books. To enter the Kiddie Corral you climbed onto the top rail and dove in, then swam to the center. You didn't care how long your mom took shopping because you had an infinite[2] supply of comics to occupy you. I believe there were kids who lived in the Kiddie Corral. Sometimes when searching for the latest issue of Rubber Man, you would find a child buried under a foot or so of comics fast asleep or perhaps just enjoying their lovely papery smell. No institution has ever done a more thoughtful thing for children. Whoever dreamed up[3] the Kiddie Corral is unquestionably in heaven now; he should have been awarded a Nobel Prize.

In our memory, things are often better than they were in reality. Read through this section again and underline all the instances where Bryson paints a rosy picture. Do these descriptions make the text more appealing to you or are they exaggerated?

[1] **corral:** eingezäuntes Areal
[2] **infinite:** unendlich
[3] **to dream up sth.:** sich etw. einfallen lassen

3 **Read the other extracts and discuss the questions below them.**

2

Dahl's had one other feature that was much admired. When your groceries were bagged (or 'sacked' in Iowa) and paid for, you didn't take them to your car with you, as in more mundane[4] supermarkets, but rather you turned them over to a friendly man in a white apron who gave you a plastic card with a number on it and placed the groceries on a special sloping conveyor belt[5] that carried them into the bowels[6] of the earth and through a flap into a mysterious dark tunnel. You then collected your car and drove to a small brick building at the edge of the parking lot, a hundred or so feet away, where your groceries, nicely shaken and looking positively refreshed from their subterranean adventure, reappeared a minute or two later and were placed in your car by another helpful man in a white apron who took back the plastic card and wished you a happy day. It wasn't a particularly efficient system – there was a line of cars at the little brick building if truth be told, and the juddering tunnel ride didn't really do anything except dangerously overexcite all carbonated beverages for at least two hours afterwards – but everyone loved and admired it anyway.

From the point of view of an eight-year-old, this system was "loved and admired". What do you think the grown-up customers thought about it? What kinds of goods deliveries are customer-friendly today?

3

It was like that wherever you went in Des Moines in those days. Every commercial enterprise had something distinctive to commend it[7]. The New Utica department store downtown had pneumatic tubes[8] rising from each cash register. The cash from your purchase was placed in a cylinder, then inserted in the tubes and fired – like a torpedo – to a central collection point, such was the urgency to get the money counted and back into the economy. A visit to the New Utica was like a trip to a future century.

Why was this kind of payment considered futuristic at that time? What are popular methods of payment today?

4

[…] Even better in terms of elevated pleasures was the Shops Building on Walnut Street. A lovely old office building some seven or eight stories high and built in a faintly Moorish style[9], it housed a popular coffee shop in its lobby on the ground floor, above which rose, all the way to a distant ceiling, a central atrium, around which ran the building's staircase and galleried hallways. It was the dream of every young boy to get up that staircase to the top floor.

Attaining[10] the staircase required cunning and a timely dash because you had to get past the coffee shop manageress, a vicious, eagle-eyed stick of a woman named Mrs. Musgrove who hated little boys (and for good reason, as we shall see). But if you selected the right moment when her attention was diverted, you could sprint to the stairs and on up to the dark eerie heights of the top floor, where you had a kind of gun-barrel view of the diners far below. If, further, you had some kind of hard candy with you – peanut M&Ms were especially favored because of their smooth aerodynamic shape – you had a clear drop of seven or eight stories. A peanut M&M that falls seventy feet into a bowl of tomato soup makes one *heck* of a splash, I can tell you.

---

[4] **mundane:** gewöhnlich, normal
[5] **conveyor belt:** Fließband
[6] **bowels of the earth:** Erdinnere (*wörtlich*: Eingeweide der Erde)
[7] **to have sth. to commend it:** etw. haben, das es auszeichnet/das es einzigartig macht
[8] **pneumatic tubes:** Rohrpost
[9] **built in a faintly Moorish style:** an die islamische Architektur Südspaniens erinnernd
[10] **to attain sth.:** etw. erreichen

You never got more than one shot because if the bomb missed the target and hit the table – as it nearly always did – it would explode spectacularly in a thousand candy-coated shards, wonderfully startling to the diners, but a call to arms[11] to Mrs. Musgrove, who would come flying up the stairs at about the speed that the M&M had gone down, giving you less than five seconds to scramble out a window and onto a fire escape and away to freedom.

Des Moines' greatest commercial institution was Younker Brothers, the principal department store downtown. Younkers was enormous. It occupied two buildings, separated at ground level by a public alley, making it the only department store I've ever known, possibly the only one in existence, where you could be run over while going from menswear to cosmetics. [...]

Younkers was the most elegant, up-to-the-minute, briskly efficient, satisfyingly urbane place in Iowa. It employed twelve hundred people. It had the state's first escalators – 'electric stairways' they were called in the early days – and first air-conditioning. Everything about it – its silkily swift revolving doors, its gliding stairs, its whispering elevators, each with its own white-gloved operator – seemed designed to pull you in and keep you happily, contentedly consuming. Younkers was so vast and wonderfully rambling[12] that you seldom met anyone who really knew it all. The book department inhabited a shadowy, secretive balcony area, reached by a pokey set of stairs, that made it cozy and club-like – a place known only to aficionados[13]. It was an outstanding book department, but you can meet people who grew up in Des Moines in the 1950s who had no idea that Younkers *had* a book department.

- **Underline the adjectives and the adverb-adjective combinations (e.g. *briskly efficient*) in extract 4. What function do they have in the text?**
- **What is the fanciest department store you have ever been to? What features would a department store need to have to attract customers in the future?**

5

But its *sanctum sanctorum*[14] was the Tea Room, a place where doting mothers took their daughters for a touch of elegance while shopping. Nothing about the Tea Room remotely interested me until I learned of a ritual that my sister mentioned in passing. It appeared that young visitors were invited to reach into a wooden box containing small gifts, each beautifully wrapped in white tissue and tied with ribbon, and select one to take away as a permanent memento of the occasion. Once my sister passed on to me a present she had acquired and didn't much care for – a die-cast[15] coach and horses. It was only two and a half inches long, but exquisite in its detailing. The doors opened. The wheels turned. A tiny driver held thin metal reins. The whole thing had obviously been hand-painted by some devoted, underpaid person from the defeated side of the Pacific Ocean. I had never seen, much less owned, such a fine thing before.

From time to time after that for years I besought them[16] to take me with them when they went to the Tea Room, but they always responded vaguely that they didn't like the Tea Room so much anymore or that they had too much shopping to do to stop for lunch. (Only years later did I discover that in fact they went every week; it was one of those secret womanly things moms and daughters did together, like having periods and being fitted for bras.) But finally there came a day when I was perhaps eight or nine that I was shopping downtown with my mom, with my sister not there, and my mother said to me, "Shall we go to the Tea Room?"

[11] **call to arms:** Mobilmachung
[12] **rambling:** weitläufig
[13] **aficionado:** Liebhaber/in; *hier:* Bücherwurm
[14] **sanctum sanctorum:** das „Allerheiligste" (*eine Anspielung auf das Marvel-Comic-Universum*)
[15] **die-cast:** aus Zinn gegossen
[16] **to beseech sb. (besought):** jmdn. anflehen

I don't believe I have ever been so eager to accept an invitation. We ascended in an elevator to a floor I didn't even know Younkers had. The Tea Room was the most elegant place I had ever been – like a stateroom from Buckingham Palace magically transported to the Middle West of America. Everything about it was starched and classy and calm. There was light music of a refined nature and the tink[17] of cutlery on china and of ice water carefully poured. I cared nothing for the food, of course. I was waiting only for the moment when I was invited to step up to the toy box and make a selection.

What is the idea of the Tea Room? What does it represent? What kind of restaurants are in your area that might fulfill the idea of the Tea Room as portrayed in the extract?

6

When that moment came, it took me forever to decide. Every little package looked so perfect and white, so ready to be enjoyed. Eventually, I chose an item of middling size and weight, which I dared to shake lightly. Something inside rattled and sounded as if it might be die-cast. I took it to my seat and carefully unwrapped it. It was a miniature doll – an Indian baby in a papoose[18], beautifully made but patently for a girl. I returned with it and its disturbed packaging to the slightly backward-looking[19] fellow who was in charge of the toy box.

"I seem to have got a *doll*," I said, with something approaching an ironic chuckle.

He looked at it carefully. "That's surely a shame because you only git one try at the gift box."

"Yes, but it's a *doll*," I said. "For a girl."

"Then you'll just have to git you a little girlfriend to give it to, won'tcha?" he answered and gave me a toothy grin and an unfortunate wink.

Sadly, those were the last words the poor man ever spoke. A moment later he was just a small muffled shriek and a smoldering spot on the carpet.

Too late he had learned an important lesson. You really should never fuck with the Thunderbolt Kid.

Can you explain why the poor man was just "a small muffled shriek and a smoldering spot on the carpet"? Why was the boy so furious with the man?

4 Choose one of these activities to do in class or at home.

1. Design a test for your classmates. Make up some true/false questions and some multiple choice questions. Provide answers for your test.
2. Make up an interview with Bill Bryson discussing the extracts.
3. Change the setting of the extracts. Imagine the events take place in your hometown today. How would everything be different?

[17] **tink:** Klang
[18] **papoose:** Babytragetuch
[19] **backward-looking:** sichtlich „geistig zurückgeblieben" (*in der geistigen Entwicklung nicht der Norm entsprechend*)

Unit 04
It's traditional

gm9pi9

In this unit you will:
- talk about what to do on New Year's Eve
- find out who likes to sleep in a graveyard
- enjoy discovering gerunds
- become familiar with new ways to talk about the past
- rediscover traditional stories
- be exciting or excited

SPEAKING **1** **a** **Talk about the pictures in pairs. What are the people doing? Why are they doing it? What could they be celebrating?**

b **Compare your answers in class, then check with your teacher.**

A

B

C

tin casting ▪ *Haka* ▪ *pancake race* ▪ *bull running* ▪ *bonfires*

D

E

2 **What might the people in the pictures be thinking or feeling? Exchange your ideas in class.**
Example: *In picture C, the man with the number 8 is really nervous and thinks, "Gosh, he's got a long tongue!"*

3 **Work in groups of four. Discuss which of these traditions you would like to take part in. Agree on a ranking from most to least attractive.**

Happy New Year!

LISTENING 4 a **What are your plans for New Year's Eve? Talk in class.**

08

b **You are going to listen to Lizzie and Hannah talking about their plans for New Year's Eve. First you will have 45 seconds to study the task below, then you will hear the recording twice. While listening, answer the questions (1–7) using a maximum of four words. Write your answers in the spaces provided. The first one (0) has been done for you.**

After the second listening, you will have 45 seconds to check your answers.

0	Where might Lizzie watch the fireworks?	in London
1	What kind of party was Steve invited to?	
2	What does Lizzie plan to do after the party?	
3	What is too expensive for Hannah?	
4	Where will Hannah spend New Year's Eve?	
5	What are the balls people swing filled with?	
6	Who do you go to when you go first footing?	
7	Why is Fergus popular on New Year's Eve?	

SPEAKING 5 **Describe the New Year traditions the girls talk about. Do you know any similar traditions?**

LANGUAGE 6 a **Talking about customs and traditions**
Which other words could you use in place of the ones underlined below? Compare in class.

L

1 It's a custom in my culture to …
2 The most popular tradition is …
3 People typically sing traditional songs …
4 It's customary to give presents to friends …
5 We usually eat fish and rice …
6 … is supposed to bring good luck.

Examples: *It's a custom in my family to … The best-known tradition is …*

b **Use the sentences to write a short description of a tradition you know about.**

SPEAKING 7 **Your English language assistant wants to know how and where you would like to spend New Year's Eve. Discuss the suggestions below with a partner and agree on three.**

- at a party at your friend's home
- at a ball/dance at a castle
- at home with your family
- at a ski lodge in the mountains
- on a cruise in the Caribbean

READING 8

pp. 22/23

Read the article about four different New Year's celebrations. Three of the celebrations have a similar idea about the New Year behind them. What is it?

Happy New Year!

You may plan your New Year's celebrations months in advance, do something impromptu or may not want to celebrate at all, but here are a few of the more unusual New Year's traditions around the world.

A Get your grapes

It's not nice to tell someone they've got a big mouth, but in Spain at New Year a big mouth would be an advantage. This is because the first 12 seconds of the Spaniards' New Year are spent eating all 12 of the 'miraculous' grapes that symbolise 12 lucky months ahead. Rare is the Spaniard who will risk poisoning their fate[1] for the coming year by skipping the grapes, one for each stroke of midnight. Eating the grapes pretty much guarantees starting off the year with a little adrenaline rush, and most likely some laughs. While the goal of getting the 12 grapes down in time can spark a contest[2] of who is 'más macho' around the table, the biggest challenge is more likely not to be gagging as you cram them in your mouth and try to swallow while laughing hysterically.

B Pants party

Did you know the pair of underpants you're wearing at New Year could bear year-long consequences? This is why yellow underwear is flying off the shelves these days in Chile, where tradition says that it brings prosperity and love if you wear it on New Year's Eve. "The yellow underwear is for love, luck, money and so that this year will go well for everyone," says Gladys Leal, a saleswoman at a lingerie stand in Santiago. This time of year, she specialises in yellow undergarments in all shapes and sizes, for women and men alike. But there's a catch, according to her colleague, Jesica Silva. "The underwear has to be given as a gift to bring luck." "Yellow," she explains, "represents the golden rays of abundance and prosperity." Some even say the undies should be worn inside-out to guarantee a year full of passion.

Many Latin American countries, such as Mexico, Peru and Ecuador, have this tradition, with slight variations. Some say you should wear red undies for love, yellow for money. Before midnight, many people change into specific coloured underwear depending on the area of life in which they're seeking improvement.

C A peaceful New Year?

At the end of the year, we try to forget the bad stuff that's happened to us and settle our differences. Each year, one area of Peru hosts the festival of Takanakuy, where there is music, dancing, drinking, eating and brightly coloured costumes. It's much like any number of festivals in Latin America – except this holiday gathering ends with a series of public fist fights. Entire towns congregate around sporting arenas to watch members of the community fight each other. People of all ages enter the ring, from young children to the elderly, women and men alike. The purpose of Takanakuy is to settle grievances[3] built up over the year in a public forum. The festival tries to resolve conflict, strengthen community bonds[4] and hopefully, result in greater peace.

---

[1] **to poison one's fate:** seine Zukunft gefährden (*wörtlich:* sein Schicksal vergiften)
[2] **to spark a contest:** einen Wettbewerb auslösen
[3] **to settle a grievance:** einen Streit/Konflikt austragen
[4] **to strengthen community bonds:** den Zusammenhalt der Gemeinschaft stärken

Takanakuy translates to 'when the blood is boiling', and people think that it's better to get everything out in the open and let their aggression out rather than living side-by-side with someone they have negative feelings towards. The fights are fully organised, with referees standing by, and there are rules, such as no biting and no hitting someone who is down on the floor. Each fight is typically very quick, sometimes lasting less than a minute. And, reflecting the intention of Takanakuy, each fight begins and ends with a hug or a handshake.

D Cemetery sleepover

One of the oddest New Year's celebrations comes from the city of Talca in Chile, where people spend New Year's Eve at their local graveyards, in the company of their deceased[5] friends and relatives. This might seem like a grim and spooky tradition, but the locals say that spending a quiet night with their dead loved ones brings peace to their souls and ensures them a lucky new year. They bring food and drinks to the graveyard and often light small fires next to the graves. This is a recent tradition which started in 1995 when a family jumped over the cemetery fence to spend New Year's Eve with their recently deceased father. Local authorities were moved by the family's decision and decided to change the local laws: until then the cemeteries were supposed to be closed on New Year's Eve, but since then they remain open and people are encouraged to decorate the graves to celebrate.

9 **Write down the main idea of each part (A, B, C and D) in a few words or a sentence. Then write supporting details for the idea around it. Compare with a partner and the class.**

They eat one grape for every month of the year.

…

In Spain, people eat grapes at midnight for good luck in the coming year.

You must eat one grape at every stroke of the bell.

This often turns into a contest.

S **Strategies box**

The **main idea** of a text can often be found at the beginning of a paragraph. It is the most general statement about the topic.

The **supporting details** generally come after the main idea. They are usually reasons, examples or descriptions relating to the main idea.

SPEAKING 10 a **How would you celebrate these four events? Could you eat twelve grapes? Who would you fight in a Takanakuy? Talk to a partner.**

b **Work in groups of four. Do some research on different customs around the world (not only on New Year's) and take notes on an unusual one. Then make up a custom yourself. In class, present both celebrations in about three minutes. Your classmates have to guess which one is real and which one you made up. Be prepared to answer a few questions!**

5 **deceased:** verstorben

LISTENING 11 09

a **Listen to part of a lecture on the importance of traditions. Why do traditions matter? Take notes.**

b **Compare your notes in class. Which argument do you agree with most and why?**

WRITING 12

Some students at your English partner school are writing articles on popular customs around the world for their school magazine. They have asked you to send them an article about a custom that is popular with many young Austrians.

In your article you should:

- present the custom
- explain where in Austria it is popular
- specify why young people like it

Write around 250 words. Give your article a title.

→ See *Writing coach, Article*, p. 178.

LANGUAGE 13 p. 26

a **Gerunds**

Gerunds are verbs used as nouns. You make gerunds by adding *-ing* to a verb.
Look at three common uses of gerunds and match them to the examples.

L

1 as the subject of a sentence	a Pat enjoys gardening.
2 after verbs, often expressing likes or dislikes	b She's good at looking after plants.
3 after prepositions	c Spending time outside is what she loves.

→ See *Grammar revisited, Gerund and infinitive*, p. 171.

b **Read text A in exercise 8 again. Find an example for each of the three uses above.**

14 **Add a gerund construction as a subject to complete the following sentences.**

1 … is a popular tradition in our family.
2 … is the most boring way to celebrate New Year's.
3 … is really bad for your health.
4 … will really annoy your neighbours.

Example: *Eating grapes at midnight is a popular tradition in our family.*

15 **Here are some examples of sentences with phrases expressing likes and dislikes. Highlight the gerunds, then change the sentences so that they are true for you and write them down.**

1 I **don't mind** spending New Year's alone as I'm not a big fan of parties anyway.
2 I **look forward to** meeting the entire family at Christmas, I rarely see them otherwise.
3 I **don't fancy** celebrating in a cemetery at night. I'd be really scared there.
4 I **am keen on** taking a trip to London soon. Maybe we could even celebrate New Year's there?
5 I **dislike** playing party games with my little cousin. He's such a bad loser.

16 **There are many more expressions that can be followed by a gerund. Complete the sentences with an expression from the box in the correct form, then highlight the gerund following it.**

admit ▪ avoid ▪ can't help ▪ consider ▪ delay ▪ get used to ▪ give up ▪ involve ▪ keep on ▪ recommend ▪ ~~suggest~~

1 Mum suggested **going** to a ski lodge for New Year's.
2 I ____________ trying to keep to my diet over the holidays. I can never keep it up.
3 James just can't ____________ living with the cold weather in Austria.
4 You should ____________ driving through the town centre. There are roadworks.

5 I ______________________ telling my friends that I don't eat meat, but they often forget.

6 She ______________________ copying her friend's homework.

7 Don't ______________________ studying for that maths test for a single second – it's tomorrow!

8 You should ______________________ going abroad for a semester to improve your English.

9 I ______________________ laughing every time she speaks. She has such a funny voice.

10 I definitely don't ______________________ going to Peru at New Year's. You could get into a fight!

11 Being really good at English ______________________ learning new vocabulary as you go along.

LANGUAGE IN USE **17 a** **Read the text about the changing tradition of Krampus. Some words are missing. Complete the text by writing <u>one</u> word for each gap (1–9) in the spaces provided. The first one (0) has been done for you.**

p. 25

Krampus is coming for you!

Crossing the Atlantic is a sinister figure wearing goatskins, horns, chains, bells and carrying wooden sticks. Yes, Krampus **(0)** ______ entering the US. From greeting cards to parties, Krampus is the latest trend. But where **(1)** ______ he actually come from?

This demonic figure goes way back, to before Christianity. He is said to be the son of the Norse goddess Hel, **(2)** ______ rules over the dead, and 'his' night was that of December 22nd, the longest **(3)** ______ of the year. Christianity paired him up with the positive figure of Saint Nicolas, who brings presents to children while Krampus delights in punishing those who misbehave by **(4)** ______ them into his bag and carrying them off. The rowdy 'Krampuslauf', when the young men of central European villages **(5)** ______ to get drunk, put on wooden masks and scare the **(6)** ______ population, is also part of this coming together of pagan and Christian traditions.

Interestingly, a **(7)** ______ custom exists in Japan. The 'namahage', demonic figures **(8)** ______ straw capes and wooden masks, walk through the villages in the north of the country and scare lazy or naughty kids. In Japan's strict society, the namahage are used to make children obey their parents. **(9)** ______ up as a Krampus, although clearly following a similar idea, also provides an opportunity to let off steam – something that seems attractive to the sophisticated urban societies of the US, where this custom is now taking hold.

0	is
1	
2	
3	
4	
5	
6	
7	
8	
9	

b **Would you like to take part in a 'Krampuslauf'? Why?/Why not?**

Once upon a time ...

READING 18 **Read the article, then discuss the questions below with a partner.**

Once upon a time ...

What's your favourite traditional tale? *Hansel and Gretel? The Tortoise and the Hare? The Pied Piper of Hamelin?* You probably used to enjoy such stories as a small child. Storytelling is an old tradition: thousands of years ago people would tell these tales to each other. However, they weren't just for entertainment, often they would carry a message or a warning for people.

The oral tradition of telling one another stories came long before the written page. Tales used to be told or performed, rather than written down, and would be handed down from generation to generation.

You will know the main elements of traditional tales, with characters who are heroes and villains, and a typical setting, such as a castle, forest or village. You will recognise the protagonist who represents good and the antagonist who is evil, and be familiar with the plots of such stories where there is always a dilemma to be resolved. Most traditional tales have talking animals, magic, spells and curses and may have a familiar beginning, such as "Once upon a time ..." or the ending "... and they all lived happily ever after."

1 Did you use to listen to traditional stories as a small child?
2 Did an adult tell you these stories?
3 Which ones did you enjoy most and why?
4 Which ones scared you and why?

LANGUAGE 19 **Talking about stories**

p. 26

Look for the following expressions in the article above. You can use them to talk about stories. Make sure you know what each of them means.

L

traditional tale ▪ for entertainment ▪ carry a message ▪ perform ▪ character ▪ setting ▪ protagonist ▪ antagonist ▪ plot ▪ resolve a dilemma ▪ beginning ▪ ending

20 a Expressing habits in the past

There are two ways of saying that someone did something regularly in the past. Look for them in the article above and then complete these sentences:

L

You probably ______________________ such stories as a small child.

Thousands of years ago people ______________________ these tales to each other.

b Now use the expressions to write sentences about your life when you were younger:

- what you played with
- who you played with
- what films you watched

READING 21 a **Take a look at Freytag's Pyramid below. It shows how to analyse the plot of a story.**

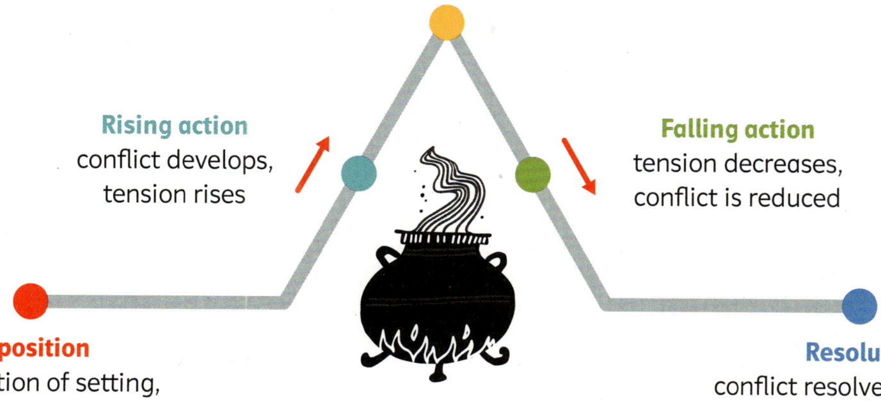

b **Read the story of *The Tortoise and the Hare* below. Use Freytag's Pyramid to help you put the parts in the right order and label them with the stages of the pyramid.**

A

The hare was embarrassed at being beaten by the tortoise and had to endure the laughter and teasing of all the other animals. "Call yourself fast?" they called to him. "You were beaten by a tortoise!"

____

B

The hare had to admit he had been boastful and proud, and he promised to change his ways. The tortoise just winked at the hare and told him, "Slow and steady wins the race!"

____

C

The next morning, the two set off for the race, watched by all the other animals. The hare thought it all a great joke and lay down under a tree for a nap, thinking he would have plenty of time to beat the tortoise later. The tortoise, meanwhile, was walking slow and steady on his way.

____

D

At midday, the tortoise passed the sleeping hare. He plodded along[6] the road and was nearing the finishing line when the hare awoke. Suddenly, he saw the tortoise about to pass the finishing line. He raced to catch up, but was just too late. The tortoise had won the race!

____

c **Many traditional tales have a message or a moral at the end. What is the moral of this story? Discuss what you think it means.**

E

Once upon a time, there was a hare who was always boasting how he could run faster than anyone else. He was forever teasing the tortoise for being slow. One day, the tortoise had heard enough and he challenged the hare to a race, which made the hare laugh aloud.

____

[6] **to plod along the road:** die Straße entlangstapfen/-trotten

WRITING 22 Work with a partner. Think of a traditional tale that you know and try to fit the plot into the pyramid. Write the story in short sections like the one in 21 and label each one.

LISTENING 23 10 p. 24

a Listen to part of a radio phone-in show on traditional stories. For each of the three callers, write down the main idea of their call. While listening a second time, check your answer and add at least one supporting detail. Remember that the main idea is the most general statement you can find while supporting details are usually reasons or examples.

	Main idea	Supporting detail
Jessica		
Trent		
Joy		

b What's your opinion? Take some notes, then make your own 'call' to a partner.

SPEAKING 24 *Individual long turn:* Prepare to talk for about five minutes by taking notes on what you want to say, but don't write down full sentences. Then talk to a partner for about three minutes.

- Compare the pictures.
- Give your opinion on whether reading stories to children is important or not.
- Suggest stories children might like.

WRITING 25 Write a PEEL paragraph on one of the following topics:

1 Is reading stories to children important today?
2 Should children be confronted with violent fairy tales?

→ See *PEEL revisited*, p. 93.

SPEAKING 26 Can you guess which stories are presented in the pictures on the right? Do you remember what happened in the stories? Share your memories with a partner or in small groups.

WRITING 27 Write down what the animals in the pictures might be thinking.

READING 28 a All cultures have traditional tales, and many traditional tales are similar. Here are two different versions of the same story. Can you guess which countries they are from?

A

Three sisters are left alone at home while their mother visits their grandmother. Lon Po Po, a grandmother wolf, comes to the house pretending to be the grandmother, but the eldest girl sees through the wolf's trick. The girls trap the wolf in a basket with gingko nuts, lift the basket up into a tree with a rope and drop the wolf to her death.

B

Because her grandmother has the flu, Petite Rouge (a duck) sets off to bring her some food. Meanwhile, a big old alligator called Claude frightens Grandma, who hides in her closet but leaves her clothes outside. Claude puts them on to trick Petite Rouge, but she throws a sausage dipped in hot sauce into the alligator's mouth. Claude has to run away to cool his mouth with water and Petite Rouge and her grandmother are safe.

b Which of these versions do you like better? Why?

STRATEGIES 29 a ***Advise* versus *persuade*: What's the difference?**

Remember the story of *The Frog Prince*. Imagine you know that if the princess kisses the frog, the frog will turn into a handsome prince. How do you *advise* or *persuade* the princess to kiss the frog? Match the function words with their definitions and examples.

1 You tell someone clearly and politely what is best to do in a certain situation by giving good reasons.

B *"I can see you are in doubt about what to do with the frog. I would recommend giving him a kiss. He has promised to turn into a prince if you kiss him. He looks serious. I would believe him."*

persuade

A *"Just look at the sweet little frog! Such a nice little guy. Why don't you just kiss him? I would if I were you. He might even turn into a handsome prince."*

advise

2 You talk or push someone into doing something by giving convincing reasons and encouraging examples.

b Write two paragraphs: One in which you advise a friend who has problems with maths to do his/her maths homework regularly, and one in which you persuade a friend to watch a good film with you.

READING 30 Read this version of *Little Red Riding Hood* and use the rhymes to guess the missing letters.

p. 24

Little Red Riding Hood and the Wolf

by Roald Dahl

As soon as Wolf began to feel
That he would like a decent (1) m__________ ,
He went and knocked on Grandma's door.
When Grandma opened it, she saw
The sharp white teeth, the horrid grin,
And Wolfie said, "May I come (2) __________ ?"
Poor Grandmamma was terrified,
"He's going to eat me up!" she (3) c__________ .

And she was absolutely right.
He ate her up in one big (4) b__________ .
But Grandmamma was small and tough,
And Wolfie wailed, "That's not (5) e__________ !
I haven't yet begun to feel
That I have had a decent meal!"
He ran around the kitchen yelping,
"I've *got* to have a second (6) h__________ !"
Then added with a frightful leer,
"I'm therefore going to wait right (7) h________
Till Little Miss Red Riding Hood
Comes home from walking in the (8) w_______ ."

He quickly put on Grandma's clothes,
(Of course he hadn't eaten (9) t__________).
He dressed himself in coat and hat.
He put on shoes, and after (10) t__________ ,
He even brushed and curled his hair,
Then sat himself in Grandma's (11) c__________ .

In came the little girl in red.
She stopped. She stared.
And then she (12) s__________ ,
"What great big ears you have, Grandma."
"All the better to hear you with,"
the Wolf replied.
"What great big eyes you have, Grandma."
said Little Red Riding Hood.
"All the better to see you with,"
the Wolf replied.

He sat there watching her and smiled.
He thought, I'm going to eat this (13) c__________ .
Compared with her old Grandmamma
She's going to taste like caviar.

Then Little Red Riding Hood said, "But Grandma,
what a lovely great big furry coat you have on."

"That's wrong!" cried Wolf. "Have you forgot
To tell me what BIG TEETH I've (14) g__________ ?
Ah well, no matter what you say,
I'm going to eat you (15) a__________ ."

The small girl smiles. One eyelid flickers.
She whips a pistol from her (16) kn__________ .
She aims it at the creature's head
And bang bang bang, she shoots him (17) d________ .

A few weeks later, in the wood,
I came across Miss Riding (18) H__________ .
But what a change! No cloak of red,
No silly hood upon her (19) h__________ .
She said, "Hello, and do please note
My lovely furry wolfskin (20) c__________ ."

LANGUAGE 31

Adjective suffixes *-ed* and *-ing*

The box below shows prefixes and suffixes you used for making word families last year. Work with a partner to find more examples for each one. Example: *music – musical – musician.*

a action	d happily	g unhappiness	j funny
b story teller	e hopeful	h activity	k cultural
c entertainment	f magician	i protagonist	l disappear

32 a Another pair of common suffixes for adjectives is *-ed* and *-ing*. Look at the sentences below. What is the difference in meaning between the two adjectives?

1 I think traditional tales are really interesting. I'd love to read more of them.
2 My teacher looked really interested during my presentation. I think I did well.

b Write down five sentences with an adjective ending in *-ing* or *-ed*. Read them to a partner without saying the adjective. Your partner has to complete the sentences.
Example: *Student A: My brother told me a really … story. Student B: Fascinating? Interesting?*

LANGUAGE IN USE 33

p. 25

Read the text on fairy tales and gender stereotypes. Some words are missing. Change the word in brackets to form the missing word for each gap (1–9). Write your answers in the spaces provided. The first one (0) has been done for you.

Fairy tales and gender stereotypes

In *The Little Mermaid*, who provides Ariel with shelter and a future life of luxury and **(0)** ______ **(happy)**? Prince Eric. In *Cinderella*, who brings her out of rags and into riches[7]? Prince Charming. Seeing a common trend? Fairy tales are part of our **(1)** ______ **(culture)** history. We read them for **(2)** ______ **(enjoy)**, but they also provide us with role models. Do we really want to teach young children that women are weak and helpless until they can be **(3)** ______ **(save)** by a man? Shouldn't we be challenging these **(4)** ______ **(worry)** gender roles to keep children more **(5)** ______ **(interest)**?

Popular books and movies mean we grow up learning from the characters we idolise[8], but these stereotypes are **(6)** ______ **(disturb)** and they don't reflect modern life. A closer study of the themes and characters in children's pop culture is needed. Some stories have made female characters more **(7)** ______ **(power)**, like Mulan, but unfortunately the stories that support the idea of strong women are often **(8)** ______ **(popular)**. If we want to get children more **(9)** ______ **(excite)** about stories that balance male and female roles so that women are not at a disadvantage, then the tales of castles and princesses may need a little tweaking.

0	happiness	5	
1		6	
2		7	
3		8	
4		9	

WRITING 34

Write a short response to the writer of this text. Do you agree or disagree with his/her views?

[7] **from rags (in)to riches:** vom Tellerwäscher zum Millionär (*rags* – wörtlich: Lumpen)
[8] **to idolise sb.:** jmdn. vergöttern

WRITING 35 a **Choose a fairy tale and write an alternative ending for it. Use as many adjectives ending in *-ed* and *-ing* as you can. Here is an example:**

The frog looked at the surprised princess with his big staring eyes and begged her, "Please, give me a kiss and I promise, I'll turn into a prince." The princess felt sorry for the scared frog. She lifted the shivering animal up to her lips and gave it an embarrassed kiss. And you will never guess what happened next: the princess turned into a frog …

b **Read out your endings in class and vote on the most creative one.**

LANGUAGE 36 **Topic vocabulary: Traditional festivals and stories**

Unscramble the words in the word map, then add more from this unit and your own ideas.

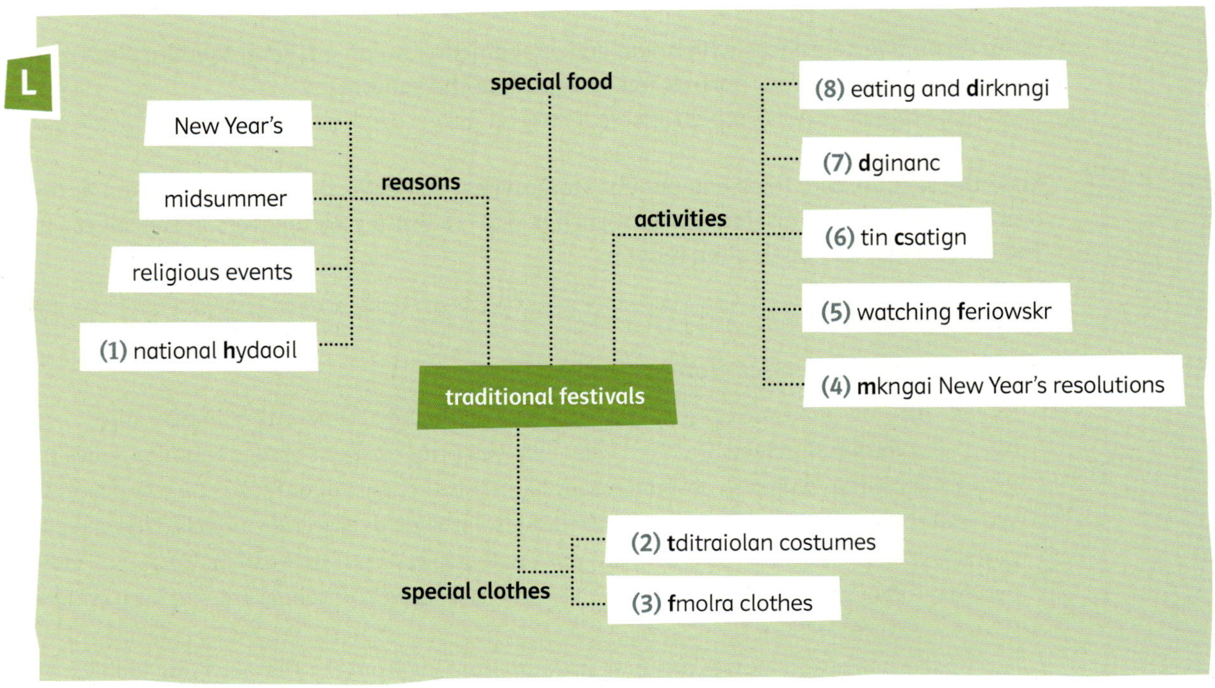

37 ***Word families.*** **Complete the table of words from this unit.**

Noun (person)	Noun (idea/concept)	Verb	Adjective
traditionalist		–	
		celebrate	celebratory
	specialisation/ speciality		
–		improve	
organiser			
	fight		
–		encourage	
			entertaining, entertained

38 **a** **Which word is the odd one out? Cross it out and write down why it doesn't fit.**

L **Talking about stories**

1 story – dilemma – tale – legend ____________________

2 protagonist – entertainment – main character – antagonist ____________________

3 exposition – climax – resolution – folktale ____________________

4 plot – drama – characters – setting ____________________

b **Now make up your own odd one out tasks and share them in class. Start with a list of words on a common topic, then add one unrelated one.**

Looking back: Learning goals of Unit 04

			✓✓	✓	!!
READING	▸▸▸ B1+	I can understand a straightforward article on the topic of tradition and change. **(ex. 8, 9, 18)**			
	▸▸▸ B1+	I can understand a description of events, feelings and wishes in a straightforward traditional tale. **(ex. 21b)**			
LISTENING	▸▸▸ B1+	I can understand straightforward factual information in clear speech on the topic of tradition and change. **(ex. 4b, 11a)**			
	▸▸▸ B1+	I can distinguish between main points and supporting detail in clear speech on the topic of tradition and change. **(ex. 23a)**			
WRITING	▸▸▸ B1+	I can write a straightforward detailed article or story on the topic of tradition and change. **(ex. 12, 22, 35a)**			
SPEAKING	▸▸▸ B1	I can express dreams, hopes and ambitions and respond to them. **(ex. 7, 10a/b)**			
	▸▸▸ B1	I can express opinions and feelings and respond to them. **(ex. 1, 2, 3, 7, 21c, 26, 28b)**			
	▸▸▸ B1	I can give a straightforward connected description on the topic of tradition and change reasonably fluently. **(ex. 5, 10b, 23b, 24, 26)**			
LANGUAGE	▸▸▸	I can use a range of verbs with gerunds correctly.			
	▸▸▸	I can use *used to* and *would* to talk about habits in the past.			
	▸▸▸	I can use a range of prefixes and suffixes to make words I need.			
	▸▸▸	I can use a sufficient range of vocabulary to express myself on the topic of tradition and change.			

A tradition worth keeping is . . .

One traditional story I would share with a younger generation is . . .

Unit 05
Wild world

86u8mt

In this unit you will:
- enjoy the beauty of nature
- do some colouring
- write traditional Japanese poetry
- take a closer look at the lives of orangutans
- learn how meat and the environment are connected

SPEAKING 1 **In pairs, talk about the photos below.**

1 What kind of landscape or environment do they show? What can you see? Describe them.
2 What does each of these areas usually feel, smell and sound like? What would you hear if you were there right now?

wild ▪ bright ▪ dry ▪ northern ▪ southern ▪ calm ▪ remote ▪ mild ▪ rough ▪ lovely ▪ wet ▪ moist ▪ natural ▪ clear ▪ clean ▪ quiet

A

B

C

D

The area in photo C could be …
This picture reminds me of …
I imagine the weather there is …

LISTENING 2 ◎11 **Listen to the different sounds and decide which sounds match which picture(s). What can you hear?**

Natural beauty

LANGUAGE 3 a Describing nature

p. 27

Look at the tree below. The words on the leaves can be used to talk about nature and the environment. Together with a partner, make sure you know what they mean. Then decide if they mostly refer to *air*, *water* or *land* and use different colour pencils to colour in the leaves. Some words can go into more than one category.

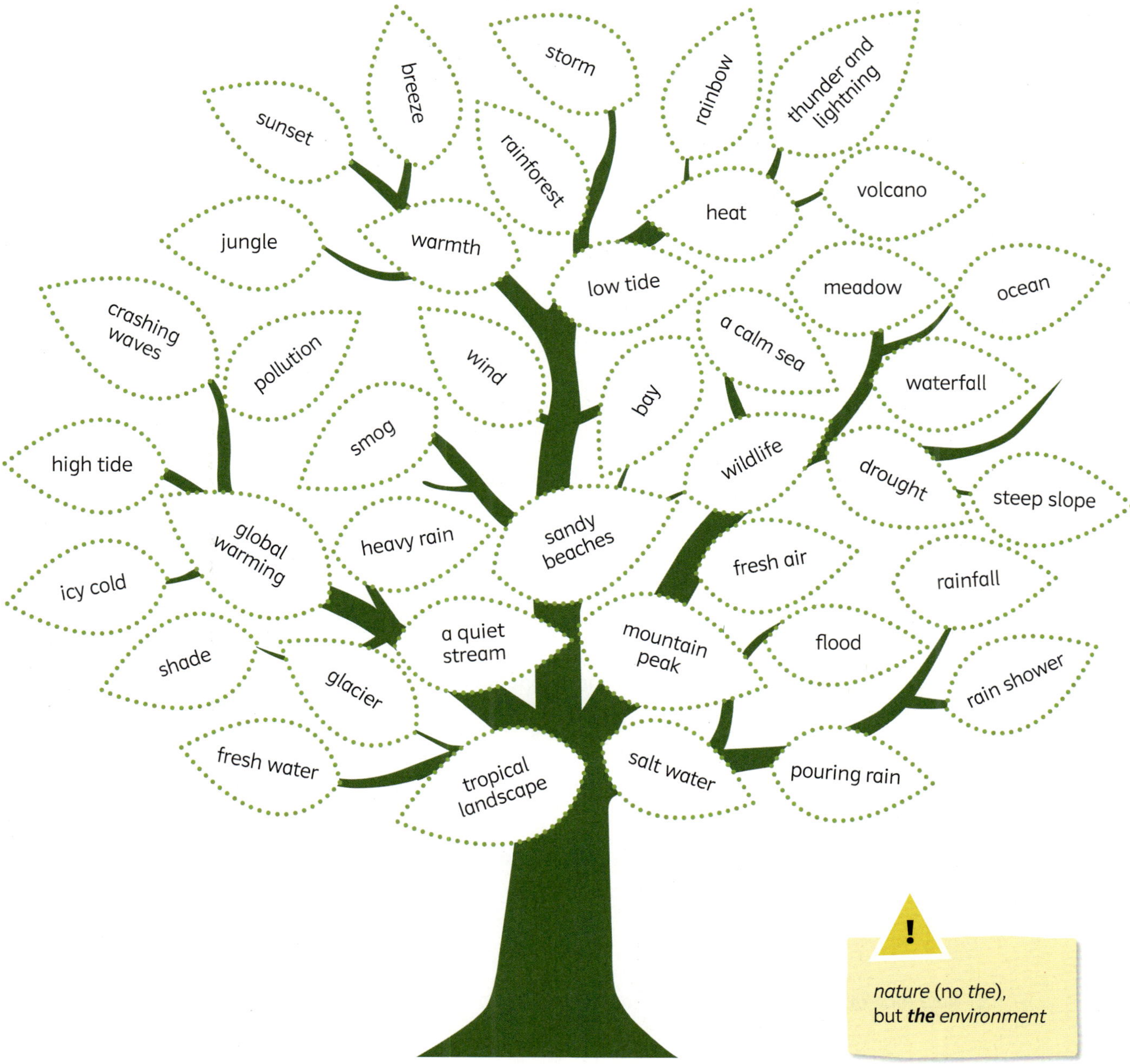

!

nature (no *the*),
but ***the*** *environment*

b **Read through the words again. Then close your book and try to write down as many as you can in one minute. Who can remember the most?**

4 **There are many different ways of describing the weather using adjectives such as *gentle*, *light*, *heavy* and *strong*, e.g. *a heavy breeze*, *strong wind*. What other weather-related collocations can you come up with? Try to use the words above and others that you can think of.**

5 **Using some of the expressions from 3a, write five positive and five negative sentences about a place in nature that you know. Read them to your classmates. Can they guess what place you are describing?**

LANGUAGE 6 p. 27

Adverbs of degree

Read the instructions on how to write a haiku poem and circle the correct expression whenever you have a choice. Sometimes both expressions are correct.

How to write a haiku

How do you capture the moment when you see something beautiful or dramatic in nature? You might take a photo, but (1) a much / an even nicer way to save it is in words, and the ideal method is a haiku poem.

A haiku is a traditional Japanese poem and is one of the (2) most / least enjoyable and challenging forms of poetry to write. The goal is to capture a specific moment in three tight lines.

A haiku has a total of 17 syllables; the first line has 5 syllables, the second line 7 and the last line 5. This means they are (3) hardly / pretty short, so the trick when writing a haiku is to choose your words (4) quite / very carefully.

Haiku poems traditionally focus on describing nature, and they emphasise simplicity and direct expression. Apart from being short, haiku poems rarely rhyme, which makes them easier to write! (By the way, the word 'haiku' is both singular AND plural.)

The main idea of a haiku is to focus on a brief moment in time and to use colourful images. The reader should be able to read your haiku in one breath and still be able to (5) rather / clearly picture what you are writing about. Ideally, a haiku should be written in the present tense.

L Language box

Adverbs of degree describe:

- the intensity
- the extent

of verbs, adjectives or adverbs in more detail.

Here are some: *not very, a bit, rather, quite, fairly, pretty, really, very, extremely, …*

Can you think of some more?

→ See *Grammar revisited, Adverbs of degree*, p. 172.

READING 7 a Read the haiku by American writer Richard Wright below.

1 Do they fit the pattern of 5-7-5 syllables?
2 What are the haiku describing? Do they give you a clear image of what is being described?

Heaps of black cherries
Glittering with drops of rain
In the evening sun.

A spring sky so clear
That you feel you are seeing
Into tomorrow.

b Now look at these haiku by the same poet. How do they give a different image?

On winter mornings
The candle shows faint markings
Of the teeth of rats.

The webs of spiders
Sticking to my sweaty face
In the dusty woods.

WRITING 8 p. 28

Your turn! Now try writing at least two haiku poems. Remember the 5-7-5 pattern and make sure you choose your words carefully – every syllable counts! Try to make the topic of your poems something to do with nature. Share your poems with your classmates.

LISTENING **9** **a** What do you enjoy about being outdoors? Talk to a partner, then collect your ideas in class.

◎ 12

b You are going to listen to four young people talking about what they enjoy doing in nature. First you will have 45 seconds to study the task below, then you will hear the recording twice. While listening, match the speakers with their statements (A–J). There are two extra statements that you should not use. Write your answers in the boxes provided. The first one (0) has been done for you.

After the second listening, you will have 45 seconds to check your answers.

Speaker 1 – Greg	0	1
Speaker 2 – Patricia	2	3
Speaker 3 – Dan	4	5
Speaker 4 – Emily	6	7

A	I enjoy watching my plants grow.	F	I love hiking in the mountains.
B	I find it fascinating that some animals can fly.	G	Sometimes I find nature immensely funny.
C	I love earning money with this hobby.	H	I only find time for my interest in nature at the weekend.
D	I'm interested in how small things in nature fit together.	I	I regularly enjoy nature programmes on TV.
E	I like to go where I rarely meet other people.	J	I find a lot of inspiration in the sky.

0	1	2	3	4	5	6	7
F							

10 Which of the ideas you collected for 9a were mentioned by the speakers?

LANGUAGE **11** **Talking about your interests**

p. 28

Look at the phrases in the box. They can all be used to talk about something you're interested in. Listen to the four people again and tick the phrases you hear.

L

- a ☐ I got involved in …
- b ☐ I'm really keen on …
- c ☐ I'm really into …
- d ☐ I love …
- e ☐ It's fascinating to …
- f ☐ I can get quite absorbed in …
- g ☐ I'm eager to …
- h ☐ I spend a lot of time …
- i ☐ I get quite a kick out of …
- j ☐ I'm hooked on …
- k ☐ I'm enthusiastic about …
- l ☐ I enjoy …

WRITING **12** Choose one of the people in 9b to write an email to. Tell him/her what your interests in nature are and how they could follow their interests in your part of the world. Use some of the phrases from exercise 11. Write about 200 words.

SPEAKING 13 a ***Individual long turn:*** **Do this speaking task with a partner. Compare either pictures A or pictures B. Then talk about bullet points 2 and 3. Your partner will give you feedback with the help of the grid below.**

A

B

- Compare the pictures.
- Give examples of beautiful places people might enjoy.
- Describe the most beautiful place in the area you live in.

Study the questions below while your partner prepares for his/her individual long turn. Tick 'Yes' or 'No' while your partner is speaking. Give honest feedback.

Did your partner ...	Yes	No
1 say what the pictures have in common and how they are different?		
2 talk about his/her opinion or feelings concerning the pictures?		
3 use present continuous when saying what the people in the pictures are doing?		
4 give reasons for his/her choice of examples of beautiful places in bullet point 2?		
5 use modal verbs (e.g. *could, might*) when talking about bullet point 2?		
6 give a clear description using positive adjectives in bullet point 3?		
7 speak fairly fluently without reading from his/her notes?		
8 speak for about 3 minutes? This means about 1 minute for each bullet point?		

b Discuss which pair of pictures (A or B) was easier to compare.

14 How would your talk have been different if bullet point 1 read "Compare the different ways of enjoying nature in the pictures" instead of "Compare the pictures"? Which version do you prefer?

Saving the planet

SPEAKING 15 **Read the statements below and discuss the following questions with a partner.**

1 What environmental issues are addressed? What do you know about them?
2 Do you agree with any of the statements? Why?/Why not?

A Why should I bother with recycling? All my carefully separated waste will just end up in a landfill somewhere anyway.

B It's important to support environmental organisations which try to protect our rainforests. We need these forests to reduce the greenhouse effect.

C In 2050 there will be more plastic than fish in the ocean, unless companies and countries stop polluting them.

D By the time my kids grow up, many endangered species, like polar bears or tigers, will have died out.

E I don't like it when environmental activists stop me on the street and tell me about climate change. I know it is natural and not man-made.

F I'm a vegetarian because I want to save the planet. After all, meat consumption is one of the biggest causes of global warming.

G I'm worried about the future. They say that extreme weather conditions and natural disasters, like floods, droughts or hurricanes, will happen more often. What will we do then? Where will it be safe?

LANGUAGE 16 a Talking about the environment

p. 28

Go through the statements again. Sort the phrases in green into 'problems' and 'solutions'. Then think of other problems and solutions which are not mentioned here and compare your findings in class.

L

Environmental problems	Possible solutions
pollution of the oceans	…
…	*protecting the rainforests*

b The statements contain three phrases that are often used to describe changes in the weather across the globe. What are they?

WRITING 17 You feel inspired by the statements on the previous page and decide to start a blog on an environmental problem that really worries you.

In your blog post you should:

- outline the problem
- explain why it worries you
- suggest a solution

Write around 250 words. Give your blog post a title.

→ See *Writing coach, Blog*, p. 182.

S Strategies box

When you **outline** a problem, you give the **main facts** about it, you describe its **general idea**.

READING 18 a How much do you know about palm oil? Take a guess at the following, then skim the text to check your answers.

1 Which of the following may contain palm oil?

☐ steak ☐ lemonade ☐ ice cream

2 How much forest has Indonesia lost to palm oil farming?

☐ 6,000 football fields ☐ 6 million football fields ☐ 60,000 football fields

3 If palm oil farming carries on in the same way, how many orangutans in Indonesia will be dead 10 years from now?

☐ 25% ☐ 50% ☐ 100%

4 After Indonesia, which country is the second-biggest palm oil producer in the world?

☐ Malaysia ☐ China ☐ the USA

b Read the text about palm oil production in Southeast Asia more closely now, then choose the correct answer (A, B, C or D) for questions 1–5. Put a cross (☒) in the correct box. The first one (0) has been done for you.

p. 30

The future of palm oil: can it be sustainable?

Palm oil is the most widely used vegetable oil in the world. It can be found in half of all packaged products on supermarket shelves, from food, such as ice cream and chocolate, to hygiene products, such as soap and make-up including lipstick. Its use is expected to increase significantly in the coming years, yet not many people know about the negative impacts of its production. It is often farmed in an unsustainable way and the results of this can be devastating[1].

B By the way

The expression 'primary forest' refers to areas of forest land which have never been touched by humans. It cannot be said for certain how much primary forest still remains in the world today, but the amount is definitely decreasing.

[1] **devastating:** verheerend

The main problem is that palm oil production is responsible for deforestation. This is particularly true in Indonesia, which lost more than 6 million hectares (more than the area of 6 million football fields) of primary forest between 2000 and 2012. As rainforests are home to more than half of the world's species of plants, animals and insects, the loss of so much forest seriously endangers much of the world's biodiversity. It has been estimated that orangutans, for example, could be extinct in 10 years if deforestation in Indonesia continues at the same rate.

Humans are also negatively affected as they are forced to make way for new plantations. The people who have lived off the forests' rich resources for generations often do not own the land they work on and, as a result, communities are destroyed.

Yet palm oil production also brings advantages to some people in developing countries. In Indonesia, for example, 11% of the country's export money is earned through palm oil. The farmers earn a stable source of income, which makes it possible for them to build homes, install running water and send their children to school. They can now afford standards of living that would not have been possible before. This is also true in Malaysia, which is the second-largest producer of palm oil and produces about 39% of the world's supply. Over the last 10 years, markets in Africa and Latin America have grown too.

However, if the oil is not produced in a sustainable way, with countries creating laws to protect the enviroment and companies acting responsibly, this growing industry could further destroy the world's rainforests. Some people have called for the production of palm oil to stop, but because many small farmers depend on it for their income, the solution is not that simple.

It is clear that many issues will need to be resolved over the coming decades: Should companies work harder to save the environment? How can governments protect their rainforests better and still support their local farmers? What do consumers need to know about the products they buy? Should everybody just stop buying products made with palm oil? These questions must be addressed if the precious tropical rainforests of Southeast Asia are to be protected.

0 Half of the things we buy

- A are not sustainable. ☐
- B contain palm oil. ☒
- C come from Southeast Asia. ☐
- D are produced in Indonesia. ☐

1 Palm oil production

- A can be done anywhere. ☐
- B is carried out responsibly. ☐
- C involves chopping down trees. ☐
- D is always sustainable. ☐

2 Rainforests are

- A a small part of Indonesia. ☐
- B where many animals and plants live. ☐
- C a big source of income for farmers. ☐
- D strictly protected in Southeast Asia. ☐

3 Palm oil farmers in Indonesia

- A now have a worse standard of living. ☐
- B are destroying the rainforests. ☐
- C cannot afford to get an education. ☐
- D have a better life thanks to palm oil. ☐

4 Sustainable palm oil production

- A is happening in Latin America. ☐
- B would also destroy the rainforests. ☐
- C is important for the future. ☐
- D can never be achieved. ☐

5 The problems of palm oil production

- A are not easy to solve. ☐
- B do not affect the poor farmers. ☐
- C can only be solved by companies. ☐
- D will be solved if we stop using it. ☐

LANGUAGE 19 **Talking about cause and effect**

Add the missing prepositions to the phrases you can use to talk about cause and effect.

L

1 Deforestation in Indonesia **is a direct result** ______ the demand for palm oil in the Western world.

2 Loss of rainforest **leads** ______ a growing number of endangered species because it **results** ______ a loss of habitat.

3 ______ **a consequence** ______ this environmental destruction, orangutans could be extinct in a decade.

4 Not buying products containing palm oil could **have a positive effect** ______ nature in Indonesia.

WRITING 20 **Design a poster about palm oil. Use information you found in the article and do some research online. You could cover the following points:**

- positive and negative sides of palm oil production
- examples of products containing palm oil
- endangered animals in areas where palm oil is produced
- suggestions to improve the situation

LANGUAGE IN USE 21 **a** **What animal or environmental organisations do you already know of? What kind of work do they do raising people's awareness and protecting animals or places?**

b **Read the text about orangutan rescue in Indonesia. Some words are missing. Complete the text by writing one word for each gap (1–11) in the spaces provided. The first one (0) has been done for you.**

Caring for our relatives

The deforestation of our planet is (0) ______ major problems for many species that make the forest their home. Happily, there are some organisations which work hard every day to rescue animals in danger and (1) ______ them from extinction. One of them is *International Animal Rescue (IAR)*, which runs a programme to rescue orangutans in Indonesia.

Orangutans spend the majority of their lives in the treetops in relative safety. However, as a (2) ______ of the 'slash and burn' techniques, in which the forests are cut and/or set on fire to make (3) ______ for the planting of oil palms, the treetops become a death trap[2]. Confused and frightened, the orangutans either remain in the trees with the fires surrounding them, (4) ______ climb down to try to escape. In both cases, the animals are then often burned alive.

As the forests are (5) ______ , the surviving orangutans are unable to get enough food and may take fruit and vegetables from farms or go into villages where they may be captured or even killed. IAR's team helps orangutans left homeless and relocates[3] these (6) ______ animals to safe areas of protected forest. Animals that can (7) ______ survive in the wild are given a permanent home at the centre.

IAR also works to rescue and care (8) ______ baby orangutans when their mothers have been killed or when they have been taken to be illegally sold as pets. Rescued baby orangutans of between the ages of two and four are taken to a baby school where they (9) ______ time in a special forest playground and

[2] **death trap:** Todesfalle
[3] **to relocate sb./sth.:** jmdn./etw. umsiedeln

are encouraged to live independently, making nests, spending more time **(10)** ______ the ground in the trees and foraging for their own food[4]. Once they finish **(11)** ______ schooling, those orangutans that are strong and independent enough are fitted with microchips, taken to a release site and set free in the wild.

0	*causing*	4		8	
1		5		9	
2		6		10	
3		7		11	

WRITING 22 **Find out ten important facts about an animal rescue or environmental organisation in Austria or in another country and make a fact sheet for the class. Here are some suggestions:**

p. 29

- when founded
- main focus
- major achievements
- recent activities
- celebrity supporters
- your own ideas

SPEAKING 23 **Discuss the two cartoons with a partner. What environmental issue is addressed in each one? How could these issues be connected?**

p. 29

24 **Eating meat can harm the environment in different ways. Look at the aspects below. How might the production of meat affect them? Talk in pairs.**

a water resources
b animal waste
c greenhouse gas emissions
d energy consumption
e land use

Cows emit methane …

Trees convert CO_2 to …

LISTENING 25 a **Listen to an FM4 interview about the environmental problems caused by eating meat. Which of the issues above does it address?**

radio FM4 13

p. 32

b **Read the statements below, then listen to the interview again. Explain what the statements mean in the context of the interview.**

Example: *"But this doesn't mean that we don't have to eat."*
→ There are still many things we can eat if we stop eating meat.

a "The good old Schnitzel is almost a national emblem."
b "But it's not efficient, it's a highly inefficient system."
c "We're trying to send out a positive message."
d "If you think of the way our grandparents lived, it was very, very different from today."

[4] **to forage for food:** nach Nahrung suchen

WRITING 26 **Write a summary of the arguments given in the interview. Try to use no more than five sentences. Then give your opinion on whether we should continue to eat meat. You could use these sentence starters:**

Animal agriculture is responsible for …
Growing animals for food needs a lot of …
That's why we should …
Instead of meat, we could …
It's possible to make this change because …

SPEAKING 27 **Find some advertisements for or against eating meat and bring them to class. You could check some magazines or search the internet. If you can't find anything you like, design an ad or a poster yourself. In small groups, decide on the most powerful ad and present it in class. The following questions will help you make your choice:**

1 What is the visual impact of the advertisement? What kind of pictures and colours are used? What is the layout like?
2 What language does it use to persuade people (not) to eat meat? Are certain words repeated? Does it use any descriptive adjectives or words appealing to your emotions?
3 Who is the target group? What makes you think so?

WRITING 28 **Surfing the internet you have come across the following blog post:**

Foodie_26

Do we have to give up on meat?

I love eating meat, and so does my family. But then we hear all these reports telling us how unhealthy meat is and that eating meat is also responsible for climate change. I just wonder, is that really true?

reply

You have decided to comment on the blog post above. In your blog comment you should:

- explain how you feel about eating meat
- point out alternative kinds of food*
- advise other bloggers what to do

Write around 250 words.

* For example, vegetarian food (mushrooms, beans and other vegetables, grains, soy, tofu, …).

→ See *Writing coach, Blog*, p. 182.

S **Strategies box**

To point out something means **to direct** somebody's **attention** towards something, especially if you think they do not know about it or have forgotten about it.

Examples: *The teacher **pointed out** the mistakes I had made in my text. But I was quick **to point out** that it wasn't my fault as my tutor had written the text for me. :-)*

29 **Look at the text and the picture on p. 72 again. Imagine you are a volunteer looking after baby orangutans. What was the scariest/best moment you've had during your time working at the centre? Write an email to one of the Whitehall students telling him/her about it.**

LANGUAGE 30 Topic vocabulary: Nature and the environment

Copy the word map into your notebook. Add the missing vowels and more phrases from this unit.

L

- **nature**
  - **places**
    - **the seaside**
      - b_y
      - the _c__n
    - mountain p__k
    - w_t_rf_ll
  - **problems**
    - d_f_r_st_t__n
    - p_ll_t__n
    - cl_m_t_ change
    - _nd_ng_r_d animals
  - **protection**
    - saving the r__nf_r_st
    - r_cycl_ng
    - eating l_ss m__t
  - **describing nature**
    - s_ft breeze
    - c_lm sea
    - r__gh climate
    - fr_sh air
    - h_m_d air

Looking back: Learning goals of Unit 05

			✓✓	✓	!!
READING	▶▶▶ B1+	I can understand a straightforward poem on the topic of nature and the environment. (ex. 7)			
	▶▶▶ B1+	I can find relevant information in a straightforward article on the topic of nature and the environment. (ex. 18a/b)			
LISTENING	▶▶▶ B1+	I can distinguish between main points and supporting detail in clear speech on the topic of nature and the environment. (ex. 9b, 25a/b)			
WRITING	▶▶▶ B1+	I can write a blog post or comment to communicate news, opinions and ideas on the topic of nature and the environment. (ex. 12, 17, 28)			
SPEAKING	▶▶▶ B1	I can enter unprepared into conversation on the topic of nature and the environment to exchange information. (ex. 1, 9a, 15, 23, 27)			
	▶▶▶ B1	I can give a straightforward connected description on the topic of nature and the environment reasonably fluently. (ex. 13a, 27)			
	▶▶▶ B1	I can make comparisons. (ex. 13a/b, 14)			
LANGUAGE	▶▶▶	I can use adverbs of degree to give more precise descriptions.			
	▶▶▶	I can use a sufficient range of vocabulary to express myself on the topic of nature and the environment.			

The environment I would like to be in right now is . . .

One aspect of the 'individual long turn' I need to improve is . . .

Unit 06
Of angst and Oscars

kb429e

In this unit you will:
- discover millions of reasons to speak English
- find out when English people speak German
- learn about issues at the Oscars
- travel to La La Land
- talk about your favourite films

SPEAKING 1 **a** **Can you recognise the English-speaking countries below? North isn't up, so rotating the book might help. Label the maps with as much information as you can: name of country, capital city/cities and any other parts of the country you know.**

b **Compare your information with a partner and your teacher.**

LISTENING 2 14 **a** **Listen to the people talking about their country. Where do you think they come from? Write their number into the maps above.**

b **Listen again. Try to describe one feature each variety of English has. (How are words pronounced differently? Is the melody or rhythm of sentences different? Do they use different words?)**

English as a world language

SPEAKING **3** **What do you need English for in your daily life? Do you think it will be important for you later in life as well? Discuss your ideas with a partner and share them with the class.**

READING **4** **Read the article below. Write down the main idea and at least one supporting detail for each paragraph.**

p. 34

Do you speak English?

Did you know there are around 7,000 different languages spoken in the world? This means there are an awful lot of people who don't share a language with you.

What do you do when you're on holiday and don't speak the local language? Chances are you might use English as a *lingua franca* (a common language) to communicate with people. There are around 360 million people who speak English as a first language, and nowadays it is almost expected that people will speak at least some English. Around one billion people speak it as an additional language, but how and why did English become the world's lingua franca?

The British colonised large parts of the world, and in the 1920s the British Empire reached its peak. At that time, a quarter of the world's land was colonised by the British. You may have heard the phrase "The sun never sets on the British Empire", and this is literally true. Britain colonised so many countries that, at its height, it was always daylight somewhere in the Empire.

As a result, some of these countries still have English as their official language despite speaking other languages too, but this is just one of the reasons why English has spread as a global language. Much of the mass media that you come across is in English. The internet (also an English term!) is full of English words, video clips, memes and so on. Advertising is another area where you will often come across English words, whether it is a language in that country or not. English is also often used when travelling – and not just by travellers; English is the official language of pilots.

So, next time you're on holiday abroad, listen carefully to find out which people use English as a lingua franca, and see how often you do this yourself!

LANGUAGE **5** **Describing language use**

Find the correct terms for these definitions in the article above.

p. 33

L

a a language used to make communication possible between people who speak different languages ____________________
b the language you learn when you are a small child because your parents speak it ____________________
c a language you learn when you are older and can already speak another language ____________________
d the language used by the government of a country, taught in schools and used for laws, etc. ____________________

SPEAKING **6** **Discuss the following questions with a partner and write down your answers:**

1 Do you think it is fair to expect people to speak English even if it isn't their first language?
2 Should English-speaking people be made to learn at least one other language well enough so that they could hold a conversation?
3 What other language(s) could be used as a lingua franca? Give reasons for your decision.

WRITING **7** **Write a PEEL paragraph on one of the following questions:**

1 At what age should children in Austria start learning English?
2 How many English lessons per week should students have?

→ See *PEEL revisited*, p. 93.

SPEAKING 8

All of the countries in exercise 1 were once part of the British Empire. Work in groups of four. Research some key facts of their history that explain their use of English, then present your findings to the class.

1 How did the country become part of the Empire? Was it settled by the British or occupied?
2 When and for how long was it part of the Empire? Why was it important for the Empire?
3 When and how did it become independent (again)?

LANGUAGE IN USE 9

Read the text about influences on the English language. Some words are missing. Complete the text by writing one word for each gap (1–10) in the spaces provided. The first one (0) has been done for you.

Can we have a word?

You may think that English and German are very (0) ______ languages, especially when you are trying to study grammar or vocabulary (1) ______ a test! However, the two languages have strong connections.

English is a Germanic language, and it (2) ______ been influenced equally by German, French and Latin. As a result, English has a much wider vocabulary (3) ______ either the Germanic languages or the Romance language family to which French belongs.

English is also very ready to take in foreign words, and as it has become (4) ______ international language, it has absorbed vocabulary from a large number of other sources. These expressions are known as 'loanwords', and many of them come from German. Did you (5) ______ that 'worry' is often known as 'angst', or that British people buy their fancy (6) ______ from a 'delicatessen'? Young British children may go to 'kindergarten', and enjoying someone else's bad (7) ______ is 'schadenfreude'.

There have been lots of other influences on the English language too. For example, the Viking invasions, which started around the (8) ______ 800, also left their mark. Not surprisingly, the (9) ______ 'anger' and 'knife' come from Old Norse, and 'Thursday' comes from 'Thor's Day', Thor being the Norse god of thunder. This connects nicely to the (10) ______ word 'Donnerstag', doesn't it?

0	*different*	4		8	
1		5		9	
2		6		10	
3		7			

SPEAKING 10

p. 33

Discuss in small groups: What loanwords in your own language can you think of? Where did they come from?
Examples: *interview, vis-à-vis, computer, …*

WRITING 11

Some students at your English partner school are writing articles on 'English as a world language' for their school magazine. They have asked you to send them an article with your ideas as a learner of English.

In your article you should:

- describe your experience with learning English
- say what you think about English as a world language
- suggest which other languages might also be important

Write around 250 words. Give your article a title.

→ See *Writing coach, Article*, p. 178.

Hollywood

READING 12

pp. 35+38

Most people in the world are familiar with Hollywood films. They are an important medium for spreading American culture and the English language across the globe. People watch films in the original English version and thus learn the language through this popular form of entertainment.

Read the article about Hollywood below. The text's three original paragraphs have been halved and then mixed up. Match the paragraph halves and decide which order the paragraphs go in. Discuss how you decided on the right order with a partner.

The making of Hollywood

A After that initial film, other producers realised that the climate in California was ideal for filming. The weather was good all year round and the sunlight was reliable. They could easily access a range of settings with the coast, forests and the desert all close by. Many filmmakers then moved from New York to California.

B There has been increasing concern about the lack of ethnic diversity in performers being nominated for and winning Oscars. In 2015 and 2016 all of those nominated for acting awards were white. Up until 2016 only 6% of the acting nominations went to non-white actors, which led to the #OscarsSoWhite protest movement. This began in 2015 and aimed to highlight the differences between the number of white and non-white people nominated for awards.

C Hollywood! What's the first thing that comes to mind when you hear the name? You probably think of films, celebrities and glamour. Hollywood must be one of the best-known places on earth, but how did it become the home of the film industry? A part of Los Angeles, it used to be called 'Hollywoodland' until 1949. The first film in Hollywood was made in 1910.

D Later in the 20th century, filmmaking progressed and thousands were produced in Hollywood. Many of them have become worldfamous, such as *Gone with the Wind*, *Avatar* and the *Star Wars* series, to name just a few. Films can cost hundreds of millions of dollars to produce, for instance, *Pirates of the Caribbean: At World's End* cost an enormous $300 million!

E In 2016, actors Will Smith and Jada Pinkett Smith boycotted the ceremony and were joined by director Spike Lee. They wanted to make a stand and campaign for more people from ethnic minorities to be both judges and nominees at the Oscars. Many other actors spoke out about this issue, such as George Clooney and Reese Witherspoon. The term 'whitewash' was used to describe the white majority deciding and winning the Oscars. It remains to be seen if their protests make a change in the future.

F So filmmaking is clearly big business. The huge sums of money and the reputation of Hollywood have drawn the finest directors, producers and actors. Since 1929, successful films and those involved in making them have been recognised with the Academy Awards, otherwise known as the 'Oscars'. These are presented in a special ceremony each year. However, in recent years there have been protests about these awards.

Body paragraph 1		
Body paragraph 2		
Body paragraph 3		

LISTENING 13 **Discuss the following questions with a partner:**

1 How many Oscar winners can you name?
2 What can you get an Oscar for?
How many different categories do you know?
3 Who decides who will get an Oscar?

14 a Before listening to an FM4 interview about criticism of how the Oscars are awarded, look at the expressions below. Match them to the correct part of the text and make sure you know what they mean.

a Academy	d demographic	g Oscars
b nomination	e organisation	h membership
c studios	f directors	i people of colour

And the Oscar doesn't go to …

The International Academy of Motion Picture Arts and Sciences (aka the (1) '☐') was formed in Los Angeles in 1927. Every year this (2) ☐ hosts the Academy Awards (the (3) '☐') to name the best actors and actresses, film (4) ☐ and producers, film music, and so on. The people and the (5) ☐ that might get an award know about their (6) ☐, but they don't know who will win.

It is really hard to get (7) ☐ of the Academy because the organisation hardly ever invites new members to join. Since the number of members is so small, not every part of the American (8) ☐ is included. There are many white male members but hardly any women or (9) ☐. This is why some people say the Academy is unfair as it is skewed towards white men getting most awards.

radio FM4
15

b You are going to listen to the FM4 interview now. First you will have 45 seconds to study the task below, then you will hear the recording twice. While listening, complete the sentences (1–6) using a maximum of four words. Write your answers in the spaces provided. The first one (0) has been done for you.

After the second listening, you will have 45 seconds to check your answers.

0	New members of the Academy are chosen _____ .	*by the existing members*
1	Most members of the Academy are _____ .	
2	Some people argue that there are fewer nominations of non-white people because _____ .	
3	The main cause of the problem is that not everyone gets _____ .	
4	The Academy ignored great performances _____ .	
5	The main question is who decides _____ .	
6	Any change to the Academy membership will _____ .	

SPEAKING 15 **The interview was conducted in 2016. How has the situation changed since then? Do some research on the internet and present your findings to the class.**

1 What changes has the Academy made to its membership?
2 Have there been more nominations of or awards for people of colour or women?
3 Are there plans for further changes?
4 What should be done in your opinion?

SPEAKING 16 **What's your favourite TV series or film of all time? Tell a partner and give them a two-minute summary. Include details, such as main characters, plot and setting, but don't share any information that gives away the ending or major events like characters dying (so-called 'spoilers').**

READING 17 **Now read about three well-known TV series and films. Which one sounds most interesting to you? Why?**

p. 35

1

One of the most successful films of all time is **La La Land**, which won an amazing six Oscars and seven Golden Globes, including 'best original score' and 'best original song'. Directed by Damien Chazelle, it stars Emma Stone as an aspiring actress and Ryan Gosling as a jazz pianist, both trying to find success in Los Angeles. The title 'La La Land' has two meanings: 'LA' stands for Los Angeles and 'to be in La La Land' is an idiom meaning 'to be detached from reality'. The movie, which can be described as a musical romantic comedy-drama, features a number of song and dance routines. Musician John Legend is a supporting actor and was also an executive producer. The film had a relatively low budget of around $30 million but made more than $400 million at the box office.

2

Some people say if you want to improve your English pronunciation, you should watch the TV series **Downton Abbey** in the original English version. This popular historical period drama portrays the lives of the British aristocratic Crawley family and their staff in the early 20th century. Downton Abbey was written by Julian Fellowes, and the cast includes a range of well-known actors and actresses, such as Hugh Bonneville and Dame Maggie Smith. The series is set in Yorkshire but filmed at Highclere Castle in Hampshire, and the episodes follow the lives of the characters between 1912 and 1926. Bonneville is the leading actor, and the show has a large supporting cast. It has won a number of Golden Globes and Primetime Emmy Awards.

3

One of the most successful film series of all time is **Star Wars**. It was first created by George Lucas in 1977, who also wrote the script for the first film. Star Wars is unusual because years after the original three films were released, prequels were made. So in order to follow the story chronologically, you have to watch the newer films before the older ones. Star Wars has been enormously successful, not just because of the films, but also due to the amount of merchandise sold. These classic sci-fi stories of good vs evil with legendary characters such as Darth Vader and Yoda are instantly recognisable all over the world. The special effects have improved with time and the soundtrack may vary, but the theme tune remains the same.

LANGUAGE 18 **a** **Talking about films**

Find the expressions in the film descriptions which match these definitions:

p. 37

L

a person playing the main male role
b visual tricks, often created by computers
c a single programme in a series
d money spent to make a film or series
e the written words to be spoken on screen
f the actors and actresses in the film
g goods sold that advertise a film
h films set in a time before the original film
i where you buy a film ticket
j the fictional people in a film or series
k the written music of a film or series
l to be happening in a particular time or place

b **Now underline any phrases and collocations dealing with films you can find in the texts.**
Examples: *to win an award, to star someone as …, to make … at the box office …, to be set in …*

LANGUAGE 19 **Choose the correct option to complete the sentences.**

1 The special effects / characters in that film were amazing. I felt like I was inside that spaceship.
2 The whole film was shot / shown in the Arctic.
3 Why does that guy always play the heroine / hero?
4 The film stars / directed Sam Rockwell, but the producer / cast really works as a team.
5 I don't like films with subtitles / music. I hate reading when I'm trying to focus on the plot / script.
6 The story is portrayed / set in India in the 19th century.

SPEAKING 20 ***Individual long turn:* Remember how to prepare for an individual long turn (see p. 23).**

p. 36

- Compare the pictures.
- Say if you prefer watching films at the cinema or on TV.
- Suggest a film you would like to see together with your friends.

Give feedback to each other. Remember what to do:

1 Start out by telling your partner what you liked about the presentation. This may include time management, body language, eye contact, the fact that your partner did not read from his/her notes, etc.
2 Have a look at the assessment grid on p. 68. The points about describing pictures apply to most individual long turns.
3 Round off your feedback by mentioning again some of the positive aspects of his/her performance and let him/her know what still needs improving.

21 ***Paired activity:* Your English language assistant wants to do a film project with your class. He/She would like to know what kind of films your class is most interested in. Discuss the ideas below with a partner and agree on two.**

- sci-fi films
- adventure films
- documentaries
- horror films
- comedies

S Strategies box

Consider the **context of the situation**. It's important what you *and* your classmates want to see. Give examples of films that you have enjoyed and give reasons why you would/would not recommend them.

STRATEGIES **22**
+ WRITING

Writing a film review

Read the information below. What other expressions can you think of for each part of a review?

S

How to write a film review	Useful expressions
Give your review a **title**. Take the title of your film or include the film title in a (provocative) question or statement.	*... makes for year's best/worst film.* *... – don't bother!* *... – the film that leaves you with a smile/mixed feelings.*
Let the reader know whether you are **recommending the film or not** – right from the beginning.	*If you want to give yourself a real treat, you should watch ...; Watching ... is a waste of time.*
Give **some general information** about the film. ▪ Outline the plot briefly, don't write a long summary, don't include any spoilers. ▪ Comment on the director or the lead role, or simply say where the film was shot, when it was released, etc.	*director, star, starring, lead role, actor/actress, main character, cast; The film is set in ...; The film is based on the book ...; The action takes place in ...;* *... was produced by...; The scenes were shot in ...;* *It's a remake of ...; It's a sequel/prequel to ...;* *... was nominated for an Oscar ...*
Give your **opinion** on the film. ▪ Say clearly what you liked or disliked. Give examples, explain what made the film special. ▪ Support your opinion with good reasons. ▪ Use descriptive adjectives to make your opinion more convincing.	*I was (pleasantly) surprised/disappointed by/with ...; The only negative thing I would say is ...; The plot is exciting/unusual/gripping/unconvincing/remarkable/unpredictable/unique/highly entertaining; The special effects are breathtaking/amazing/realistic; The scenes are spectacular; The dialogue is excellent/weak ...; The soundtrack is moving/dull/lively ...*
Make a clear **recommendation** for people who might want to watch the film.	*I would definitely (not) recommend seeing ...;* *If you get the chance to see it, ...; The film speaks to people of all ages/is especially suited for...;* *All things considered, I'd recommend ...; It's a must for anyone interested in ...*

23 **Study paragraphs A and B below.**

1 Can you guess the films that are being reviewed?
2 Which one is clearly a positive recommendation? Find the positive and negative expressions that might help you to write a recommendation yourself.

A

Otherwise, this is a pacy, witty film that creatively expands the story world while still keeping the fans happy. It has an emotional resonance[1] – heightened[2] by Carrie Fisher's last turn as Leia – and even asks a few questions about who really benefits from war.

Well worth seeing, hype and all.

B

If you remember the story – and many people will have seen at least one previous version – this doesn't have much new to offer beyond nice cinematography. The sheer size of the cast means that the top-notch actors don't really get to exercise their talents, and it's lacking in suspense. An attempt to give Hercule some emotional backstory also doesn't really work.

Still, it's pleasant enough family viewing. Especially if the more aged family members have lost this particular plot.

[1]**to have an emotional resonance:** (starke) Gefühle hervorrufen
[2]**to heighten sth.:** etw. verstärken

LANGUAGE + WRITING **24** a **Complete the film review below by filling in the words from the box.**

based on ▪ characters ▪ dialogue ▪ favour ▪ highly ▪ lead roles ▪ must ▪ pleasantly surprised ▪ plot ▪ recommend ▪ soundtrack ▪ starring ▪ suited to

Want to see a classic film?

Try 10 Things I Hate About You!

There are some films you just have to see, and *10 Things I Hate About You* is one of them.

A 1999 classic **(1)** ______________ Heath Ledger and Julia Stiles in the **(2)** ______________, the film's action takes place in an American high school. Loosely **(3)** ______________ Shakespeare's play *The Taming of the Shrew*, the **(4)** ______________ follows two sisters whose father refuses to let them date boys. One of the sisters, Bianca, desperately wants to start dating. The other, Kat, is especially bad-tempered and stubborn, so what guy would want to date her anyway? Finally, their father decides that Bianca can date, but only if Kat is dating someone too. Some guys plan to pay a boy to date Kat. Their choice: Patrick Verona, a bad boy with a mysterious reputation. Will he win Kat's heart?

I think you'll love this film as it's **(5)** ______________ entertaining. There are lots of high school teen movies, but I was **(6)** ______________ to find this one is different. The plot is unpredictable and the **(7)** ______________ is genuinely funny. The **(8)** ______________ are believable, and Heath Ledger is really amusing in the role of Patrick. Also, the **(9)** ______________ is lively and fits the film well. You will have to wait till the end to find out where the film gets its title.

I would definitely **(10)** ______________ seeing *10 Things I Hate About You*. It's a **(11)** ______________ for anyone who wants to watch a fun film with witty dialogue. It's particularly **(12)** ______________ a teenage audience, but parents will enjoy it too. Do yourself a **(13)** ______________ and watch this film. I promise, you won't regret it!

5

b **Now write your own review of a film you have seen recently.**

LANGUAGE 25 Topic vocabulary: Talking about films

Copy the word map below into your notebook, then add more collocations and expressions from the unit to the categories.

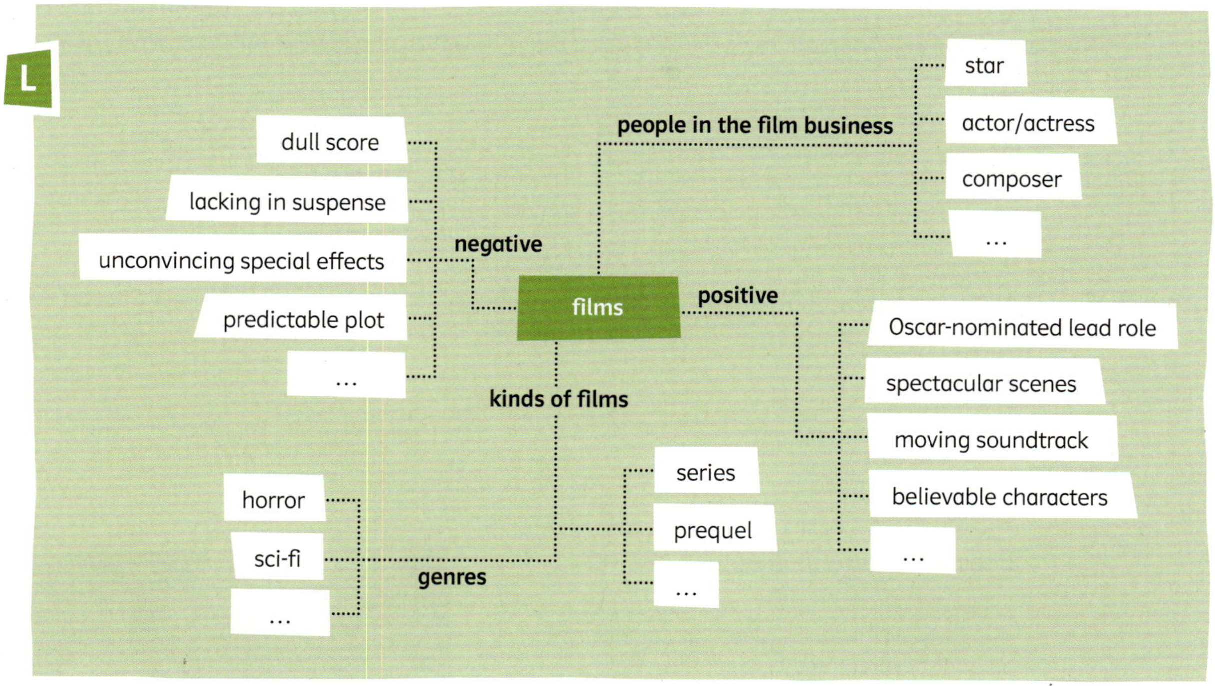

Looking back: Learning goals of Unit 06

			✓✓	✓	!!
READING	▸▸▸ B1+	I can understand a straightforward article on the topics of English as a global language and films. **(ex. 4, 12, 17)**			
LISTENING	▸▸▸ B1+	I can understand straightforward factual information in clear speech on the topic of films. **(ex. 14b)**			
WRITING	▸▸▸ B1+	I can write an article to communicate news, opinions and ideas on the topic of English as a global language. **(ex. 11)**			
SPEAKING	▸▸▸ B1	I can enter unprepared into conversation on the topics of English as a global language and films to exchange information. **(ex. 3, 21)**			
	▸▸▸ B1	I can give a straightforward connected description on the topics of English as a global language and films reasonably fluently. **(ex. 8, 16, 20)**			
LANGUAGE	▸▸▸	I can use a sufficient range of vocabulary to express myself on the topics of English as a global language and films.			

Five words which German has 'borrowed' from English are ...

I would give an Oscar to ...

Semester check 01

What's your progress with the learning goals of this semester? Make a mark on the line that shows where you see yourself, then do the tasks. Don't forget to check your answers with the key on p. 205.

	✓✓	✓	!!
LESEN ▸▸▸ B1+ Ich kann unkomplizierte Texte über vertraute Themen mit befriedigendem Verständnis lesen und wichtige Informationen auffinden.			

READING 1

Read the text about how shopping centres are changing in the UK, then choose the correct answer (A, B, C or D) for questions 1–5. Put a cross (☒) in the correct box. The first one (0) has been done for you.

k_white

Lifestyle centre or shopping centre?

Last weekend, my Sunday morning began the same way it always does; an unbelievable amount of scrambled eggs, coffee, and a discussion with my partner about how we were going to spend the day. With pouring rain and no hope of a barbecue, we decided to head to the Trafford Centre in Manchester to check out the shops, have dinner and see a film.

As I work in shopping centre management, I am no longer able to mindlessly wander round shopping centres. Oh no, I'm looking at the mix of shops, analysing the organisation of the place and observing other visitors! This time, reflecting on the reasons for my own visit made me think about the way that we use shopping centres. My partner and I hadn't purely come to shop. We firmly intended to spend time at the centre's 'Great Hall' – home to a wide range of fast food restaurants and casual dining spaces alongside a 20-screen cinema, Laser Quest and rock climbing venue and entertainment arcade. There's a gym, but it doesn't have a pool.

Changes in retail have made shopping centre owners think about how they entice customers in and how they improve the guest experience. The better the experience for visitors, the longer they will stay and the more money they will spend. Logical, right? Research shows that people who eat and drink at a shopping centre stay 86% longer than those who do not. So, lots more places selling food and drinks and leisure activities is the answer to a more successful shopping centre. Food is no longer seen as 'fuel' to keep shoppers going, but it becomes part of the experience. According to data, more and more people are ignoring traditional mealtimes, which makes it even more important to have a range of places within shopping centres offering fast food, healthy pick-me-ups and other dining options.

However, a rounded 'lifestyle' experience cannot be achieved through retail and food and drink alone. Carefully placed cinemas, bowling alleys, amusement arcades or, in the case of the Trafford Centre, more adventurous destinations such as Sea Life and Legoland Discovery Centre, mean families can enjoy the shopping centre into the late evening.

'Shopping centre' or 'lifestyle centre'? The retail landscape is rapidly changing and shopping centres will fail if they do not move on from only offering shopping. They need to be experience centres offering entertainment, sports and dining. I am interested to know if you agree!

reply

0 The blogger went to the shopping centre

- A just to look for clothes. ☐
- B for shopping and entertainment. ☒
- C to have a big breakfast. ☐
- D to wait until the weather improved. ☐

1 Due to her job, the blogger

- A usually tries to avoid shopping centres. ☐
- B only shops with her partner. ☐
- C likes to go window-shopping. ☐
- D can't help studying shopping centres. ☐

2 At the Trafford Centre one can

- A only eat fast food. ☐
- B play Laser Quest and swim. ☐
- C eat, play games and watch a movie. ☐
- D choose from 20 different cinemas. ☐

3 A study showed that

- A people like to eat whilst doing leisure activities. ☐
- B 86% of customers eat at shopping centres. ☐
- C shoppers stay longer if they can eat. ☐
- D restaurants are cheaper at centres. ☐

4 In future, the best shopping centres will

- A offer customers more things to do. ☐
- B cut down on the number of restaurants. ☐
- C serve food at regular mealtimes. ☐
- D just serve fast food to customers. ☐

5 Families visiting the Trafford Centre

- A all go to the Sea Life Centre. ☐
- B might like to go swimming. ☐
- C are all very adventurous. ☐
- D can stay there until late. ☐

HÖREN ▸▸▸ B1+ Ich kann unkomplizierte Sachinformationen über gewöhnliche alltags-, berufs- oder ausbildungsbezogene Themen verstehen und dabei Hauptaussagen und Einzelinformationen erkennen, sofern klar artikuliert und mit vertrautem Akzent gesprochen wird.

✓✓	✓	!!

LISTENING 2

16
yt8w9q

You are going to listen to a podcast about an exhibition. First you will have 45 seconds to study the task below, then you will hear the recording twice. While listening, complete the sentences (1–6) using a maximum of four words. Write your answers in the spaces provided. The first one (0) has been done for you.

After the second listening, you will have 45 seconds to check your answers.

0	The name of the exhibition is 'A history of the world _____'.	in 100 objects
1	The items on display come from _____ .	
2	You can find out more about the exhibition both from a radio programme and _____ .	
3	The presenter remembers going to the British Museum _____ .	
4	The presenter's opinion on mummies _____ .	
5	Researchers have discovered what the mummy _____ .	
6	The light bulb was invented by _____ .	

✓✓	✓	!!

SPRACH-VERWENDUNG IM KONTEXT ▸▸▸ Ich kann ein hinreichend breites Spektrum an sprachlichen Mitteln, die eher vorhersehbare Situationen beschreiben, korrekt erkennen und anwenden.

LANGUAGE IN USE 3

Read the text about St Patrick's Day. Some words are missing. Complete the text by writing one word for each gap (1–11) in the spaces provided. The first one (0) has been done for you.

Music, dancing, and a whole lot of green!

Does the colour green suit you? If so, then **(0)** ______ will really enjoy the tradition of celebrating St Patrick's Day on 17th March. This Irish festival often involves **(1)** ______ on green clothes, painting your face green and even drinking green milkshakes! If you are wondering why the colour green, it is often associated with Ireland. In fact, Ireland is known as the 'Emerald[1] Isle', a name **(2)** ______ partly comes from the green countryside on this beautiful island.

So who was St Patrick? He was a 5th-century bishop and is the patron saint[2] of Ireland. It is believed he **(3)** ______ born in England, but in his teens, he was captured by pirates and taken to Ireland, where he was put to work looking after cattle. After escaping, he **(4)** ______ 30 years setting up schools, churches, and monasteries across Ireland, and St Patrick's Day was established in his honour.

St Patrick's Day is celebrated all over the world, but outside Ireland it is probably most popular in the USA, where many people are proud of **(5)** ______ Irish heritage[3]. In America, there are parades and parties, and in Chicago, the whole river is dyed green for the day. This is done with vegetable dye and it only lasts a few hours, but it looks very impressive. One of the largest parades is in New York City, where **(6)** ______ are closed off to traffic and thousands of people march through the city centre, passing St Patrick's Cathedral **(7)** ______ the way.

On this day, it is customary **(8)** ______ enjoy a bowl of Irish stew made with lamb or beef and a pint of the world-famous Guinness beer. People typically eat traditional soda bread or a **(9)** ______ made from mashed potatoes and cabbage called 'colcannon'. Cookies made **(10)** ______ the shape of a shamrock, a three-leaved plant, are also popular **(11)** ______ the shamrock is often used as a symbol of Ireland.

There is a saying that 'Everyone is Irish on St Patrick's Day', so get out your green clothes, ready for 17th March!

0	you	6	
1		7	
2		8	
3		9	
4		10	
5		11	

[1] **emerald:** smaragdgrün; **the Emerald Isle:** die Grüne Insel
[2] **patron saint:** Schutzpatron/in
[3] **heritage:** Erbe *(Geschichte, Hintergrund)*

✓✓	✓	!!

SCHREIBEN ▶▶▶ B1+ Ich kann unkomplizierte, detaillierte Beschreibungen zu einer Reihe verschiedener vertrauter Themen verfassen.

WRITING 4

The school magazine of your English partner school is publishing articles about the dangers of posting personal information on social networks. You have decided to send them an article on posting selfies.

In your article you should:

- explain why you or your friends like posting selfies
- give examples of selfies people should not post
- point out why posting selfies might be dangerous

Write around 250 words. Give your article a title.

✓✓	✓	!!

SPRECHEN ▶▶▶ B1 Ich kann relativ flüssig eine unkomplizierte, aber zusammenhängende Beschreibung zu vertrauten Themen geben.

▶▶▶ B1 Ich kann ohne Vorbereitung an Gesprächen über vertraute Themen teilnehmen und Informationen austauschen.

SPEAKING 5 a <u>Individual long turn (3 minutes)</u>

Prepare for about 8 minutes, then do the task below. Your partner will give you feedback with the checklist in the key.

- Compare the pictures.
- Give examples of what young people like buying.
- Recommend a shop you really like.

b <u>Paired activity (7 minutes)</u>

Your English language assistant wants to know how students of your class best learn English. Discuss the ideas below with a partner and agree on three.

- watching films/TV shows in English
- listening and singing to English pop songs
- chatting online with international friends
- doing an online English course
- reading and writing blog comments on the internet

Unit 07
The story of my life

y2839f

In this unit you will:
- discuss what's important for teenagers
- PEEL longer than ever before
- discover if justice can really be blind
- find out what people with disabilities want
- improve your adjectives
- learn how a cat helps a homeless man

SPEAKING 1 **Look at the signs below and talk about these questions in pairs:**

1 Where could you find signs like these?
2 Who are the signs meant for?
3 Do you think they are appropriate/fair?

A

B

C

D

You might see a sign like that …
- *on the door to a restaurant*
- *at a museum* ▪ *at a car park*

The sign could be for…
- *guests* ▪ *students* ▪ *customers*

I think the sign is …
- *unfair* ▪ *not OK* ▪ *important*

because …

E

WRITING 2 **Look at one of the signs above more closely. How do you feel about it? What is your immediate reaction to it? Write an inner monologue of about 200 words.**

S **Strategies box**

Writing an **inner/interior monologue** means **writing down your thoughts**, emotions and sensations **as they occur** when you see one of these signs. You may use elements of direct speech ("Ah, what's this?") and incomplete sentences ("I just wonder … I don't like that sign. It's offensive.").

Young living

SPEAKING 3 **Discuss the quotes below with a partner.**

1 Can you guess the authors of these quotes? **a** Socrates **b** Oscar Wilde **c** J. K. Rowling
2 What do they say about your age group? Do you agree? Why?/Why not?

"Youth cannot know how age thinks and feels. But old men are guilty if they forget what it was to be young."

"The children now love luxury. They have bad manners, contempt for authority[1]; they show disrespect for elders and love chatter in place of exercise."

"The youth of the present day are quite monstrous. They have absolutely no respect for dyed hair."

WRITING 4 **a** **In pairs, come up with your own quote about being young today and compare it in class.**

b **Choose one of the quotes from 3 and comment on it in around 70 words.**

LISTENING 5 **a** **In exercise 6 you will listen to Pam (Lizzie's stepmother) and two teachers from Whitehall talking about a school project. All the expressions below are used in the conversation. Match the two parts of the expressions and then find their definitions.**

Example: *1 to create + c involvement + 5 to get people to take part in something*

~~1 to create~~	a accepted	1 to do what most people do
2 to commit (oneself)	b pressure	2 to think about your decisions and try to find the best solutions for you and the people around you
3 to follow	~~c involvement~~	3 to have the feeling that most people agree with you or like you
4 to feel	d responsibility	4 to invest money, time or effort into a plan
5 to take	e against something	~~5 to get people to take part in something~~
6 peer	f the crowd	6 to openly show that you disagree with something
7 to protest	g to (doing) something	7 the strong influence of a group on all its members

b **What do you think the school project could be about? Use the expressions to talk about your ideas.**

[1]**contempt for authority:** Verachtung für Autorität

LISTENING 6 ◎ 17

Now listen to the first part of the conversation and take notes to answer the questions below.

1 What will the project at Whitehall be about?
2 What steps in the project are the teachers planning?
3 What are Ms Anderson and Mr Jackson asking Pam to do?
4 Why have the teachers decided to do this project?
5 What should the students in years 11 and 12 learn from the project?
6 What is Pam going to focus on?

7 a The second part of the discussion focuses on youth culture today and on what has changed since the hippie and punk movements. Write down three things that you think have changed for your generation. Compare your lists in small groups.

◎ 18

b Look at the expressions below and guess what Ms Anderson says (underline it in one colour) and what Mr Jackson says (underline it in another colour). Then listen to the conversation and write down the words that you hear before and after these phrases.

1 protests against all sorts of things
2 change your identity really quickly
3 not enough commitment
4 you get instant feedback

WRITING 8 a Use your notes from 7b to reconstruct the opinion of each teacher.

b Do you agree with them? Write a response to either Mr Jackson or Ms Anderson.

LANGUAGE 9

Talking about youth culture

Look at the expressions below. Choose three that you think are the most important for talking about youth culture, and give reasons for your choice. Then add your own ideas and justify them.

L anti- ▪ acceptance ▪ clothes ▪ commitment ▪ counter-culture ▪ developing identity ▪ hairstyle ▪ involvement ▪ music ▪ outsider ▪ participation ▪ peer group ▪ peer pressure ▪ sense of belonging

SPEAKING 10

Discuss the cartoon on the right with a partner, then compare your ideas in class.

1 **What is happening?**
Describe what you can see in the picture.

2 **What are they saying?**
Who is talking? Explain what is being said in your own words.

3 **What does it mean?**
Explain what the cartoonist is trying to say with this cartoon. Why could it be funny?

4 **What do you think about it?**
Comment on the opinion expressed in the cartoon. Do you agree with it? Why?/Why not?

"Look at those dang fool teenagers, wearin' their pants hangin' down low like a coupla idiots!"

STRATEGIES 11 Writing a paragraph – the PEEL strategy revisited

Remember how the PEEL strategy can help you to structure a paragraph clearly:

S

P	Start your paragraph by stating your **point** with a 'topic sentence'. This is the sentence that expresses the key idea of your opinion.
E	Support your opinion with **examples** or **evidence** you have found. Include details such as facts, statistics, stories, etc.
E	Provide an **explanation** for the example/evidence you have given. Develop your ideas starting with words such as *furthermore*, *in fact*, *in addition to*, or *first*, *secondly*, etc.
L	Conclude your paragraph by summarising what you have written. Your last sentence should be a **link** back to your point, but avoid using exactly the same words.

READING 12

p. 39

a Study the text bits below and find out which part is the POINT, which one gives an EXAMPLE, which one provides an EXPLANATION and which one summarises what has been said before by LINKING it back to the point. Draw lines.

How important are social networks for you and your classmates?

For example, we can set up groups on applications like WhatsApp and exchange information there.

Therefore, it can be said that social networks are essential for successfully working together in class.

Social networks are the best way to study with your friends and get organised.

P E E L

That way everybody shares their knowledge, and people who didn't understand something in class can get help from other students. Furthermore, we can also remind each other about homework or other tasks we have to remember.

b The PEEL paragraph above is around 80 words. Which part(s) would be easiest to stretch if you wanted to write around 100 to 120 words?

S **Strategies box**

How can you count the number of words you have written?

Take the average number of words you have written in your first couple of lines and multiply it with the number of lines you have filled with your text.

WRITING 13 a Now study a longer version (115 words) of the same PEEL paragraph. Number the sentences and decide how they follow the PEEL structure.

- a That way everybody shares their knowledge, and people who didn't understand something in class can get help from others.
- b This is especially useful when a test is coming up.
- c For example, teenagers can set up class groups on applications like WhatsApp and study together.
- d Also, if someone wasn't in school because they were sick, this is a really good way to catch up with missed work.
- e From all the evidence provided it is obvious that social networks help students to study and organise their workflow.
- 1 f Social networks are a great way to study with your friends and get organised. POINT
- g What's more, teenagers can also remind each other about homework or other tasks they have to remember.

b Which parts are longer than in the first example? What words are used to develop the ideas?

14 Look at another version of the same text. Fill in the missing words from the box and draw lines. How is it different from the versions above?

additionally ▪ avoided ▪ do ▪ else ▪ example ▪ feel ▪ off ▪ only ▪ unfair ▪ which ▪ why

This is (1) __________ I am afraid that teenagers might get hurt, and therefore they should really stay (2) __________ social networks.

This makes teenagers (3) __________ disappointed and leads to them being unhappy and feeling alone. (4) __________, people often use photo editing software to make themselves look good, and this is (5) __________ and unnatural. They only show themselves in a positive way, (6) __________ is unrealistic as everyone has bad days.

PEEL

For (7) __________, frequently looking at pictures on Instagram only makes teenagers feel bad about themselves. They think everyone (8) __________ is having more fun than them and that everybody looks better than they (9) __________.

Social networks (10) __________ bring problems for young people, and, for this reason, they should be (11) __________.

WRITING 15 a The version above is around 115 words. Write a shorter version of 70 to 80 words taking the same view. Which parts can you shorten?

b Write a paragraph of 100 to 120 words on one of the following topics:

1. Should young people listen to adults when starting a relationship?
2. What is the biggest problem teenagers are facing today?
3. Is peer pressure a problem in your class?

Living with a disability

SPEAKING 16 **What does it mean when a person is disabled? Talk in pairs.**

LANGUAGE 17 a Disabilities

The box below shows a range of expressions connected with physical/sensory disabilities. Sort the words into four categories.

L

blindness	paralysed	hard of hearing	deaf
hearing	mute	vision	amputated
amputee	deafness	blind	muteness

b Discuss in pairs what life must be like for a person with these disabilities. Take notes.

1 What problems might occur?
2 What might being a disabled teenager be like?
3 What kinds of jobs could be easy/hard/impossible/… to perform with these disabilities?

LISTENING 18 a In 18b you will listen to an FM4 interview with a blind judge who works at the Michigan Supreme Court. Before you listen, try to come up with some questions that you might like to ask Justice Bernstein if you could meet him. After listening, see if they were answered in the interview.

19

b You are going to listen to the interview with Judge Bernstein now. First you will have 45 seconds to study the task below, then you will hear the recording twice. While listening, choose the correct answer (A, B, C or D) for each question (1–5). Put a cross (☒) in the correct box. The first one (0) has been done for you. After the second listening, you will have 45 seconds to check your answers.

0 Bernstein thinks that being able to see as a judge

- A makes the job easier. ☐
- B can be a disadvantage. ☒
- C gives you a neutral picture of people. ☐
- D is as important as being well-dressed. ☐

1 Bernstein believes that how people look can

- A influence what we think of people. ☐
- B help us know who we are dealing with. ☐
- C keep us from listening closely. ☐
- D be a sign of innocence or guilt. ☐

2 Bernstein says that blind people

- A know what discrimination feels like. ☐
- B have problems picking up sounds. ☐
- C can hear if someone is lying. ☐
- D are the most open-minded people. ☐

3 Bernstein's election to the Supreme Court was

- A unusual. ☐
- B similar to many others. ☐
- C not carried out in a fair way. ☐
- D financed by a big company. ☐

4 Before the election, people were asked

- A if they were going to vote. ☐
- B why they were voting for Bernstein. ☐
- C which candidate they didn't like. ☐
- D how they decided on their vote. ☐

5 The people who voted for Bernstein

- A were mainly college-educated. ☐
- B had no idea who he was. ☐
- C didn't like older judges. ☐
- D said he could understand them best. ☐

19 **In the interview, Judge Bernstein said, "Justice is supposed to be blind." Discuss with a partner what you think he meant by that. Do you agree with him? Why?/Why not?**

LANGUAGE 20 a **Word order**

p. 39

Look at the sentence below and circle the different parts of the sentence (subject, verb, etc.).

I often scan the newspaper headlines quickly at the breakfast table in the mornings.

b **How many rules for building sentences in English can you remember? Talk in pairs.**

c **Use the rules to put the sentence parts below in the correct order. If more than one order is possible, write all possible sentences.**

1 very few blind people / have been elected / in the US / as judges / .
2 many spectators / the Paralympics / in Tokyo / attracted / last year / .
3 Mum / for Mother's Day / got / a great present / I / .
4 is / late / Tim / always / when / we / for project work / meet / in the afternoon / .
5 understand / he / never / can / why / annoyed / get / about this / I / .
6 because / doesn't like / she / her brother / , / as much as possible / avoids / him / she / .
7 when / meet / my friends / in the evening / I / , / often / go to / a pub / in town / we / .

d **Translate sentences 5 and 6 into German. How does the word order change?**

→ See *Grammar revisited, Word order*, p. 173.

READING 21 a **Before reading the article below, take notes on the following questions:**

1 What mental disabilities do you know of?
2 What do you think are right or wrong ways to respond to people with a disability?

b **Read how Robyn Lambird describes what it feels like to live with a disability and complete the sentences (1–6) using a maximum of four words. Write your answers in the spaces provided. The first one (0) has been done for you.**

What you should know about living with a disability

Disabled people make up the world's biggest minority – that includes sensory, physical, mental or intellectual disabilities. As a young woman living with cerebral palsy, a neurological condition affecting movement and muscle tone[2], I often notice that disabled people could benefit from more meaningful representation. Because there's such an unacceptable lack of visibility in mainstream media, disabled people are still very much misunderstood. I recently shared my feelings about the disabled identity on the wonderful *Body Pos Project*, an online platform for sharing stories about overcoming issues regarding body positivity. People responded with so much love. Still, there are some things I wish they knew.

First of all, we can't be summed up with a wheelchair symbol. Although a wheelchair is the universal symbol for accessible facilities, this is not suitable as the actual community is so much broader than that! Some disabilities are visible, some aren't. A disability might be the result of an accident or illness, or people may have just been born this way. Having the wheelchair symbol represent the entire disabled community is unhelpful as it often means that individuals who have 'invisible disabilities' face discrimination. Many of my disabled friends, when not using mobility aids, have received negative comments and stares when taking a priority seat on public transport. This is because we appear to be young able-bodied individuals, and our mobility and balance problems aren't obvious, so please be careful what you say.

As long as you are polite and respectful, I'm more than happy to answer your questions about my situation. I understand the natural curiosity, and the more you understand about my disability, the more I actually benefit. If people are willing to sit and listen to our stories and challenges, that goes a long way in making us feel valuable and empowered. We want to be seen. It's validating to see someone who looks like you on screen, on a billboard or in a magazine. Unfortunately, this rarely happens for disabled people. But if we have representation, disability will be normalized, and negative attitudes (like fear and bias) can be changed. Some brands are including disabled models in advertising, but there is more work to be done. Still, I'm hopeful.

[2] **muscle tone:** Muskelspannung

Please, don't call us 'brave'. Having a disability doesn't make us exceptional or inspirational or brave. In fact, those words actually come across as careless and condescending. I shouldn't be seen as remarkable because I use a wheelchair, but rather because of my achievement in athletics or because I work to raise awareness for my community. Disabled people are reasonable, we just want the same things as everyone else: employment, relationships, and the opportunity to go out and experience the world in the same way as our able-bodied peers.

0	Disabled people represent _____ .	the world's biggest minority
1	In Lambird's view, people with a disability should _____ .	
2	The wheelchair is not a suitable symbol for the community of disabled people because _____ .	
3	Sometimes when people with a 'hidden' disability occupy priority seats, they _____ .	
4	Disabled people are willing to share their stories because they _____ .	
5	Companies should show people with a disability in advertisements because this _____ .	
6	People with a disability don't want to be called 'brave' because it _____ .	

WRITING 22 a **Work in pairs. Use the information from the article to write down five suggestions on how to respond to people with a disability.**

b **In the article, Robyn Lambird says, "As long as you are polite and respectful, I'm more than happy to answer your questions about my situation." Come up with three questions you would like to ask her.**

1 ______________________________

____

2 ______________________________

____

3 ______________________________

____

LANGUAGE 23 **Adjectives ending in *-ful*, *-able* and *-less***

In the article above there are 12 adjectives ending in *-ful*, *-able* and *-less*. Copy the words into your notebook. For how many of them can you find an opposite?

LANGUAGE 24 Adjectives ending in *-ful*, *-able* and *-less*

You can use the suffixes *-ful*, *-able* and *-less* to make a range of adjectives from verbs and nouns. Study the information in the box and do the task below.

Suffix	Examples	Function	Meaning
-ful	to hope → hopeful spoon → spoonful	verb to adjective noun to adjective	'having this quality' 'as much as can fit'
-able	to comfort → comfortable fashion → fashionable	verb to adjective noun to adjective	'having this quality'
-less	to help → helpless child → childless	verb to adjective noun to adjective	'not having this quality'

Which suffixes can be used with the words below? Sometimes more than one is possible.
Example: *meaning → meaningful/meaningless*

a success c use e forget g suit
b enjoy d prefer f colour h care

! The suffix *-ful* is spelt with only one *l*, unlike the word *full*.

LANGUAGE IN USE 25

p. 42

a What sports events for disabled people do you know about? Talk in class.

b Read the text about the Paralympic Games. Some words are missing. Change the word in brackets to form the missing word for each gap (1–9). Write your answers in the spaces provided. The first one (0) has been done for you.

The Paralympics

The Paralympic Games take place in the same year as the Olympic Games and are an international sports event for athletes who are **(0)** ______ **(able)** in some way. Participants may be paraplegic, blind or have had limbs amputated, but all are **(1)** ______ **(skill)** sportsmen and women who are competing for gold medals. These **(2)** ______ **(fear)** competitors take part in a wide range of disciplines from badminton to football, from wheelchair basketball to canoeing – the list is **(3)** ______ **(end)**. Sometimes assistance is needed; for example, blind **(4)** ______ **(run)** have a 'buddy' attached by the wrist with a short piece of rope who runs with them. Some cycling competitions would be **(5)** ______ **(suit)** for blind athletes, so tandems are used with a sighted partner who rides at the front. One sport which is exclusive to the Paralympics is goalball. Goalball involves two teams of blind and visually impaired **(6)** ______ **(play)** on an indoor court. The object is to throw a heavy ball filled with bells into the opposing team's net while the other team tries to block its progress with their bodies. In the weight-lifting contest the **(7)** ______ **(power)** competitors are able to lift up to an amazing 100 kg or more. The Paralympic Games provide non-stop **(8)** ______ **(act)**, and they are without doubt an **(9)** ______ **(forget)** experience for the athletes taking part.

0	disabled	5	
1		6	
2		7	
3		8	
4		9	

26 **Make a list of the differences between Paralympic disciplines and 'regular' Olympic ones.**

Living on the street

SPEAKING **27** **a In pairs, come up with a definition of 'homelessness'.**

b Study the pie chart on homelessness in the USA.

p. 41

1 What does it tell you about the different groups of homeless people?
2 The chart is from 2010. Do you think it would look different today? If so, how?
3 What could the situation in Austria be like? Do some research and discuss the results in class.

c What could everyday life be like for homeless people?

28 ***Paired activity:*** **Go back to p. 22 to refresh your memory about what a good paired activity should be like. Work in groups of three so a classmate can give you honest feedback based on the grid below.**

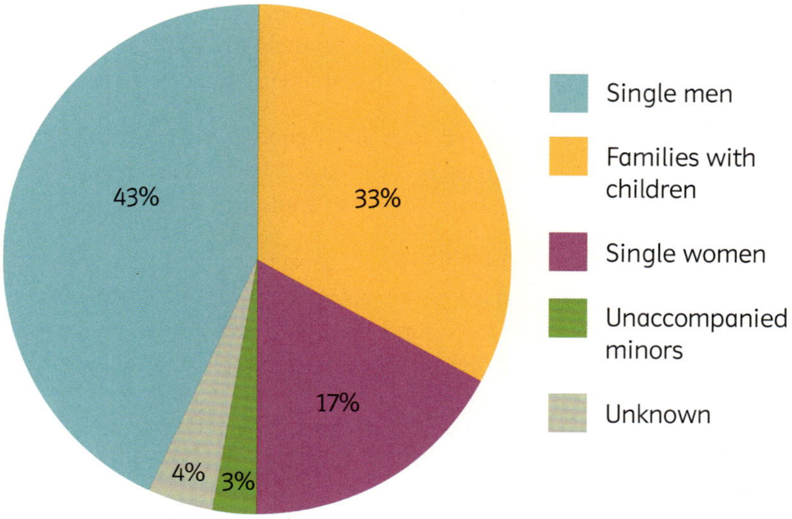

Your English language assistant is doing a social studies project with your class. Your class wants to donate money to an organisation helping homeless children. Now your language assistant would like to know how the money can be raised. Discuss the options below with a partner and agree on three.

- selling toys and clothes at a flea market after school
- selling home-made cakes during breaks
- donating 10% of students' monthly pocket money
- organising a singing competition – audience pay an entry fee
- organising a sports event – admission fee for visitors

Student A ...	Yes	No
considers the situational context.		
listens to what B says.		
invites B to give his/her opinion.		
reacts to B's arguments politely and competently.		
gives good examples for all bullet points.		
speaks fluently.		
doesn't dominate the discussion.		

Student B ...	Yes	No
considers the situational context.		
listens to what A says.		
invites A to give his/her opinion.		
reacts to A's arguments politely and competently.		
gives good examples for all bullet points.		
speaks fluently.		
doesn't dominate the discussion.		

READING 29 **a** Look at the picture on the right. How could having an animal help a homeless person?

p. 40

b You are going to read an extract from the book *A Street Cat Named Bob*. It's an autobiographical story about James Bowen, who has a rough childhood, becomes a drug addict and ends up on the streets of London. But then he befriends a street cat, and this changes his life …

Read the following episodes of James' growing up and put the paragraphs into the right order.

A [1] The answer to how people like me end up on the streets is always different, of course. But there are usually some similarities. Often drugs and alcohol play a big part in the story. But in an awful lot of instances, the road that led them to living on the streets stretches all the way back to their childhoods and their relationship with their family. That was certainly the way it was for me.

B [ ] Life in Australia was pretty good. We lived in several large houses over the years, each of which had vast garden areas at the back. I had all the space a boy could want to play in and explore the world and I loved the Australian landscape. The trouble was that I didn't have any friends.

C [ ] Predictably, I got into drugs, at first sniffing glue, probably to escape from reality. I didn't get addicted to it. I only did it a couple of times after seeing another kid doing it. But it was the start of the process. After that I started smoking dope. It was all connected, it was all part of a cycle of behaviour, one thing led back to another, which led back to another, and so on. I was angry. I felt like I hadn't had the best breaks.

D [ ] Around my 18th birthday, I announced that I was going to move back to London to live with my half-sister from my father's previous marriage. It marked the beginning of the downward spiral.

E [ ] By the time I was in my mid-teens, I'd pretty much quit school. I left because I was just sick to death of the bullying I encountered there. I became a tearaway, a wild kid who was always out late, always challenging my mother and generally thumbing his nose at[3] authority, no matter what form it took.

F [ ] I went to stay with my half-sister in South London. My brother-in-law wasn't too happy about my arrival. As I say, I was a rebellious teenager who dressed like a goth and was – probably – a complete pain in the arse[4], especially as I wasn't contributing to the household bills. In Australia I'd worked in IT and sold mobile phones, but back in the UK I couldn't find a decent job. Eventually, my half-sister kicked me out. I started sleeping on friends' floors and sofas. Soon I was leading a nomadic existence, carrying my sleeping bag with me to various flats and squats around London. Then, when I ran out of floors, I moved to the streets.

G [ ] I found it very hard to fit in at school, mainly, I think, because we'd moved a lot. The chances of settling into life in Australia disappeared when I was nine and we moved back to the UK. I enjoyed being back in England and have some happy memories of that period. I was just getting back into life in the northern hemisphere when we had to move yet again – back to Western Australia, when I was around twelve.

H [ ] I lived quite a rootless childhood, mainly because I spent it travelling between the UK and Australia. I was born in Surrey, but when I was three my family moved to Melbourne. My mother and father had separated by this time.

I [ ] Things headed downwards fast from there. Living on the streets of London takes away your dignity, your identity – your everything, really. Worst of all, it takes away people's opinion of you. They see you are living on the streets and treat you as a non-person. They don't want anything to do with you. Soon you haven't got a real friend in the world.

[3] **to thumb your nose at sb./sth.:** jmdn./etw. nicht respektieren
[4] **pain in the arse** *(infml.)*: Nervensäge, Ärgernis

SPEAKING 30 What are the reasons why James Bowen became homeless? What are other possible reasons why people might become homeless? What can society do to help homeless people?

READING 31 Now read this extract from later in the book. How does Bob change James' life?

Ordinarily, no one would engage or even exchange a look with me[5]. I was a busker and this was London. I didn't exist. I was a person to be avoided, shunned even. But as I walked down Neal Street that afternoon, almost every person we passed was looking at me. Well, more to the point, they were looking at Bob.

One or two had strange, slightly confused looks on their faces, which was understandable, I guess. It must have looked slightly incongruous, a tall, long-haired bloke walking along with a large, ginger tomcat on his shoulders. Not something you see every day – even on the streets of London.

Most people, however, were reacting more warmly. The moment they saw Bob, their faces would break into broad smiles. It wasn't long before people were stopping us.

'Ah, look at you two,' said one well-dressed, middle-aged lady laden down with shopping bags. 'He's gorgeous. Can I stroke him?'

'Of course,' I said, thinking it would be a one-off event.

She plonked down her bags and placed her face right up to his.

'What a lovely fellow you are, aren't you,' she said. 'He's a boy, isn't he?'

'He is,' I said.

'Isn't he good to sit there on your shoulders like that? Don't see that very often. He must really trust you.'

WRITING 32 Imagine Bob, the cat, is writing a diary. Write a diary entry about a typical day with James.

33 Your partner school in Cambridge is doing a literature project on outsiders in society. They have asked you to send them an article recommending a book or film that deals with this topic.

In your article you should:

- present a book/film dealing with outsiders
- point out what makes life difficult for the outsider
- convince students at your partner school that the book/film is worth reading/watching

Write around 250 words. Give your article a title.

→ See *Writing coach, Article*, p. 178.

S **Strategies box**

Convince (*überzeugen*), **persuade** (*überreden*), **advise** (*etwas raten*), **recommend** (*empfehlen*) and **suggest** (*vorschlagen*) are not the same, but have a similar function: You want to achieve something or **make someone do something** by offering good reasons, evidence and examples.

The following expressions might help: *Why don't you … ?; You could/should/might …; Wouldn't it be great to … ?; You simply have to …; I'm certain …; You will definitely see …; It's quite obvious …; What needs to be done …; Don't miss …; You won't believe …; Wouldn't you agree … ?; Don't you think … ?; It's crystal clear …; If I were you, I'd …*

[5] **to not exchange a look with sb.:** jmdn. keines Blickes würdigen

LANGUAGE 34 a Topic vocabulary: Social groups

Add the phrases from the box to the word map, then improve it with your own ideas.

developing identity ▪ homeless people ▪ loss of dignity ▪ misunderstanding ▪ peer pressure ▪ people with disabilities ▪ physical ▪ raising awareness

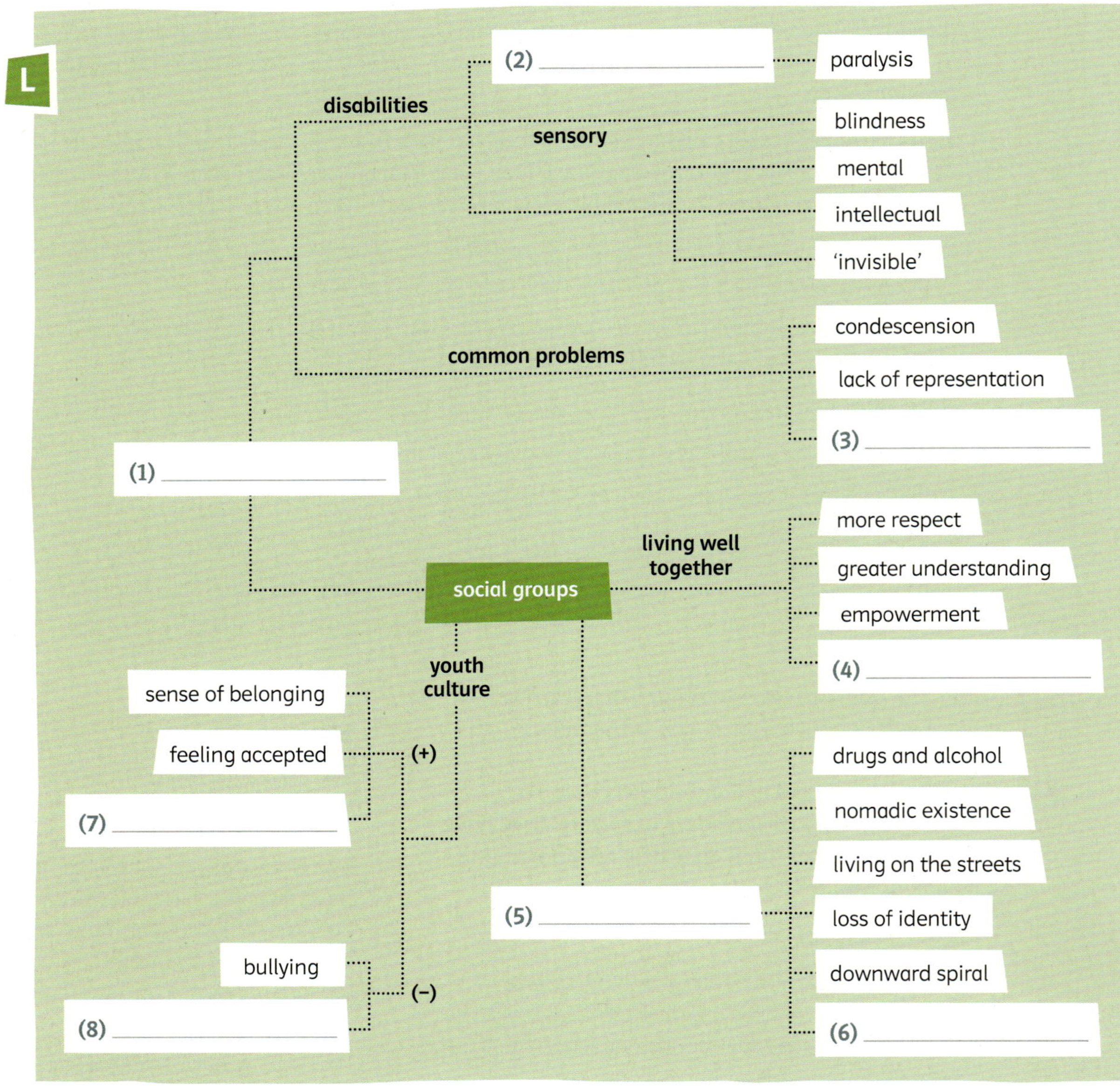

b **Copy the word family below into your notebook. Then create your own for the words 'comfort', 'fear' and 'care'. Compare with a partner and your teacher.**

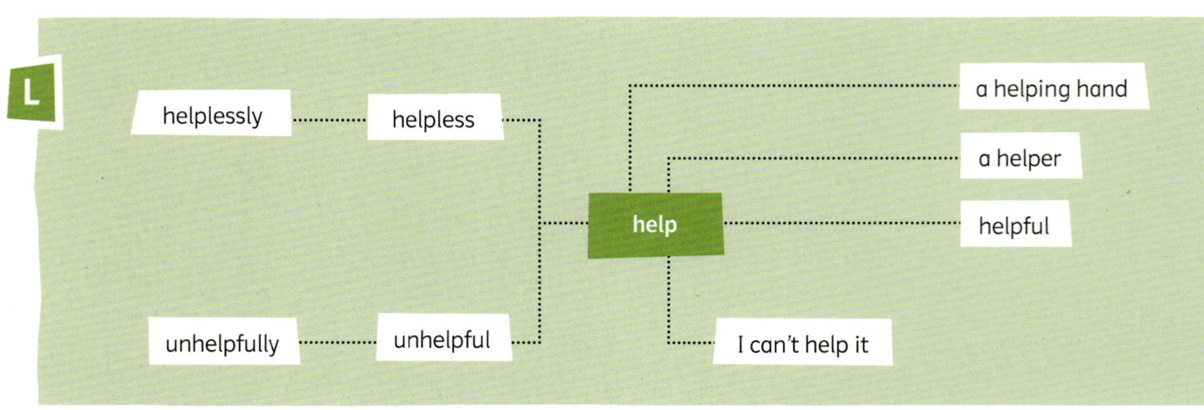

STRATEGIES **35** a **New goals for the summer term**

Welcome to the summer term! This is the first time that the learning goals are changing during a school year and not just in between years. Study the table with learning goals below and compare it with the ones from the past six units. Highlight any differences. Then share your findings in class.

1 What differences can you find?
  I can express and exchange ideas about …
2 Which learning goals now have more difficult tasks for you to deal with?
  I can understand most of …
3 Which learning goals have similar tasks, but now expect your results to be better?
  I can enter into conversation …

b **Discuss the following questions with a partner. Then write down your three main goals and how you plan to achieve them.**

1 Which of the new goals might be challenging for you?
2 What are you going to do to achieve these goals?

Looking back: Learning goals of Unit 07

			✓✓	✓	!!
READING	▸▸▸ B1+	I can scan a longer text on the topic of social groups for relevant information. **(ex. 21b)**			
LISTENING	▸▸▸ B1+	I can understand a large part of a radio programme on the topic of social groups when the delivery is relatively slow and clear. **(ex. 18b)**			
WRITING	▸▸▸ B1+	I can write an article to communicate information and ideas on a cultural topic like a book or film. **(ex. 33)**			
	▸▸▸ B1+	I can write a text to explain a problem somewhat precisely. **(ex. 15b)**			
SPEAKING	▸▸▸ B1+	I can express and exchange ideas about more abstract, cultural topics such as social groups. **(ex. 1, 3, 10, 16, 17b, 19, 27b, 30)**			
	▸▸▸ B1+	I can enter unprepared into conversation on the topic of social groups with some confidence. **(ex. 10, 17b, 28)**			
LANGUAGE	▸▸▸	I can use a wider range of suffixes to make adjectives I need.			
	▸▸▸	I can put the parts of longer, more complex sentences in the correct order.			
	▸▸▸	I can use a sufficient range of vocabulary to express myself with reasonable precision on the topic of social groups.			

One thing I learned about disabled people is …

One interaction skill I need to work on is …

Unit 08
Read all about it!

a5g8jy

In this unit you will:
- learn of a hamster's dangerous journey
- read about lucky escapes
- revise the passive voice
- write a report
- watch a video about books
- discuss what young people read

SPEAKING 1 **Talk about memes A–C in pairs. What issues do they address?**

A

B

C

D

2 **Discuss the following questions with a partner:**

1 Do you sometimes share memes on social media? Why?/Why not?
2 What are some of your favourite memes? Why do you like them? Describe them.
3 What makes a good meme?
4 What is the difference between a picture and a meme? How can you use them differently?

WRITING 3 **Create a meme by using picture D and adding your own text. Share your memes in class and vote on the best one.**

It's in the news

LANGUAGE 4 Kinds of media

Read the text below. Use the expressions in green to start a word map on 'news and the media'. Improve it with your own ideas and concrete examples (e.g. names of social media sites), then share it in class. Keep adding more words to it as you work through this unit.

L

It all started with **word of mouth**: Sharing exciting news about family members, friends or neighbours. Maybe sometimes a trader or traveller would bring fascinating stories from faraway places. Then, with the invention of the printing press, came **newspapers** as the first kind of **mass media** and with them a range of news from all over the world. As technology improved and more and more people learned to read, **magazines** and other **print media** were able to bring even more news to their readers. The 20th century saw the invention of **broadcast media**: first the **radio** and then **television**, which made it possible to see news events live, just as they were happening. Then the **internet** changed the game yet again and **media outlets** of all kinds now struggle to stay relevant in the online age. With the arrival of **social media**, it seems we have come full circle: once again it's not only professional journalists but regular people sharing news of their everyday lives.

SPEAKING 5 p. 43

Discuss the following questions in groups of three. Agree on a single sentence as your group statement for each question and share the statements with your class.

1 Why is it important to know about events happening around the world?
2 What should news media do to be interesting for a teenage audience?
3 How can you decide if you should believe something you read?

LISTENING 6 20

a **Newspaper headlines try to attract the attention of the readers and make them read the article. Read the headlines and make notes on what the stories could be about. Do they make you curious?**

A **Skywalkers in Korea cross Han Solo**

B **Escaped tiger tamed**[1]

C **Delivery man attacked by ninjas**

D **Clean getaway**[2]

b **Now listen to a radio report on three of these news stories. Put them in the order they appear.**

WRITING + SPEAKING 7

a **Rewrite the headlines as full sentences. What was removed to create a headline?**

b **Write your own news report for the one headline you didn't hear about. Record your reports and share them in class.**

[1] **tamed:** gezähmt, ungefährlich gemacht
[2] **getaway:** Flucht (*nach einer Straftat*)

READING 8 a Look at the four texts below, but only read the first sentence of each one. What problem did the people face? How could it have ended?

b Now read the whole texts about people who had a lucky escape. Choose the correct texts (A–D) for each question (1–10). You can use a text more than once. Write your answers in the boxes provided. The first one (0) has been done for you.

Text A

A passenger plane was left stuck dangerously on the side of a cliff in Turkey after it skidded off a runway. It was reported that all 162 passengers and crew on board the Boeing plane miraculously escaped, and no serious injuries were caused following the incident. Authorities have not yet worked out what led the airplane to veer off the runway shortly after landing.

Panicked passengers were evacuated from the aircraft early on Sunday after emergency services and fire crews were called to the scene. One passenger told the media they stayed inside the plane "for at least 20 minutes" waiting for help to arrive. "There was a smell of fuel inside, so we all thought the plane would explode, but thankfully it did not happen," she said. Another passenger said, "The plane had been tipped to the side, and the back was up. There was panic and people were shouting and screaming, some of them in tears." Another passenger said it was a miracle that they survived the ordeal. "The plane could have caught fire and exploded. Thank God it didn't."

Text B

A shocking sight was waiting for the owner of a house in Manchester when she returned home to find a man hanging out of her bathroom window. The man had been trying to burgle the house but got his head wedged in the small window which had been left open by the owner. Police said he was lucky to survive getting stuck around five metres above the ground. The man was freed after the fire brigade was called.

A prison sentence was given to the man at a court hearing. A police spokesman said, "It's the first time we've seen this happen. Burglars have got stuck in windows before, but they usually manage to free themselves."
A photo of the man was shared by the police to serve as a warning to the public about burglars in the area. "People think that if no ladders are left lying around, burglars can't get up. But such burglaries are common in this area, and money and jewellery are often stolen."

Text C

It has been reported that a woman in Thailand had a lucky escape after taking an unexpected swim when her bungee jump went badly wrong. According to witnesses, the distance between the bridge and the water was not measured properly before the woman was allowed to jump. The bungee rope was too long to work properly.

A TV advert was being filmed with the woman when she jumped off the bridge. However, instead of bouncing back up after her jump, her head hit the water and she was almost completely submerged. In the video clip, the woman can be seen being pushed from the platform before dropping 15 metres and hitting the water head first.

Luckily, the company's safety team were on hand and the woman was immediately pulled out of the water. She was taken to hospital after the incident, but she did not suffer any serious injuries. A complaint was made by her lawyers, who are considering whether to sue the bungee sports company for carelessness after the incident. For the moment, all jumps have been cancelled.

Text D

WORLD NEWS

A group of people on a skiing trip in Kashmir, India, got a shock when they spotted something in the snow as they skied down a steep mountain. They came across a rare snow leopard which had been hiding out of sight in the deep snow. The leopard was straight in the path of the off-piste skiers, lying camouflaged in the snow. Luckily, it was seen in time for the group to stop.

The leopard jumped out of the snow, began chasing one of the ski guides and then ran into the woods. One of the group said, "It stayed for about a minute checking us out, then a loud roar was heard and it chased the guide for a short time before running away down the slope. We weren't sure if it was going to attack us or not, so we all stood really still."

The experience left the skiers shocked as it was totally unexpected. These animals are rarely seen since the snow leopard is an endangered species, with only around 4,000 still in existence. The ski guides said that in future great care would be taken in this area.

In which news story ...

did someone nearly drown?	0	
was someone committing a crime?	1	
were people doing a risky sport?	2	3
did someone spot the danger just in time?	4	
was a large number of people saved?	5	
was a distance not measured correctly?	6	
was the fire service needed?	7	8
were people yelling and crying?	9	
did someone get stuck in a small space?	10	

0	1	2	3	4	5	6	7	8	9	10
C										

SPEAKING 9 **Think of a lucky escape you had or heard about. Make some notes, then tell a partner about it in around 90 seconds. Answer any questions your partner has after you have finished.**

LANGUAGE 10 **Crime**

p. 44

Texts B and C contain eleven expressions connected with crime, such as *police* or *court hearing*. Write them into your notebook, together with an example sentence and a translation.

LANGUAGE **11** a **The passive**

pp. 43/44

Underline all passive structures (e.g. *was left*, *had been tipped*) in the articles in 8. Can you work out the rules for how to make passive sentences from these examples? Check your ideas with *Grammar revisited*, p. 174.

b **Determine the tense used in the sentences below, then fill in the corresponding passive form on the right.**

L

1 A wild animal chased the guide down the hill. Tense: ______	The guide ______ down the hill.
2 Most people expect planes to be on time. Tense: ______	Planes ______ to be on time.
3 A teacher has called off the next school council meeting. Tense: ______	The next school council meeting ______.
4 We could have avoided the problem if we had talked about it. Tense: ______	The problem ______ if we had talked about it.
5 The woman will sue the bungee jumping company for carelessness. Tense: ______	The bungee jumping company ______ for carelessness.

→ See *Grammar revisited, The passive*, p. 174.

12 **We often use the following expressions to make passive structures:**

21

~~be supposed to~~ ▪ be told to ▪ be asked to ▪ be expected to ▪ be allowed to ▪ be required to

Listen to Dan and Hannah and complete the sentences with the expressions above in the correct tense.

1 The school magazine was supposed to come out after half-term.

2 Dan ______ move the deadline forward.

3 The magazine ______ deal with the youth group project.

4 The editorial team of the school magazine ______ fill eight pages.

5 Mark ______ write about immigration by Mr Jackson.

6 This time, the editorial team ______ use the school's copying system.

13 **Work in small groups. Take turns to describe an object in your classroom starting each sentence with 'It'. The others have to guess which object you are describing.**

Example: *It is used for …*

Media use of young people

SPEAKING 14 Take a look at your word map on media again (see exercise 4). Which kinds of media do you use regularly? Compare your results with a partner.

LANGUAGE 15 **Reading statistics**

Match the percentages to the phrases on the right.

L

1	5%	☐	a	slightly more than half
2	20%	☐	b	less than a third
3	25%	☐	c	more than three quarters
4	30%	☐	d	half
5	35%	☐	e	almost two thirds
6	45%	☐	f	less than a quarter
7	50%	☐	g	hardly anyone
8	55%	☐	h	all
9	65%	☐	i	almost half
10	70%	☐	j	almost all
11	75%	☐	k	a quarter
12	80%	☐	l	three quarters
13	90%	☐	m	less than three quarters
14	100%	☐	n	a bit more than a third

SPEAKING 16 **a** Look at the two charts below. The bar chart on the left shows social media use of US teenagers according to a survey done in 2015. The pie chart on the right is based on a survey recently done among 16-year-old students at a school in Denmark. Describe both charts using the phrases above. Then talk about them using expressions like *the majority*, *about twice as many*, *a small percentage*, *only a minority*, *one out of ten*, *approximately one fifth*, etc.

pp. 45/46

Social media use of 13- to 17-year-old US teenagers

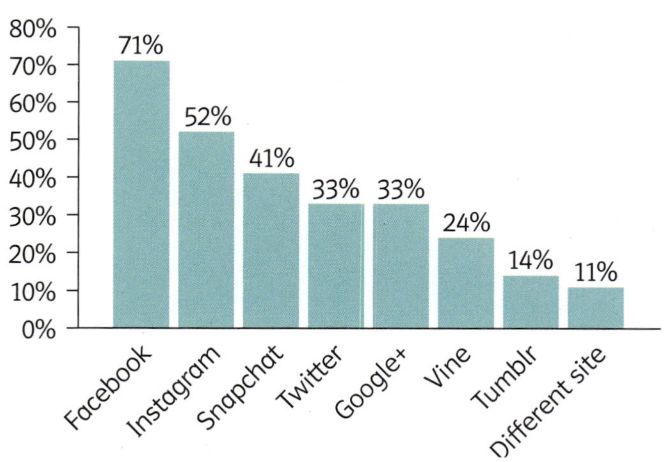

16-year-olds' favourite social media (Denmark)

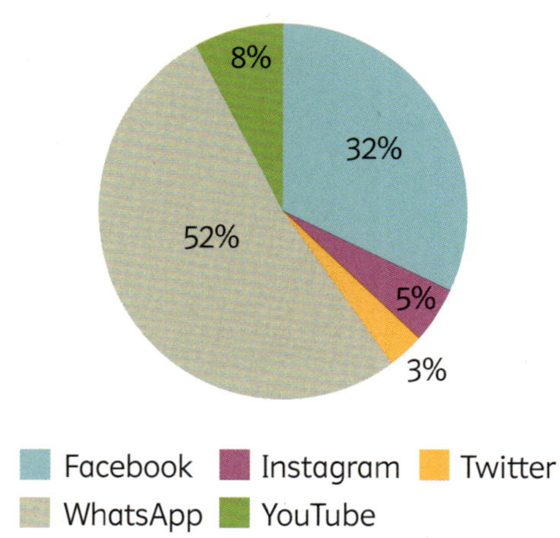

b Conduct a survey of social media use in your class. Which social media are most popular among your classmates? What are they mainly used for? Compare the results with the charts above.

STRATEGIES + WRITING **17** **a** **Writing a report**

What is a report? Find out by completing the diagram below with the words in bold given in the box.

It's written for a particular (1) ______ (e.g. an institution, a person in charge).	It presents information and (2) ______ based on research and evidence.
What is a report?	
It ends with a summary, a future outlook, or, quite often, with a (4) ______.	It has a clear (3) ______, making use of sections and headings.

S **Strategies box**

recommendation – your report helps to deal with an issue or solve a problem
audience – somebody wants your report to deal with an issue or solve a problem
structure – it makes it easy to follow the information
facts – should be to the point:
A – accurate
B – brief
C – concise

b **Study the text production features below and decide whether they are characteristic of an article (A) or a report (R). Highlight the features of reports and articles with different colours.**

p. 44

S

What is the purpose of the text?	To inform, persuade, engage, entertain the reader	A
	To write about facts, events, projects, research, etc.	R
Who reads the text?	Someone who makes decisions, often a superior or an institution	
	Readers of an (online) magazine	
What is the layout of the text like?	**From:** who is writing it **Subject:** what it is about **Date:** … Paragraphs with headings	
	Title Paragraphs	
How should the text be organised?	Catchy title Introduction – to catch the reader's attention Paragraphs Ending – gives the reader something to think about	
	Introduction – to explain the purpose of it Paragraphs (sections with headings) Conclusion – may be a summary, a recommendation or a future outlook	
What are the stylistic features of the text?	Formal, no contractions, factual, concise, to the point	
	Informal (or semi-formal), (rhetorical) questions, reader should be addressed	

→ See also *Writing coach*, *Report*, p. 180.

WRITING **18** **Read the writing prompt and the tips on the next page. Then write the report. Exchange your text with a partner. Did you write similar things?**

Your English language assistant wants to do a project on electronic media with students in your class. For this reason, he/she would like to know which electronic media are most popular among the students. You have been asked to do a survey among your classmates and hand in a report.

Students' favourite electronic media activities (n[3] = 20)

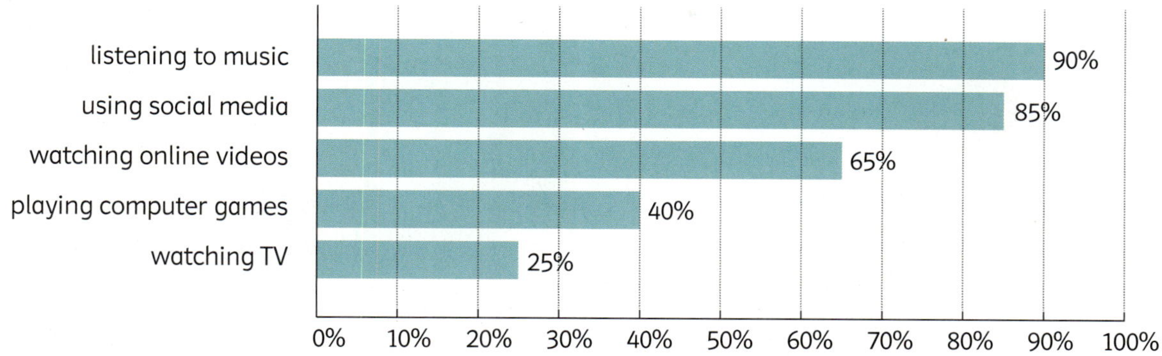

In your report you should:

- present the results of your survey
- give possible reasons for the results
- suggest what kind of media project might be successful with students in your class

Write around 250 words. Divide your report into sections and give them headings.

From: … (your name)
Subject: Ideas for the electronic media project
Date: …

This is the **layout** of a report. It has to be clear who's writing it and what it is about.

Introduction
The aim of this report is to make suggestions for the electronic media project based on students' favourite media activity.

In the **introduction**, you give details of what the report is about. You could also give details of your methods of research or the test group.

Students' favourite media activities
- Point out important information for the reader of the report. For instance, listening to music and using social media sites are more popular than watching TV.
- Use **quantifiers** (*most of the, the majority of, some of them, less than, twice as many, only a few/one third/a quarter, …*).
- Don't forget about **linking words** (*whereas, on the one/other hand, while, yet, …*).

Start each of your **paragraphs** (bullet points) with a **heading**.

Possible reasons for these results
- Explain why listening to music and using social media sites are popular. For instance, listening to music can be done easily, on their mobile …
- Use **gerunds** (*listening*), **passives** (*can be done*), **modals** (*could discuss lyrics*) and **conditionals** (*If students discuss lyrics, …*).

Recommendations for the project
- Suggest what the language assistant can do to make the project work with your classmates. For instance, discuss lyrics or ask students to give presentations, etc.

[3] **n:** number of students asked in the survey

The changing face of reading

SPEAKING 19 **Which of these pictures illustrates your reading experience best? Why? Talk in pairs.**

LANGUAGE + SPEAKING 20 Talking about books and literature

Choose the correct option to complete the questions. Then discuss them in class.

L
1 Who is your favourite e-reader / author / bestseller?
2 Would you say you are a bookworm / page-turner / printing press?
3 What's the best place to read an audiobook / e-book / address book?
4 "You can't judge a book by its dust jacket / font / cover." What does this mean?
5 Would you prefer your English textbook to only come in digital form / content / paperback?

21 **Below you can find some helpful expressions for talking about literature. Which of them are positive and which ones are more negative?**

p. 45

L
Plot: fascinating, boring, (un)realistic, predictable, frustrating ending, confusing, satisfying ending
Characters: believable, stereotyped, flawed, dynamic, well-developed, unique, unbelievable
Author's style: descriptive, lively, full of action, dull, filled with clichés, passionate, critical

SPEAKING 22 **Prepare a short presentation (about two minutes) about your favourite book. Say what it is about and why you like it so much. Persuade your audience to read it. Do your presentations in groups of four, give feedback and then choose the best one to share with the rest of the class.**

LISTENING + VIEWING 23 **Match the beginnings of the sentences with their endings. Use a dictionary to find out the meaning of the underlined words.**

1 The printing press was a real turning point
2 My family are real book lovers. We must
3 If things are easily accessible to me,
4 Many people enjoy the convenience of
5 The author almost stopped writing because
6 A beautiful cover can increase a book's
7 Young people's lives changed with the
8 It's frustrating when a novel and its sequel

a she had an argument with her publisher.
b having all their information on a computer.
c in the history of the Western world.
d advent of social media in the 2000s.
e are years apart and you have to wait for it.
f have over a thousand paperbacks on our shelves.
g appeal so that more people will buy it.
h I will probably use them too.

24 a **Before you watch the BBC video about books and reading, try to guess the answers to the questions below. Discuss them with a partner. Then watch the video to check your answers.**

BBC 04

p. 46

1 Remember from history class: When was the printing press invented?
2 Which country publishes the most books in the world per year?
3 How many paperbacks can a modern printing press produce in a month?
4 What is the 'paperback revolution'?
5 What is the name of the novel by George Orwell predicting the future?
6 What arguments for paperback books do book lovers make?

b **You are going to watch the video again. First, study the task below. Then, while watching, complete the sentences (1–7) using a maximum of four words. Write your answers in the spaces provided. The first one (0) has been done for you.**

After watching, take some time to check your answers.

0	One of the key turning points in history was the invention of the _____ .	*printing press*
1	A modern printing press can print four million _____ .	
2	The publisher *Penguin* had a huge impact on the book industry in _____ .	
3	Paperback books were successful because they _____ .	
4	Unlike a physical book, an electronic reading device can _____ .	
5	It's better to read a physical book rather than an electronic one when _____ .	
6	Reading a printed book is compared to having _____ .	
7	Books make it possible for people to communicate _____ .	

SPEAKING **25** a **Get together with a partner and come up with positive and negative sides of e-books and printed books. Take notes.**

b **Decide whether you prefer the e-book or the printed book. Do you think it makes a difference whether you read a novel or a book on cooking? Support your view with good arguments.**

LANGUAGE 26 a Genres

Match the literary genres to the book titles. There are three genres you won't need.

L

a autobiographies	c coming-of-age novels	e romance	g short stories
b crime	d fantasy	f sci-fi	h historical novels

(1) ______	(2) ______	(3) ______	(4) ______	(5) ______
▪ The Hobbit ▪ Harry Potter ▪ A Song of Ice and Fire	▪ Flawed ▪ The Outsiders ▪ The Perks of Being a Wallflower	▪ Murder on the Orient Express ▪ In Cold Blood ▪ Rebecca	▪ The Tell-Tale Heart ▪ The Necklace ▪ The Open Window	▪ Boy: Tales of Childhood ▪ The Life and Times of the Thunderbolt Kid ▪ A Street Cat Named Bob

b **Find more examples of the five categories above and the three you didn't need.**

c **Which of these books and stories do you know? Try to remember as much about them as you can and share your knowledge in class.**

d **Which of the titles that you don't know yet sound interesting to you?**

S **Strategies box**

Don't only discuss what you and your partner would like to read, **consider the other classmates** as well. Remember to support your arguments with details and examples. Draw from your own reading experience.

SPEAKING 27

***Paired activity*: Your English language assistant wants to do a reading project with your class. He/She wants to know what kind of books your class would be interested in. Discuss the options below with a partner and agree on three.**

- collection of short stories
- crime
- coming-of-age novel
- sci-fi
- fantasy

WRITING 28

Your English language assistant couldn't listen to all paired activities. For this reason, he/she has asked you to write a report on the kind of books your class would be interested in based on the results of your discussion in exercise 27.

In your report you should:

- specify what you agreed on
- give reasons for your decision
- suggest activities for the reading project

Write around 250 words. Divide your report into sections and give them headings.

→ See *Writing coach, Report*, p. 180.

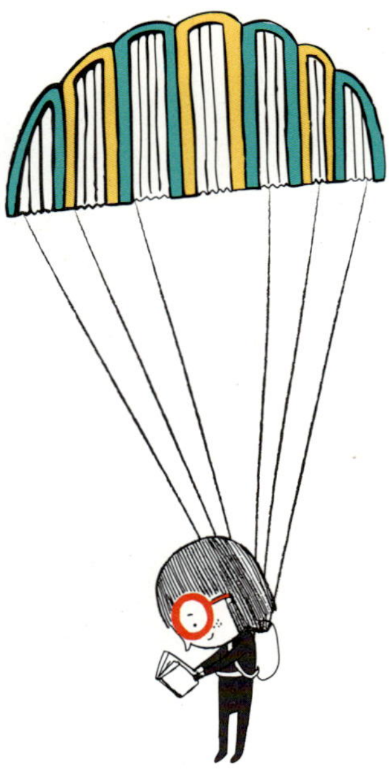

LANGUAGE **29** a **Topic vocabulary: Media and crime**

Get the word map you've made on media while working on this unit and put it on your desk. Then walk around in class and 'steal' words from your classmates' maps to improve your own.

b **Start a word map on 'crime' using the information below. Then add the words you found in the first part of this unit. When you're done, compare your maps in pairs and ask your teacher for a model.**

Categories:

L
- people
- places
- events
- actions

Expressions:

arrest sb. ▪ court of law ▪ criminal ▪ get away with sth. ▪ jail ▪ police officer ▪ prison ▪ prisoner ▪ prison sentence ▪ rob sb. ▪ punish sb.

Looking back: Learning goals of Unit 08

			✓✓	✓	!!
READING	▸▸▸ B1+	I can scan a longer text on the topic of media for relevant information. (ex. 8)			
	▸▸▸ B1+	I can compile information from several texts on the topic of media. (ex. 8)			
LISTENING	▸▸▸ B1+	I can understand straightforward factual information in clear speech on the topic of media. (ex. 6b, 12)			
	▸▸▸ B1+	I can understand a large part of a TV programme on the topic of media when the delivery is relatively slow and clear. (ex. 24b)			
WRITING	▸▸▸ B1+	I can write a report to communicate information and ideas on the topic of media. (ex. 18, 28)			
SPEAKING	▸▸▸ B1+	I can express and exchange ideas about more abstract, cultural topics such as media. (ex. 1, 5, 16, 24a, 25a)			
	▸▸▸ B1+	I can express and exchange ideas about my experiences, feelings and reactions. (ex. 2, 9, 14, 19, 22, 25b, 26c/d, 27)			
LANGUAGE	▸▸▸	I can use passive structures with reasonable precision.			
	▸▸▸	I can use a range of language to express percentages.			
	▸▸▸	I can use a sufficient range of vocabulary to express myself on the topic of media with reasonable precision.			

What I need to remember about writing reports is . . .

Printed books will/will not go out of fashion because . . .

Unit 09
Make a change!

xv5p4s

In this unit you will:
- find out about the subject 'government and politics'
- improve your linking words
- hear about new ways of organising political power
- decide if you should follow the leader
- learn about volunteering

READING + SPEAKING

1 a Read the facts below and guess which countries they are about.

Brazil ▪ the USA ▪ Iraq ▪ South Africa ▪ New Zealand ▪ China ▪ India

Who knew?

A
Since 2001 it has been a custom for the president of ______ to 'pardon' a turkey, which means that this particular turkey gets a name and is not going to end up on the traditional Thanksgiving dinner table.

B
The first black president of ______, Nelson Mandela, spent 27 years in prison considered a terrorist.

C
In 2003, then US president George W. Bush was holding a speech in ______, when suddenly a reporter got up and started throwing his shoes at him as a sign of protest.

D
The country of ______ has had debates about changing its flag, which looks too similar to its neighbouring island's flag. In 2016 the country held a public flag design competition and received 10,000 suggestions.

E
About one third of the world's population live in the two countries ______ and ______.

F
______ has a long-standing tradition of introducing mock-candidates in their elections. The most famous one was a rhinoceros which was voted into the city council of São Paulo in 1959.

b Research some more 'fun facts' about politics at home and make one up. Then present them to your class and let your classmates guess which ones are real and which ones are fake.

Who should lead us?

SPEAKING 2 **Read the statements and work on tasks 1–3 with a partner.**

1 What opinions are expressed below? Put them in your own words.
2 Do you agree or disagree with the statements? Give reasons.

A I think it's sad many students don't take the **election** of the **class representative** or the **head student** seriously. Good **candidates** can really make a difference in school!

B Young people today have more influence on who will be in **government** than ever before. Here in Austria, we can **vote** for a **party** as soon as we turn 16.

C I have no idea who the **mayor** or the **president** is. It doesn't have anything to do with me or my life.

D **Politicians** should do more to make young people interested in **politics**. Does it have to be so boring?

LANGUAGE 3 **a** Talking about politics

Take turns explaining the expressions in green to your partner. Can he/she guess the expressions?

p. 47

b **Start a word map on 'politics' with the expressions from above.**

c **Match the parts to make expressions dealing with politics. You can use most of the parts more than once. Make sure you know what the expressions mean.**

L

1 to hold	a a town/city/country
2 to elect	b vote
3 to vote for	c a leader
4 to come to	d (a) mayor
5 to register to	e a council meeting
6 to be in	f the majority
7 to have	g an election
8 to become	h power
9 to run	i a party
	j an agreement
	k (an) office

d **Now work with a partner to think of more words connected with politics. Look up the English words if you don't know them. Share your results in class and use them to improve your word map.**

SPEAKING 4 **Would you like to have a subject at school that only deals with politics? What would you expect to learn there? Discuss your ideas with a partner and share them in class.**

LANGUAGE IN USE 5 **Read the article that Hannah wrote for the school magazine at Whitehall. Some words are missing. Choose the correct answer (A, B, C or D) for each gap (1–10). Put a cross (☒) in the correct box. The first one (0) has been done for you.**

SCHOOL

Why choose 'government and politics'?

Like all of us in Year 11, in addition to our GCSE worries, I now have to decide on the range of subjects to choose for my A levels. I can tell you, this is not an easy **(0)** ______, but I've finally made up my mind on one subject I'm going to take: government and politics.

I think the deciding point for me was the last **(1)** ______, when I felt rather excluded. My feelings were probably shared by a lot of other young people who were not old enough to vote. Another problem of course was the fact that many young people simply did not care about casting their votes. I was really worried that older, rather disgruntled people were deciding over my fate as a future **(2)** ______ of the UK and was quite disappointed by the result. The party that won will be making big decisions that will change my life, yet I know nothing about these people and how the system works.

Another thing that got me going was the fact that I found out, through relatives living on the Continent[1], that electoral systems differ from country to country. I think it's interesting how most Western **(3)** ______, even though they stress that they are exactly that – a democracy – have different systems of **(4)** ______. In Britain, we are used to electing somebody who represents us directly in Parliament, our 'MP', but this is not the case in other countries where people **(5)** ______ for a party, not a person. There are countries where the president is just a symbolic head of state, a bit like our Queen – or King –, and there are countries where he or she is the most powerful person in the **(6)** ______, like in France or the US.

I've always been interested in finding out how society works, why some people have more power or wealth than others and how we could achieve a more just balance. I'm also interested in the different **(7)** ______. Communism, for example, on paper looks really good, so I'm hoping to find out why it failed so spectacularly in Europe. And I'm wondering why, in a world that is starting to be really small, people focus on nationality more than global citizenship. I think if more young people became interested in **(8)** ______ on their own, and not just vote, if they vote at all, for the same party their parents vote for, politicians might be a little less comfortable and a little more on edge when it comes to pushing through reforms, and that would be a good thing.

All this I'm hoping to understand by the time I have finished my A levels. It doesn't mean that I'll love politics, but it will let me participate fully and hopefully meaningfully in the **(9)** ______ processes of this country. It will still be difficult to decide who to vote for once I've reached **(10)** ______ age, but at least it's going to be an informed decision.

14

[1]**the Continent:** the mainland/continent of Europe except for the British Isles

0	A decision ☒	B idea ☐	C step ☐	D option ☐
1	A election ☐	B poll ☐	C elections ☐	D votes ☐
2	A participant ☐	B citizen ☐	C native ☐	D member ☐
3	A democracy ☐	B country ☐	C democracies ☐	D states ☐
4	A parties ☐	B elections ☐	C representation ☐	D politics ☐
5	A stand ☐	B decide ☐	C vote ☐	D elect ☐
6	A world ☐	B parties ☐	C politics ☐	D government ☐
7	A ideologies ☐	B states ☐	C parties ☐	D societies ☐
8	A policies ☐	B politicians ☐	C participation ☐	D politics ☐
9	A decision ☐	B political ☐	C citizen ☐	D democrat ☐
10	A mature ☐	B voting ☐	C driving ☐	D school ☐

SPEAKING 6 **Discuss Hannah's article in small groups. Talk about the following questions:**

1 What are her reasons for choosing the subject 'government and politics'?
2 What do you think about her decision? Do you agree with her? Why?/Why not?
3 Should students be allowed to choose if they want to learn about politics or not? Give reasons.

LANGUAGE 7 a **Linking devices – part 1**

p. 47

Linking devices are used to mark relationships between ideas, sentences or parts of sentences. They are also used to connect paragraphs within a text. Match the explanations on the left with the examples on the right.

L

1 You have given some information and want to **add more information.**
2 You have made a statement and want to **give a reason** for it.
3 You want to **arrange** your ideas **in a logical order.**
4 You have made a statement and want to **support it with an example.**

a *for instance, such as, namely, in other words, …*
b *also, moreover, apart from, besides, furthermore, … too, …*
c *because, since, …*
d *first (of all), secondly, then, finally, next, another idea, also, in conclusion, to summarise, lastly, to sum it up, …*

b **What other linking devices can you find in Hannah's article?**

WRITING 8 **As Whitehall's school magazine is also published in electronic form, readers are invited to leave comments on articles. You have decided to comment on the 2nd paragraph (the paragraph starting with "I think the deciding point for me…").**

p. 48

In your comment you should:

- say how you feel about older people deciding on the future of your country
- explain whether it is a good idea that Austrians are allowed to vote at 16
- suggest how young people can be motivated to vote in elections

Write around 250 words.

SPEAKING 9 If you were the mayor of your town, what would you change and why? Write down three changes and find good arguments why they should be made. Then get together with another student and discuss your ideas. Agree on one change you would both like to see.

p. 50

LISTENING 10 Read the information below, then discuss it with a partner. What do you think of this idea?

p. 49

US political scientist Benjamin Barber has a radical idea. He says that today's problems, such as climate change, terrorism and poverty, cannot be solved by politicians of nation states or traditional international organisations. He argues that cities and the mayors who run them are much more likely to succeed if they can work together and take responsibility for the larger issues. Barber proposes a 'World Parliament of Mayors' in which the world's cities work together to improve the situation for everyone.

11 a You are going to listen to an FM4 interview with Benjamin Barber. Write down three questions you have about his ideas. Then listen to the interview. Does he answer any of them? What does he say?

radio FM4

22

b You are going to listen to the interview again. First, study the task below. Then, while listening, answer the questions (1–8) using a maximum of four words. Write your answers in the spaces provided. The first one (0) has been done for you.

After listening, take some time to check your answers.

0	What part of the world's population lives in cities?	the majority
1	Why can't mayors solve the big problems now?	
2	What are mayors like, in Barber's opinion?	
3	Which group of people do mayors have to work with? (Give one answer.)	
4	What does Barber say the world is like today?	
5	What percentage of the US population lives in cities?	
6	What should cities fight for?	
7	What percentage of the US population are white people?	
8	Who controls the world, in Barber's opinion?	

SPEAKING 12 Collect Barber's ideas on the board and discuss them in class. Do you think a class from a school that is in a different area of Austria – a city or the countryside – would agree with you?

WRITING 13 Do you agree that cities and their mayors should have more influence in politics? Write a PEEL paragraph of around 100 words on your opinion.

→ See *PEEL revisited*, p. 93.

Being a leader

SPEAKING 14 **Can you think of a person you'd say is a good leader? Maybe an athlete, a politician, a teacher or a class representative? Describe him/her to a partner and convince your partner of your choice.**

LANGUAGE 15 The qualities of a leader

p. 49

Which of these qualities do you think a leader should/should not have? What would you add?

L

To be ...

a good communicator ▪ a risk taker ▪ calm under pressure ▪ caring ▪ creative ▪ decisive ▪ fair ▪ good-looking ▪ honest ▪ manipulative ▪ open-minded ▪ respectful ▪ self-confident ▪ strong ▪ trustworthy

READING 16 a **In the classic novel *Lord of the Flies* by William Golding, a group of schoolboys become stranded on a deserted island. In the extract below, the boys choose a leader. Which qualities does Ralph show that make him a good leader?**

Merridew turned to Ralph.

"Aren't there any grownups?"

"No."

Merridew sat down on a trunk and looked round the circle.

"Then we'll have to look after ourselves."

[...]

"We've got to decide about being rescued."

There was a buzz. One of the small boys, Henry, said that he wanted to go home.

"Shut up," said Ralph absently. He lifted the conch[2]. "Seems to me we ought to have a chief to decide things."

"A chief! A chief!"

"I ought to be chief," said Jack with simple arrogance, "because I'm chapter chorister and head boy[3]. I can sing C sharp."

Another buzz.

"Well then," said Jack, "I –"

He hesitated. The dark boy, Roger, stirred at last and spoke up.

"Let's have a vote."

"Yes!"

"Vote for chief!"

Let's vote –"

[...] Jack started to protest but the clamour changed from the general wish for a chief to an election by acclaim[4] of Ralph himself. None of the boys could have found good reason for this; what intelligence had been shown was traceable to Piggy while the most obvious leader was Jack. But there was a stillness about Ralph as he sat that marked him out: there was his size, and attractive appearance; and most obscurely, yet most powerfully, there was the conch. The being that had blown that, had sat waiting for them on the platform with the delicate thing balanced on his knees, was set apart.

"Him with the shell."

"Ralph! Ralph!"

"Let him be chief with the trumpet-thing."

Ralph raised a hand for silence.

"All right. Who wants Jack for chief?"

With dreary[5] obedience the choir raised their hands.

"Who wants me?"

[2] **conch:** Gehäuse einer Meeresschnecke, Trompetenmuschel
[3] **head boy:** Schulsprecher
[4] **by acclaim:** durch (öffentliche) Abstimmung
[5] **dreary:** gelangweilt, unglücklich

Every hand outside the choir except Piggy's was raised immediately.

Then Piggy, too, raised his hand grudgingly[6] into the air.

Ralph counted.

"I'm chief then."

The circle of boys broke into applause. Even the choir applauded; and the freckles on Jack's face disappeared under a blush of mortification. He started up, then changed his mind and sat down again while the air rang.

b Later in the novel, Ralph's leadership is challenged by Jack, who has become a violent and dangerous hunter. Does Jack show different qualities? Read on and see for yourself.

The boys ranged themselves in rows on the grass before him but Ralph and Piggy stayed a foot lower, standing on the soft sand. Jack ignored them for the moment, turned his mask down to the seated boys and pointed at them with the spear.

"Who's going to join my tribe?"

Ralph made a sudden movement that became a stumble. Some of the boys turned toward him.

"I gave you food," said Jack, "and my hunters will protect you from the beast. Who will join my tribe?"

"I'm chief," said Ralph, "because you chose me. And we were going to keep the fire going. Now you run after food –"

"You ran yourself!" shouted Jack. "Look at that bone in your hands!"

Ralph went crimson[7].

"I said you were hunters. That was your job."

Jack ignored him again.

"Who'll join my tribe and have fun?"

"I'm chief," said Ralph tremulously. "And what about the fire? And I've got the conch."

"You haven't got it with you," said Jack, sneering.

"You left it behind. See, clever? And the conch doesn't count at this end of the island –"

All at once the thunder struck. Instead of the dull boom there was a point of impact in the explosion.

"The conch counts here too," said Ralph, "and all over the island."

"What are you going to do about it then?"

Ralph examined the ranks of boys. There was no help in them and he looked away, confused and sweating. Piggy whispered.

"The fire – rescue."

"Who'll join my tribe?"

"I will."

"Me."

"I will."

"I'll blow the conch," said Ralph breathlessly, "and call an assembly."

"We shan't hear it."

Piggy touched Ralph's wrist.

"Come away. There's going to be trouble.

c Now compare the leadership qualities of Ralph and Jack. Who would you rather have as a leader? Discuss your ideas with a partner and try to come to an agreement.

WRITING 17 **What do you think will happen next? Write the next 200 words of the story. Then get together in groups of four and share your texts.**

SPEAKING 18 **Can you think of any films or books in which one of the characters is a good leader? Prepare to give a short description of the character and his/her actions in the story. How can you tell they are a good leader? Then work in pairs and present the character to each other.**

---

[6] **grudgingly:** widerwillig
[7] **crimson:** dunkelrot

LANGUAGE 19

p. 47

Linking devices – part 2

Match the explanations on the left with the examples on the right.
Choose one phrase from each group and use it in the speaking task below.

L

1 You have given some information and want to **point out the result or the consequence** that follows.
2 You want to make a **general statement.**
3 You have made a **statement** and want to **contrast it with another statement.**
4 You want to **compare two ideas.**

a *not only – but also, compared to, just like, also, both, either – or, neither – nor, instead, in contrast to, …*
b *on the whole, as a rule, in most cases, usually, generally, in general, …*
c *so, as a result, therefore, consequently, this means that, for this reason, so that, as a consequence, that is why, …*
d *but, although, even though, however, nevertheless, while, whereas, despite, in spite of the fact, …*

SPEAKING 20

***Individual long turn*: Do this task with a partner. One person compares pictures A, the other one compares pictures B. Both of you talk about the other two bullet points as well. Give each other feedback.**

A

B

- Compare the pictures.
- Point out what a successful leader should be like.
- Explain who you would consider to be a good leader.

Volunteering

SPEAKING 21 **Look at the pictures below and talk about the following questions with a partner:**

1 What are the people in the pictures doing?
2 How many charitable organisations and/or activities can you name?
3 Can you imagine helping any of them? Why?/Why not?

LISTENING 22 23

a Listen to the different people talking about their volunteering experience. Which of the speakers goes with which picture?

A

B

C

b You are going to listen to the people again. First, study the task below. Then, while listening, match the speakers with their statements (A–J). There are two extra statements that you should not use. Write your answers in the boxes provided. The first one (0) has been done for you.

After listening, take some time to check your answers.

D
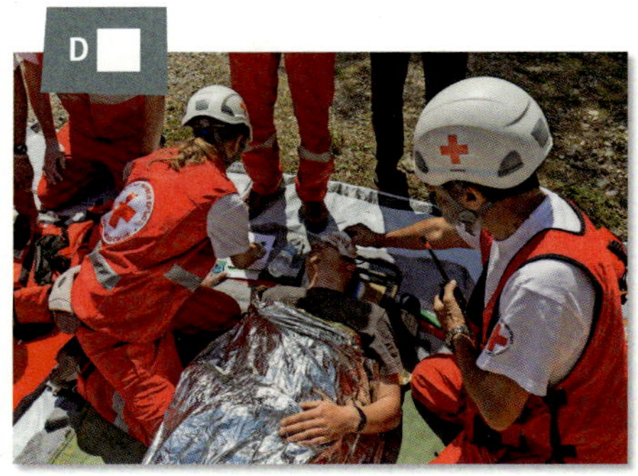

Speaker 1 – Emily	0	1
Speaker 2 – Jacob	2	3
Speaker 3 – Greg	4	5
Speaker 4 – Lizzie	6	7

A	I'm also interested in another project.	F	I looked after other people's children.
B	My mother made me start this job.	G	I'm really into sports.
C	An event got me started in this activity.	H	A friend introduced me to this activity.
D	I'm learning some useful skills.	I	Saturday is when I usually study for school.
E	I taught the kids some important things.	J	I made sure people had enough to drink.

0	1	2	3	4	5	6	7
F							

SPEAKING 23 **Look at the pictures in exercise 22 again. What might have happened before and after the pictures were taken? Make up some stories.**

LANGUAGE 24 a Articles – and when *not* to use them

p. 49

You already know how to use articles in English. Explain how they are used in these examples:

1 In picture B, people are building **a** house.
2 **The** people in picture C are handing out food.
3 **An** event got me started in my job.

b Knowing when *not* to use an article can be tricky because some of the rules for this case are different to German. Translate the sentences below to see the difference:

1 I spend a lot of time at school. ☐
2 Volunteers are building a house on Market Street. ☐
3 I came here by car. ☐
4 The most important thing in my life is art. ☐

c Study the rules on when not to use an article below. Match them to the examples above.

L

You do *not* use an article with:
a plural nouns or uncountable nouns expressing general ideas (*in nature*)
b many names of countries, towns, streets or mountains (*on Mount Everest*)
c nouns for certain places, when talking about the purpose you use them for (*in court*)
d nouns for some forms of transport (*on foot*)

→ See *Grammar revisited, Articles*, p. 174.

25 a Cross out the wrong articles in the sentences below. Explain why they are wrong.

1 The injured man was quickly taken to ~~the~~ hospital.
→ *It's not about the hospital as a building, but about what they do there (the purpose).*
2 Did the schoolboys get to the island by the boat?
3 Ralph and Jack fight for the control of the group.
4 My brother is a volunteer firefighter in the town.
5 A new soup kitchen has opened on the Abbey Road.
6 We read the book *Lord of the Flies* together in the class.
7 Problems like the climate change can only be solved by working together.
8 I generally go to the bed far too late.

b Which two sentences go together and why?

1 Robert and Marie first met at college.
2 Robert and Marie first met at the college.

a There were lots of good coffee shops nearby.
b They were both studying biology at the time.

26 Use each of the words below in a sentence. Think carefully about whether you need an article, this will depend on the sentence you write. Check your sentences with your teacher.

a education
b Oxford Street
c bike
d university

WRITING 27

The English language assistant at your school is involved in a WWF project to clear the woods surrounding your area from plastic waste. He/She is looking for volunteers to help and wants to know how to best motivate the students at your school to support this project. You have decided to do a survey and hand in a report.

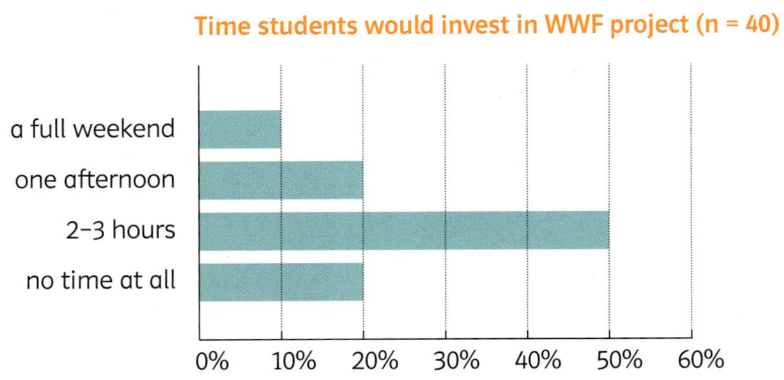

In your report you should:

- describe the results of your survey
- give possible reasons for the results
- suggest ways to motivate students to help with the WWF project

Write around 250 words. Divide your report into sections and give them headings.

→ See *Writing coach, Report*, p. 180.

LANGUAGE 28

Topic vocabulary: Politics and leaders

***Word families.* Complete the table below.**

Noun (person)	Noun (idea/concept)	Verb	Adjective
	politics	–	
		volunteer	
		–	democratic
–		elect	
			voting/voted
	leadership		
–			successful
	communication		

29 a **Share your word maps on politics in class and add as many words as possible to your own.**

b **Sort the adjectives below into pairs of opposites.**

> **L** attractive ▪ calm ▪ caring ▪ close-minded ▪ decisive ▪ dishonest ▪ disrespectful ▪ emotional ▪ honest ▪ indecisive ▪ open-minded ▪ respectful ▪ self-confident ▪ self-conscious ▪ strong ▪ unattractive ▪ uncaring ▪ weak

c **Which of the adjectives apply to good and which to bad leaders? Some could go into both categories.**

Looking back: Learning goals of Unit 09

			✓✓	✓	!!
READING	▸▸▸ B1+	I can identify the main conclusions in a clearly signalled argumentative text. (ex. 6)			
	▸▸▸ B1+	I can compile information from several literary texts. (ex. 16a/b/c)			
LISTENING	▸▸▸ B1+	I can distinguish between main points and supporting detail in clear speech on the topic of politics. (ex. 11b, 22a/b)			
	▸▸▸ B1+	I can understand a large part of a radio programme on the topic of politics when the delivery is relatively slow and clear. (ex. 11b)			
WRITING	▸▸▸ B1+	I can write straightforward connected texts to describe feelings and reactions on the topic of politics. (ex. 8, 13, 17)			
	▸▸▸ B1+	I can write a report to explain a problem somewhat precisely. (ex. 27)			
SPEAKING	▸▸▸ B1+	I can express and exchange ideas about more abstract, cultural topics such as politics. (ex. 2, 4, 6, 12, 20, 21)			
	▸▸▸ B1+	I can express and exchange ideas about my experiences, feelings and reactions. (ex. 4, 6, 9, 14, 18, 21)			
LANGUAGE	▸▸▸	I can use a range of linking devices to structure texts with reasonable precision.			
	▸▸▸	I can use articles with reasonable precision.			
	▸▸▸	I can use a sufficient range of vocabulary to express myself on the topic of politics with reasonable precision.			

I would make a great leader because ...

Three linking devices I will use from now on are ...

Literature along the way

The Lottery

by Shirley Jackson

1 **What comes to mind when you hear the word 'lottery'? Take one minute to write down all the things it makes you think of. Then compare your list with a partner. Which words do you have in common?**

2 **Read the first extract from a short story called 'The Lottery' by Shirley Jackson, an American writer (1916–1965). Discuss these questions with a partner:**

1 Where and when does the story take place?
2 How do you think the story is going to continue? Will it have a good or bad ending? Underline all the expressions that make you think it will have a good ending in blue, and the ones that make you think the ending might be bad in red. Compare what you've underlined with your partner.

The morning of June 27th was clear and sunny, with the fresh warmth of a full-summer day; the flowers were blossoming profusely[1] and the grass was richly green. The people of the village began to gather in the square, between the post office and the bank, around ten o'clock; in some towns there were so many people that the lottery took two days [...], but in this village, where there were only about three hundred people, the whole lottery took less than two hours, so it could begin at ten o'clock in the morning and still be through in time to allow the villagers to get home for noon dinner.

The children assembled first, of course. School was recently over for the summer, and the feeling of liberty sat uneasily on most of them; they tended to gather together quietly for a while before they broke into boisterous[2] play, and their talk was still of the classroom and the teacher, of books and reprimands. Bobby Martin had already stuffed his pockets full of stones, and the other boys soon followed his example, selecting the smoothest and roundest stones; Bobby and Harry Jones and Dickie Delacroix [...] eventually made a great pile of stones in one corner of the square and guarded it against the raids of the other boys. The girls stood aside, talking among themselves, looking over their shoulders at the boys, and the very small children rolled in the dust or clung to the hands of their older brothers or sisters.

Soon the men began to gather, surveying their own children, speaking of planting and rain, tractors and taxes. They stood together, away from the pile of stones in the corner, and their jokes were quiet and they smiled rather than laughed. The women, wearing faded house dresses and sweaters, came shortly after their menfolk. They greeted one another and exchanged bits of gossip as they went to join their husbands. Soon the women, standing by their husbands, began to call to their children, and the children came reluctantly[3], having to be called four or five times. Bobby Martin ducked under his mother's grasping hand and ran, laughing, back to the pile of stones. His father spoke up sharply, and Bobby came quickly and took his place between his father and his oldest brother.

[1] **profuse:** übermäßig, üppig
[2] **boisterous:** wild, laut, übermütig
[3] **reluctant:** widerwillig

The lottery was conducted – as were the square dances, the teen club, the Halloween program – by Mr. Summers, who had time and energy to devote to civic activities. He was a round-faced, jovial[4] man and he ran the coal business, and people were sorry for him, because he had no children and his wife was a scold[5].

When he arrived in the square, carrying the black wooden box, there was a murmur of conversation among the villagers, and he waved and called. "Little late today, folks." The postmaster, Mr. Graves, followed him, carrying a three-legged stool, and the stool was put in the center of the square and Mr. Summers set the black box down on it. The villagers kept their distance, leaving a space between themselves and the stool, and when Mr. Summers said, "Some of you fellows want to give me a hand?" there was a hesitation[6] before two men, Mr. Martin and his oldest son, Baxter, came forward to hold the box steady on the stool while Mr. Summers stirred up the papers inside it.

3 **The author singles out one character, Mrs Hutchinson, in the next two paragraphs. Write down three details that you think stress the 'normality' of the situation, and three details that make you feel a bit uneasy.**

Just as Mr. Summers finally left off talking and turned to the assembled[7] villagers, Mrs. Hutchinson came hurriedly along the path to the square, her sweater thrown over her shoulders, and slid into place in the back of the crowd. "Clean forgot what day it was," she said to Mrs. Delacroix, who stood next to her, and they both laughed softly. "Thought my old man was out back stacking wood," Mrs. Hutchinson went on, "and then I looked out the window and the kids was gone, and then I remembered it was the twenty-seventh and came a-running." She dried her hands on her apron, and Mrs. Delacroix said, "You're in time, though. They're still talking away up there."

Mrs. Hutchinson craned her neck to see through the crowd and found her husband and children standing near the front. She tapped Mrs. Delacroix on the arm as a farewell and began to make her way through the crowd. The people separated good-humoredly to let her through: two or three people said, in voices just loud enough to be heard across the crowd, "Here comes your Missus, Hutchinson," and "Bill, she made it after all." Mrs. Hutchinson reached her husband, and Mr. Summers, who had been waiting, said cheerfully, "Thought we were going to have to get on without you, Tessie." Mrs. Hutchinson said, grinning, "Wouldn't have me leave m'dishes in the sink, now, would you, Joe?" and soft laughter ran through the crowd as the people stirred back into position after Mrs. Hutchinson's arrival.

4 **In the story, the lottery now proceeds with every head of family taking a piece of paper out of the black box. Read the next paragraphs and make a list of the words and phrases that describe the atmosphere and compare it with a partner. Then finish reading the extract.**

A sudden hush fell on the crowd[8] as Mr. Summers cleared his throat and looked at the list. "All ready?" he called. "Now, I'll read the names – heads of families first – and the men come up and take a paper out of the box. Keep the paper folded in your hand without looking at it until everyone has had a turn. Everything clear?"

The people had done it so many times that they only half listened to the directions: most of them were quiet, wetting their lips, not looking around. Then Mr. Summers raised one hand high and said, "Adams." A man disengaged himself from the crowd and came forward. "Hi, Steve." Mr. Summers said,

---

[4] **jovial:** heiter, fröhlich
[5] **scold:** zänkisches Weib, (Haus-)Drachen
[6] **hesitation:** Zögern, Unentschlossenheit
[7] **assembled:** versammelt
[8] **A sudden hush fell on the crowd:** Die Menge verstummte schlagartig

and Mr. Adams said, "Hi, Joe." They grinned at one another humorlessly and nervously. Then Mr. Adams reached into the black box and took out a folded paper. He held it firmly by one corner as he turned and went hastily back to his place in the crowd, where he stood a little apart from his family, not looking down at his hand. […]

With the last name, "Zanini", the lottery is finished.

After that, there was a long pause, a breathless pause, until Mr. Summers, holding his slip of paper in the air, said, "All right, fellows." For a minute, no one moved, and then all the slips of paper were opened. Suddenly, all the women began to speak at once, saying, "Who is it?," "Who's got it?," "Is it the Dunbars?," "Is it the Watsons?" Then the voices began to say, "It's Hutchinson. It's Bill," "Bill Hutchinson's got it."

5 **What do you think Bill Hutchinson has got? Write an ending to the story and compare the different versions in class. Then read the actual ending of the story below.**

People began to look around to see the Hutchinsons. Bill Hutchinson was standing quiet, staring down at the paper in his hand. Suddenly, Tessie Hutchinson shouted to Mr. Summers. "You didn't give him time enough to take any paper he wanted. I saw you. It wasn't fair!"

"Be a good sport, Tessie." Mrs. Delacroix called, and Mrs. Graves said, "All of us took the same chance."

"Shut up, Tessie," Bill Hutchinson said. […]

"How many kids, Bill?" Mr. Summers asked formally.

"Three," Bill Hutchinson said. "There's Bill, Jr., and Nancy, and little Dave. And Tessie and me."

"All right, then," Mr. Summers said. "Harry, you got their tickets back?"

Mr. Graves nodded and held up the slips of paper. "Put them in the box, then," Mr. Summers directed. "Take Bill's and put it in."

"I think we ought to start over," Mrs. Hutchinson said, as quietly as she could. "I tell you it wasn't fair. You didn't give him time enough to choose. Everybody saw that."

Mr. Graves had selected the five slips and put them in the box, and he dropped all the papers but those onto the ground, where the breeze caught them and lifted them off.

"Listen, everybody," Mrs. Hutchinson was saying to the people around her.

"Ready, Bill?" Mr. Summers asked, and Bill Hutchinson, with one quick glance around at his wife and children, nodded.

"Remember," Mr. Summers said, "take the slips and keep them folded until each person has taken one. Harry, you help little Dave." Mr. Graves took the hand of the little boy, who came willingly with him up to the box. "Take a paper out of the box, Davy," Mr. Summers said. Davy put his hand into the box and laughed. "Take just one paper," Mr. Summers said. "Harry, you hold it for him." Mr. Graves took the child's hand and removed the folded paper from the tight fist and held it while little Dave stood next to him and looked up at him wonderingly.

"Nancy next," Mr. Summers said. Nancy was twelve, and her school friends breathed heavily as she went forward switching her skirt, and took a slip daintily from the box. "Bill, Jr.," Mr. Summers said, and Billy, his face red and his feet overlarge, near knocked the box over as he got a paper out. "Tessie," Mr. Summers said. She hesitated for a minute, looking around defiantly, and then set her lips and went up to the box. She snatched a paper out and held it behind her.

"Bill," Mr. Summers said, and Bill Hutchinson reached into the box and felt around, bringing his hand out at last with the slip of paper in it.

The crowd was quiet. A girl whispered, "I hope it's not Nancy," and the sound of the whisper reached the edges of the crowd. […]

"All right," Mr. Summers said. "Open the papers. Harry, you open little Dave's."

Mr. Graves opened the slip of paper and there was a general sigh through the crowd as he held it up and everyone could see that it was blank. Nancy and Bill, Jr., opened theirs at the same time, and both beamed and laughed, turning around to the crowd and holding their slips of paper above their heads.

"Tessie," Mr. Summers said. There was a pause, and then Mr. Summers looked at Bill Hutchinson, and Bill unfolded his paper and showed it. It was blank.

"It's Tessie," Mr. Summers said, and his voice was hushed. "Show us her paper, Bill."

Bill Hutchinson went over to his wife and forced the slip of paper out of her hand. It had a black spot on it, the black spot Mr. Summers had made the night before with the heavy pencil in the coal company office. Bill Hutchinson held it up, and there was a stir in the crowd.

"All right, folks," Mr. Summers said. "Let's finish quickly."

Although the villagers had forgotten the ritual and lost the original black box, they still remembered to use stones. The pile of stones the boys had made earlier was ready; there were stones on the ground with the blowing scraps of paper that had come out of the box. […] And someone gave little Davy Hutchinson a few pebbles.

Tessie Hutchinson was in the center of a cleared space by now, and she held her hands out desperately as the villagers moved in on her. "It isn't fair," she said. A stone hit her on the side of the head. Old Man Warner was saying, "Come on, come on, everyone." Steve Adams was in the front of the crowd of villagers, with Mrs. Graves beside him.

"It isn't fair, it isn't right," Mrs. Hutchinson screamed, and then they were upon her.

6 Talk about the following questions in class.

1 Should traditions always be continued? In the story, nobody questions what is happening.
2 What do you think the author's attitude towards tradition and change was? What in the story makes you think this?
3 What strikes you about the names the author uses?
4 Which of these statements best summarises the story for you?
  a Traditions should not be followed uncritically.
  b Groups may be wrong in their decisions.
  c People should stand up to authority when authority is wrong.
  d Everybody is capable of evil under pressure and needs to fight against this.

7 Choose one of these activities to do in class or at home.

1 Imagine you are a tourist from Mars. What would you write about this 'lottery' in a letter home?
2 Think of three questions you would like to ask Ms Jackson, the author, in an interview. Do some research on her on the internet and write her answers.
3 Watch a YouTube video about the story and write a summary of it for your classmates.
4 Work in groups to create a poster on 'The Lottery'. You can include information on the author, the public's reaction to the story when it was published in 1948, your own and your classmates' opinion about it, follow-ups (films, series), books with similar content – and anything else you can think of.

Unit 10
Bigger, better, faster, stronger

k8z22e

In this unit you will:
- learn more about your body
- find help at the doctor's
- consider the pros and cons of self-driving cars
- speculate how AI will change our future

SPEAKING 1 **What inventions and discoveries do the unit title and the box above make you think of? Make a list and share it with a partner. Then discuss how and why these inventions and discoveries have changed our world.**

2 a Compare the nature of a human being (e.g. emotional, warm, ...) to the nature of a robot (rational, cold, ...).

b Discuss whether a human or a robot would be of more help in the following situations:

a picking out a nice outfit
b improving your grades at school
c moving to a new house or flat
d helping you when you are ill
e travelling to a foreign country
f cheering you up when you're feeling down

c Think of more situations in which either a robot or a human being might be helpful. Give reasons for your choices.

Ouch!

LANGUAGE 3 **Body parts**

Match the words from the box to the body parts (a–r) on p. 132.

L ankle ▪ cheek ▪ chest ▪ chin ▪ elbow ▪ eyebrow ▪ forehead ▪ heel ▪ hip ▪ jaw ▪ knee ▪ shin ▪ shoulder ▪ stomach ▪ thigh ▪ thumb ▪ waist ▪ wrist

READING 4 **Read the article about health below. Which facts do you find the most interesting?**

p. 52

How your body works

Your brain

You might make jokes about your brain not working properly, but did you know that by the age of eighteen your brain stops **growing**? From that age onward it starts losing more than 1,000 brain cells every day. The typical brain weighs only about 1.4 kg, but it can come up with almost 50,000 thoughts in a day! Some people **suffer** a loss of blood supply to the brain, possibly **resulting** in a **stroke**. This is a serious condition and needs immediate medical treatment. If you get thirsty and become too **dehydrated**, this can **affect** brain function and cause **headaches**. Your brain works continuously and never rests, even when you're asleep.

Your heart

Did you know that on average your heart **beats** 40 million times per year? Over your lifetime that adds up to two billion, six hundred million heartbeats **pumping** between 5 and 7 litres of blood per minute – that's over 7,000 litres per day. **Heart disease** is the world number one cause of death, and an unhealthy lifestyle, poor diet and being overweight can lead to a **heart attack**. However, with modern treatment nowadays many people **recover**.

Your lungs

Whilst the heart pumps your blood around, your **lungs** transport oxygen from the air you **breathe** into your bloodstream and take away carbon dioxide. An average person breathes in around 11,000 litres of air every day. We all know that **smoking** can cause **lung cancer**, but it can cause other lung diseases too, such as **emphysema**, so it makes sense for smokers to quit! **Asthma** is a common disease that affects the lungs. Asthma attacks happen when your airways narrow, and this makes **breathing in** air more difficult.

Your liver

The liver is a truly remarkable organ as it has the ability to grow back almost completely if you lose part of it. This is good news as it **performs** more than 500 different functions, including **storing** glucose, **cleaning** your blood, producing antibodies and recycling hormones. Your liver weighs about the same as a small chihuahua, around 1.5 kg, and is about the size of a football, although 96 percent of this is water.

Some lifestyle choices can have a serious effect on this vital organ. For example, the liver can only handle a certain amount of alcohol at any given time, so **drinking** too much or too quickly means the liver cells have difficulty **processing** it. This can also seriously affect the **kidneys**. Regular and heavy drinking over time can lead to **liver disease**. Similarly, drugs can also **injure** the liver and **disrupt** its normal function, **causing** liver disease to **develop**. Symptoms of liver disease include tiredness, weakness, **stomach ache**, loss of appetite and yellowing of the skin (known as **jaundice**).

LANGUAGE 5 **Medical vocabulary**

p. 52

Copy the table into your notebook and put the green expressions from the text in the correct categories. Then add words you already know and share them in class.

L

Organs	Medical conditions	Verbs

LISTENING 6 a Listen to four conversations with people who need medical help. Which of the expressions below are used in which conversation? Add the numbers. Three expressions are not used in any conversation.

24

☐ allergic to cat hair	☐ medication	☐ scar
2 bandages	☐ open wound	☐ sore throat
☐ get stitches	☐ painkillers	☐ sprained ankle
☐ GP	☐ plaster cast	☐ swollen
☐ have a fever	☐ prescription	☐ unconscious
☐ ligament	☐ runny nose	☐ X-ray

b Work in pairs. Do you know what all of these expressions mean? Look them up if necessary.

7 Listen again and say where the conversations could be taking place. Write the numbers next to the places:

hospital: __________ , general practitioner's surgery: __________ , pharmacy: __________

SPEAKING 8 Discuss with a partner: Which of these medical facilities do you have in your region? Where would you go in what situation?

LANGUAGE 9 Health problems

p. 52

Combine words from the boxes so that you can complete sentences 1–10.

L

brain ▪ heart ▪ liver ▪ lung ▪ medical ▪ open ▪ pollen ▪ runny ▪ sore ▪ stomach ▪ torn

ache ▪ allergy ▪ attack ▪ cancer ▪ cells ▪ disease ▪ ligament ▪ nose ▪ wound ▪ throat ▪ treatment

1 To avoid infection, you should cover a/n ______________________ with a clean bandage.

2 Even if you don't smoke, breathing in other people's cigarette smoke can cause ______________________ .

3 If you fall off your bicycle and cut yourself badly, you will need to get ______________________ .

4 Many people start to notice their ______________________ in the spring when the trees start to flower.

5 The footballer was tackled hard by another player and ended up with a/n ______________________ in his knee, even though you couldn't see a wound.

6 Being overweight and lack of exercise can lead to a/n ______________________ , which is a major cause of death worldwide.

7 Regularly drinking too much alcohol and abusing drugs can result in ______________________ .

8 Getting plenty of sleep and cutting down stress can speed up your body's ability to produce new ______________________ .

9 If you have a cold and a/n ______________________ , you'll probably have a/n ______________________ too.

10 If someone gets a/n ______________________ every time they drink milk, it could mean that they have a dairy allergy.

WRITING 10 Write three sentences about people having a health problem using the phrases from p. 134. Exchange your sentences with a partner and write down what the people should do about it.

SPEAKING 11 Do a simulation in groups of four. This is the scenario: Your class is visiting your partner school in Cambridge. You and your classmates are cycling to school. One of your classmates falls trying to avoid a collision with a car. His/her knee is slightly swollen and hurts terribly. Also, he/she seems to be in shock. You and your classmates try to help. What would you suggest doing first?

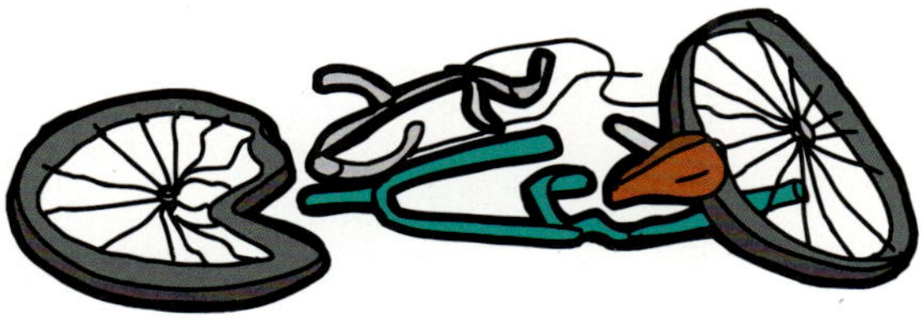

Choose one of the options and prepare arguments to convince the others. Also, consider possible counter-arguments that might come up during the discussion. Try to convince the others to accept your view. Prepare for about 5 minutes and discuss the situation for about 8–10 minutes.

Get in touch with the host family.
Possible counter argument: The host mother has an appointment in London on this day.

Call an ambulance.
Possible counter argument: You are on a cycle path and don't know your exact location.

Suggest calling his/her parents in Austria.
Possible counter argument: You don't want to upset them before you know what the problem really is.

Get help at a nearby pharmacy.
Possible counter argument: You can only guess what might be good for your injured classmate.

B

By the way: Take your medicine

If you stop a British person on the street and ask where the nearest *drugstore* is, they will most likely give you a funny look. Medication in general is referred to as *drugs* in the US but *medicine* in the UK. The Brits get their medicine from the *chemist* or *pharmacy*.

There are several other British English/American English differences you should know about if you need medical items. If you cut your finger, for example, you will need a *plaster* in the UK but a *Band Aid* in the USA. *Band Aid* is a brand name but has become a generic term in American English. If you're looking after a baby, you will need *nappies* in the UK and *diapers* in the US. If someone is ill in the States, they will say they are *sick*, but *to be sick* in the UK means *to vomit*.

Hopefully you'll never need to pay a visit to the hospital, but if you do, you could end up in the *ER (Emergency Room)* in the US and at *A and E (Accident and Emergency)* in the UK. You may need an injection, which is called *getting a shot* in the US but *a jab* in the UK. If you need fluids intravenously, you'll get *a drip* in the UK and *an IV* in the US. Any broken bones will land you in the *operating room* in America or the *operating theatre* in the UK. But don't worry, thanks to the American *anesthesiologist* or British *anaesthetist*, you won't know a thing about it!

Make a table of the phrases in American and British English and add German translations. Then tell a partner a story and use some of the words.

Smart technology changing the world

LANGUAGE + SPEAKING **12** a **Talking about inventions**

Match the inventions to the two areas of technology below. Then add your own ideas.

L
a heart monitors
b CT/MRI scans
c power steering
d engines
e self-driving cars
f GPS navigation
g vaccinations
h X-ray machines

technology in cars

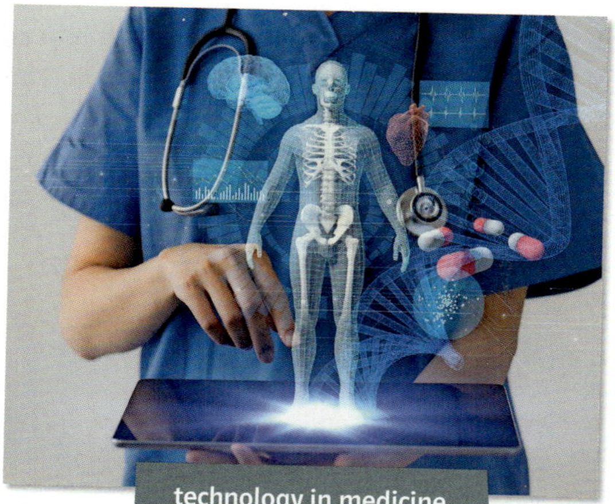

technology in medicine

b **Talk about the inventions with a partner. Why are they useful?**

… has a positive effect on … ▪ … improves our life because … ▪ … allows us to … ▪ … helps people to … ▪ We can't imagine living without … ▪ … has changed the way people … ▪ We couldn't get by without …

SPEAKING **13** a **On your own, think of all the inventions that have changed the way humans live, work and communicate with each other, such as the computer or the car. Write down three that you think are really important.**

b **Work in groups of three. Each group needs to agree on the three most important inventions. Then each member of the group presents one invention to the class. In your presentation you should convince your audience of your choice by giving good reasons why the invention is so important.**

LISTENING + VIEWING **14** BBC 05 p. 53

a **You are going to watch the first part of a BBC documentary on vehicles. Before watching, discuss these question in pairs:**

1 Which of the following vehicles are the most common on the world's streets? Agree on a ranking from 1 (the most) to 4 (the least): private car – motorbike – taxi –truck
2 Take a guess: How many cars are there in the world today?
3 Looking at the picture on the right, what do you think will be discussed in the video?
4 What kinds of drive-through services do you know? Have you got any in your area?

b **Now watch the video to find some answers to the questions. Which facts were most surprising for you?**

15 **Watch the video again and find out how these expressions are used. What do they mean?**

can't get enough ▪ engine ▪ laundry ▪ never-ending circle ▪ parking lot

BBC 06

p. 54

16 **a** **You are going to watch the second part of the BBC documentary now. First you will have 45 seconds to study the task below, then you will watch the video twice. While watching, match the beginnings of the sentences (1–6) with their sentence endings (A–I). There are two extra sentence endings that you should not use. Write your answers in the spaces provided. The first one (0) has been done for you.**

After the second watching, you will have 45 seconds to check your answers.

0	One of the problems with cars today is that our roads ____ .	B
1	Shelley is able to ____ .	
2	Many people will have difficulties ____ .	
3	Race car drivers go very fast while ____ .	
4	It's possible for two people to ____ .	
5	The prototype car's special quality is ____ .	
6	It will need a lot of work before the car can ____ .	

A	sit up front	F	go faster than human drivers
B	are too full	G	read maps and drive at the same time
C	using satellite navigation	H	trying to stay as safe as possible
D	combining a lot of everyday technology	I	drive on a road with other cars
E	accepting a car that can drive itself		

b **What do you think of this car? Would you go around a race track with it? Why?/Why not?**

SPEAKING **17** ***Paired activity:*** **Your English language assistant is doing a project on safe ways of travelling. He/She wants to know which means of traffic you consider the safest. Discuss the options below with a partner and agree on two.**

- (regular) cars
- self-driving cars
- buses
- trains
- airplanes

S **Strategies box**

Don't forget to discuss the **advantages *and* disadvantages** of each of these options.
Try to support your view by making use of the PEEL strategy.

READING 18 **a** **You've seen a self-driving race car, but what do you think are the challenges and possible benefits of having self-driving cars in normal traffic? Make a list, then collect your ideas in class.**

b **You are going to read four opinions on self-driving cars. Match texts A, B, C and D to the sentences on the next page.**

p. 52

A

The advantages of self-driving cars? Top of the list must be an increase in road safety. Worldwide, 1.2 million people are killed each year in traffic accidents. Studies have shown that even partial automation of driving could significantly reduce these deaths, making the roads safer for everyone. Already, cars with forward collision warning systems that alert drivers or automatically brake are involved in far fewer crashes. Automating driving would also bring with it the benefit of decreased traffic. As connected vehicles and driverless vehicles communicate with each other and their surroundings, they are able to identify the optimum route, which helps spread demand for scarce road space. Separate vehicles move together as a unit, reducing unnecessary accelerating and braking, which are often the cause of traffic congestion. And as automated vehicles decrease the number of accidents, traffic will be increasingly lighter since accidents are one of the biggest causes of congestion.

B

Self-driving cars don't drink and drive, fall asleep at the wheel, text or talk on the phone while driving. With their sensors and processors, they navigate roads without any of these human failings that can result in accidents. But there is something self-driving cars do not yet deal with very well – the unexpected. The human brain is still better than any computer at making decisions in the face of sudden, unforeseen events on the road – a child running into the street, a swerving cyclist or a fallen tree branch. Computers can ensure that self-driving cars obey the rules of the road – making them turn, stop and slow down, but this technology can't control the behaviour of other drivers. Added to this, snow, rain, fog and other types of weather make driving difficult for humans, and it's no different for driverless cars, which stay in their lanes by using cameras that track lines on the pavement.

C

One of the biggest advantages of self-driving cars has to be decreased traffic congestion. Let's face it, one of the leading causes of traffic jams is selfish behaviour among drivers. It has been shown when drivers space out and allow each other to move freely between lanes on the highway, traffic continues to flow smoothly, regardless of the number of cars on the road. In fact, we have the capability of pretty much eliminating traffic jams right now. All we'd have to do is allow three to four car lengths of space between our car and the car in front of us, even in slow-moving traffic. The way we drive now, when traffic gets heavy, if someone needs to change lanes to exit the motorway, or if someone needs to enter the motorway, everybody has to stop to let it happen because we drive packed so tightly together. And, there's no other way to say it, we do this out of selfishness. Self-driving cars can be programmed to space out automatically, thereby eliminating the problem.

D

Self-driving cars sound like a great idea, but it has been reported that millions of driving jobs are at risk from autonomous vehicles. This includes truck, bus, delivery and taxi driving jobs that could be lost if fully autonomous vehicle technology is adopted in a short period of time, according to a new report. With more than 30 companies – including automakers BMW, Daimler and Ford and technology giants Apple, Uber and Google – developing autonomous vehicle technology, the idea that transportation workers will be replaced by these innovations is no longer science fiction. Not everyone agrees driverless trucks are around the corner and many believe regulations and costs will influence how quickly the technologies are out on the road, but research into autonomous vehicles is in high gear, with Google and car makers at the forefront and in some cases already manufacturing products.

Which two people ...

1 agree on one aspect of how self-driving cars will change traffic on the road? ☐ + ☐
2 are not sure self-driving cars will have positive consequences? ☐ + ☐

Which person ...

3 thinks people still make better decisions than a computer in an emergency? ☐
4 is concerned that self-driving cars will result in mass unemployment? ☐
5 thinks that this new technology has the double benefit of less traffic and increased safety? ☐
6 is unhappy with the egotistical way people drive? ☐

19 **Which person do you agree with most? Give reasons for your choice.**

LANGUAGE **20** **Opposites**

Find the opposites of the following words in the texts. Sometimes more than one answer is possible.

Text A

1 to increase ______________________
2 disadvantage ______________________
3 full/complete ______________________

Text B

4 predictable ______________________
5 upright ______________________

Text C

6 selfless ______________________
7 creating ______________________
8 loosely ______________________

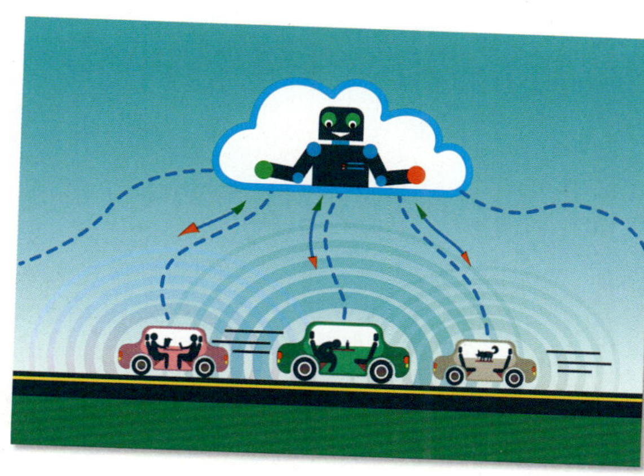

Text D

9 disagree ______________________
10 gained ______________________

WRITING 21 The physics department of your English partner school wants to do a project on the future of cars together with your school. They are interested in your ideas and are asking for a report. You have asked your classmates for suggestions and done a survey.

Students' project preferences (n = 20)

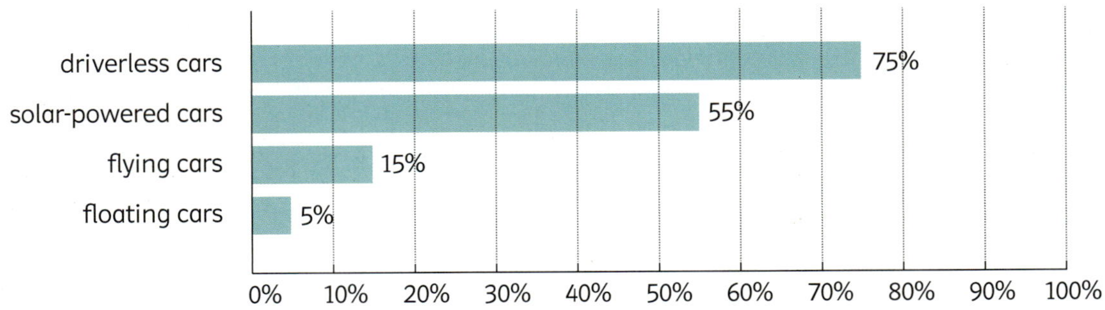

Write a report based on the results of your survey.
In your report you should:

- explain the results
- outline advantages of driverless cars
- suggest what your class can do to make the project work

Write around 250 words.
Divide your report into sections and give them headings.

→ See *Writing coach, Report*, p. 180.

S Strategies box

When you **explain** the **results**, you **describe** them and **give** possible **reasons** for them.

SPEAKING + LISTENING 22

a **Self-driving cars are not the only kind of modern technology relying on AI (artificial intelligence) to solve problems for their human users. How could AI be useful in medicine? Discuss in class.**

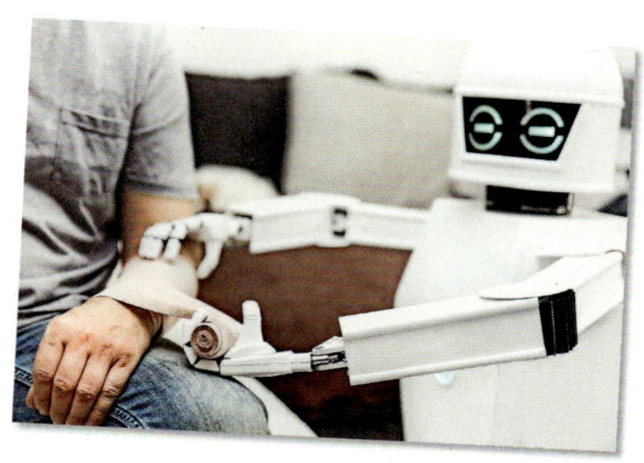

25

b **You are going to listen to an expert explaining how AI can help in medicine. Read the ideas below. While listening for the first time, circle the four main ideas he mentions. Compare in class.**

How AI can support medicine

- predicting health problems
- diagnosing problems
- improving emergency medicine
- preventing patients from falling off bed
- creating images to find injuries
- finding correct medication much faster
- predicting risk for heart attack
- finding the right therapy
- preparing staff in hospital
- dealing with Ebola
- supporting decision-making
- improving first aid

c **Now copy the four main ideas into your notebook. Listen again and add two supporting details from the list above to each main idea.**

LANGUAGE IN USE **23** **a** Read the text about the film *The Matrix*. Some words are missing. Choose the correct answer (A, B, C or D) for each gap (1–8). Put a cross (☒) in the correct box. The first one (0) has been done for you.

p. 55

The Matrix – The Fight for the Future

What if virtual reality wasn't just for fun, but was being used to imprison you? That's the dilemma (0) ______ faces mild-mannered computer freak Thomas Anderson (Keanu Reeves) in *The Matrix*. It's the year 1999, and Anderson is a man living two lives. By day he is an average computer programmer (1) ______ in an office, and by night he is a hacker known as Neo. Neo has always questioned his reality, but the truth is far beyond his imagination.

After (2) ______ a mysterious message on his computer, Neo ends up in a nightclub where he is contacted by another hacker, Trinity (played by Carrie-Anne Moss). Trinity (3) ______ about the mysterious Morpheus (Laurence Fishburne) and says that he should (4) ______ him. When Neo is taken to see Morpheus, he learns the terrible truth: First of all, the year is actually closer to 2199, and (5) ______, the real world is a post-apocalyptic wasteland. Most of humanity (6) ______ by a race of machines that live off the humans' body heat and electrochemical energy and imprison their minds within an artificial reality. As a rebel against the machines, Neo must return to the matrix and confront the 'Agents': super-powerful computer programs (7) ______ aim is to get rid of Neo and the entire human rebellion. Neo will (8) ______ if they catch him, but Morpheus is convinced Neo is 'The One' who can crack open the matrix and bring his people to both physical and psychological freedom.

0	A this	☐	B that	☒	C what	☐	D who	☐
1	A working	☐	B that's being	☐	C is bored	☐	D that's	☐
2	A received	☐	B saw	☐	C had got	☐	D receiving	☐
3	A tells him	☐	B says him	☐	C is telling him	☐	D warning him	☐
4	A met	☐	B have met	☐	C meet	☐	D meeting	☐
5	A however	☐	B secondly	☐	C despite that	☐	D differently	☐
6	A is capturing	☐	B has captured	☐	C was captured	☐	D has been captured	☐
7	A who's	☐	B which	☐	C whose	☐	D their	☐
8	A be killed	☐	B have killed	☐	C be killing	☐	D to die	☐

b Do you know the film? If so, do you think this is an accurate description of it? Why?/Why not? If you don't know the film, would you like to see it now? Why?/Why not?

c Do you know any other films that deal with the topic of artificial intelligence? Is it shown in a positive or negative way?

WRITING **24** Use the text above as a model to write a similar description of a sci-fi film or book you have recently read. Don't give away the ending though!

WRITING 25

Write a PEEL paragraph of about 100 words about one of these topics:

- the greatest technical achievement of today
- the most dangerous technical achievement of today
- the most dangerous disease of today
- the most important invention ever made

→ See *PEEL revisited*, p. 93.

LANGUAGE 26

Topic vocabulary: Body parts

Complete the crossword with the correct organs and body parts.

Across

2 connects hand and arm
3 bottom of face
4 transport 11,000 litres of sth. per day
5 between throat and stomach
8 back of foot
10 short and thick finger
11 hair above eyes
12 where arm meets chest
13 also affected by alcohol
16 friends kiss here
17 important to bite and chew
18 connects leg to rest of body

Down

1 connects foot and leg
2 between chest and hips
4 weight of small chihuahua
6 hurts if you eat too much
7 gets hot when you have a fever
8 transports 7,000 litres of sth. per day
9 front of lower leg
13 connects the two parts of the leg
14 connects the two parts of the arm
15 upper part of leg

27

p. 54

Topic vocabulary: Collocations

Which word does *not* collocate with the one in bold? Cross it out.

L

1 self-driving – driverless – driver **cars**
2 light – heavy – strong – decreased **traffic**
3 black – autonomous – careful **driving**
4 sudden – unforeseen – scarce **event**

28

Topic vocabulary: Health and medicine

Complete the word map on the next page with these phrases and add your own ideas.

give medical treatment ▪ headache ▪ liver disease ▪ lung cancer ▪ open wound ▪ painkillers ▪ pharmacy/drugstore ▪ prescriptions ▪ runny nose ▪ sore throat ▪ sprained ankle ▪ treat patients

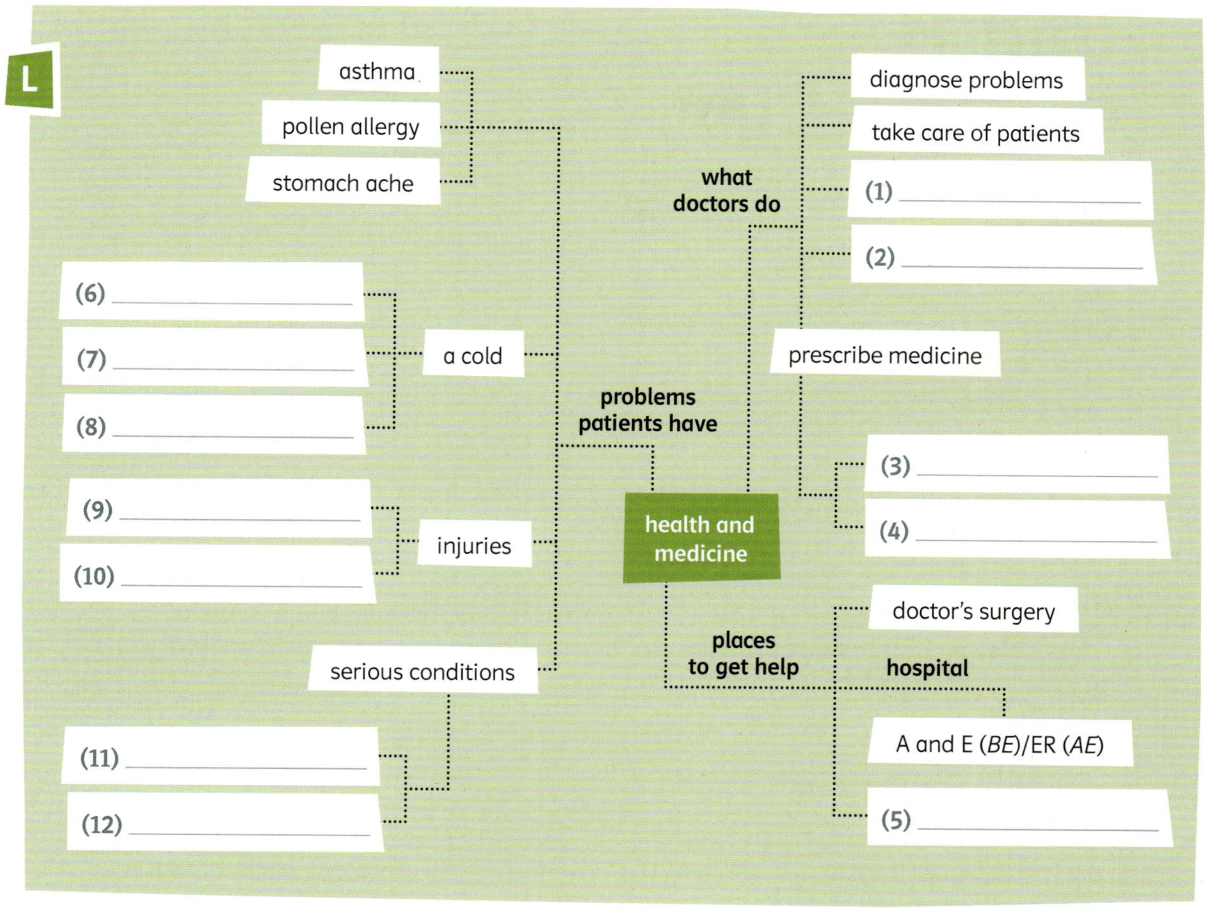

Looking back: Learning goals of Unit 10

			✓✓	✓	!!
READING	▶▶▶ B1+	I can compile information from several texts on the topic of science and technology. **(ex. 18b)**			
	▶▶▶ B1+	I can identify the main conclusions in a clearly signalled argumentative text. **(ex. 18b)**			
LISTENING	▶▶▶ B1+	I can distinguish between main points and supporting detail in clear speech on the topic of science and technology. **(ex. 22b/c)**			
WRITING	▶▶▶ B1+	I can write a report, summary or paragraph to communicate information and ideas on the topic of science and technology. **(ex. 21, 24, 25)**			
SPEAKING	▶▶▶ B1+	I can enter unprepared into conversation on the topic of science and technology with some confidence. **(ex. 2, 8, 11, 12b, 13b, 17)**			
LANGUAGE	▶▶▶	I can use a sufficient range of vocabulary to express myself on the topic of politics with reasonable precision.			

AI will make/break humankind because . . .

I would/wouldn't want a self-driving car because . . .

Unit 11
Culture is key

9p356a

In this unit you will:
- think about some misunderstandings
- find out why not all rugs can be stepped on
- hear what language assistants think of Austria
- learn about Austria's secret national anthem

SPEAKING **1** **a** **Are you aware of cultural differences and pitfalls or do walk right into them? Take our quiz to find out. Circle your answers, then check with the key below.**

1 *In Thailand, if you show someone the soles of your feet,*
- **A** they will be very offended – it's rude.
- **B** they will laugh at you – it's humorous.
- **C** they will show you their feet – it's a greeting.

2 *In Japan, you should blow your nose*
- **A** loudly in public – no one cares.
- **B** only in private – it's disgusting!
- **C** only when other people are blowing their noses.

3 *If someone shakes their head at you in India,*
- **A** they mean 'no'.
- **B** they mean 'yes'.
- **C** they mean 'I don't know'.

4 *The Maori people of New Zealand greet each other by*
- **A** bumping shoulders together.
- **B** slapping each other on the face.
- **C** pressing their noses together.

5 *Tipping the waiter or waitress in the USA*
- **A** is expected – it's the main part of their earnings.
- **B** is only necessary if the bill is over $20.
- **C** is not expected at all.

6 *If you show someone the 'OK' sign in Brazil,*
- **A** they will expect you to buy them a drink.
- **B** they will get upset and shout at you. It's like showing your middle finger.
- **C** they will show you the 'OK' sign back – it's a way of saying 'hello'.

Answers:
1 A, 2 B, 3 B, 4 C, 5 A, 6 B

5 or 6 correct answers:
Congrats! You're a pro at knowing how to behave around the world. What are you waiting for? Happy travelling!

3 or 4 correct answers:
Yay! You have a pretty good idea of how to fit in on your travels. You still have a few things to learn, though!

1 or 2 correct answers:
Uh-oh! You could easily offend someone – find out more about the places you're visiting before you go travelling!

b **Discuss the quiz with a partner.**

1. Which of these rules do you find surprising?
2. Which rules are similar in Austria?
3. What tips would you give someone in order to avoid social pitfalls in Austria? Make a list of ideas and share them in class.

Misunderstandings

READING 2 a Read the forum post. Can you guess what the missing word is?

Boccadiaa	**German custom of leaving ____________ outside front doors**
Joined: 02 Feb 2016 Posts: 236	According to a recent Reuters news report, more than 100 ____________ were stolen by a fox. They had been left outside their doors by the inhabitants of Föhren. My question: why did so many people leave them outdoors? Is this a common German habit/custom? What happens if it rains?

b What would your answer to this post be?

LANGUAGE 3 a Describing intercultural experiences

Read the reactions of the other forum users. Use the sentence parts in the box to complete them.

L

a I remember vividly how surprised we were
b I've not been disrespectful
c I find it strange
d I'm being respectful
e the custom is understandable
f everyone looks at us as if we're
g people are too polite to point it out
h it really felt very foreign

Sjoren Joined: 16 Nov 2014 Posts: 521	***> Boccadiaa wrote: German custom …*** As a rule, Germans take their shoes off before entering someone's home. They may be left on the front stoop[1] (assuming there is a roof over it in case of rain).
epscohost Joined: 1 Jan 2015 Posts: 1207	***>> Boccadiaa wrote: German custom …*** I know people who take theirs off in my hall before coming any further, and (1) ☐. It's never been suggested to me that I take mine off before going into someone's house or flat. I hope (2) ☐.
Sjoren Joined: 16 Nov 2014 Posts: 521	***> epscohost wrote: I know people …*** Perhaps (3) ☐, epscohost, and have patiently been waiting for you to notice the shoes gathered by the door and the bare feet of all their other guests.
here_US Joined: 20 May 2015 Posts: 622	***>>> Boccadiaa wrote: German custom …*** It's not generally done in the US. But (4) ☐ to encounter it in Hawaii, perhaps because sand really makes a mess indoors. Our relatives seemed distinctly[2] annoyed if we didn't take our shoes off inside, which we kept forgetting to do because (5) ☐ to us. I think (6) ☐, but it didn't endear itself to me[3]. There are other ways I can show (7) ☐.
Totempole Joined: 6 June 2014 Posts: 332	***>>>> Boccadiaa wrote: German custom …*** After living in Austria for 15 years, we're totally used to taking our shoes off. So we do it all the time when we get home to New York, and (8) ☐ completely nuts.

b Use the sentence parts from the box to write about your own experiences with other cultures.

[1] **front stoop** (*AE*): Veranda
[2] **distinctly:** merklich, deutlich
[3] **it didn't endear itself to me:** ich konnte mich nicht damit anfreunden

WRITING 4 **Choose one of the statements below and write a post to the forum expressing the idea.**

a "I've got a hole in my sock – I want to keep my shoes on."
b "Ugh, people walking into the loo without their shoes on!"
c "Gosh, it must be really uncomfortable to keep your shoes on all the time."

SPEAKING + WRITING 5 a **Some students from the Whitehall partner school have asked what cultural practices they should know about when they come to Austria. Should they bring a gift for their host family, for example?**

In pairs, discuss some of the everyday things Austrians do and give advice on what to expect and how to behave in these situations in Austria:

a when you meet somebody
b when a family sits down to eat
c when you give somebody a gift
d when you use public transport

b **Choose an everyday activity from 5a and write an informal email to one of your friends in Cambridge. Give advice on how to do this in Austria. Write around 200 words.**

SPEAKING 6 **In pairs, talk about these points:**

1 Which of the following do you do/don't you do? Explain why/why not.
   a take off your shoes when you go into someone's home
   b shake hands with people when you meet them
   c greet people with a hug and a kiss on each cheek
   d haggle[4] when buying something in a shop or at a market
   e applaud when your plane lands safely
   f say something like 'bless you' when someone sneezes
2 Have you ever misunderstood the local customs in an unfamiliar place? If so, what happened?
3 How important do you think is it to know about the local customs in a new place/country you are visiting?

READING 7 pp. 56–58

Read the text by Maya Angelou. First decide whether the statements (1–7) are true (T) or false (F) and put a cross (☒) in the correct box. Then identify the sentence in the text which supports your decision. Write the first four words of this sentence in the space provided. There may be more than one correct answer; write down only one. The first one (0) has been done for you.

Maya Angelou was an African-American author well known for her writing about intercultural issues. She campaigned for civil rights for black people in the USA. Here she describes a visit to a friend's house in Senegal.

Samia was a famous actress from Senegal who dressed in glamorous flowing clothes. I met her on a trip to Paris. [...] Samia said she and her husband Pierre lived most of the year in Dakar, the capital of Senegal, and I would always be welcome in their home. Years passed before I did visit Senegal, but the telephone number they had given me still worked. I was invited for dinner.

I entered a beautifully furnished living room to the sound of people laughing and glasses clinking with ice. The guests were integrated. As many Europeans as Africans were enjoying a full-blown party. Samia introduced me to a small group near the door and stayed talking to us until a server offered me a drink.

I wandered from group to group. Samia's first language was Serer, but I did not speak Serer and the Senegalese accent made the French which was spoken hard for me to comprehend. I passed an open door where people stood along the wall, careful not to step on the beautiful Oriental rug in the center of the room.

[4] **to haggle:** feilschen *(einen günstigeren Preis aushandeln)*

I had known a woman in Egypt who would not allow her servants to walk on her rugs saying that only she, her family and friends were going to wear out her expensive carpets. Samia plummeted in my estimation[5]. Obviously she had informed her guests that she would not look favorably on them if they stepped on her rug. I wondered what words did one use to inform a guest how to behave? I decided to find out.

I went into the room and in the guise of looking closely at some paintings on the wall, I walked across the center of the rug, then turned and walked back to another painting. I must have stepped on the rug four or five times. The guests who were bunched up on the sidelines smiled at me weakly. They might be encouraged to admit that rugs were to be walked on.

A Senegalese woman in a white brocade gown smiled at me and engaged me in conversation. She was a writer and we began talking about books. I became so interested I nearly missed the next scene. Two maids came and rolled up the rug I had walked on and took it away. They returned immediately with another equally as beautiful. They spread it, and patted it until it was smooth. They then put glasses on the carpet and huge serving spoons, folded napkins and silverware, wine and pitchers of water. Finally a bowl of steaming rice and chicken was placed on the carpet. Samia and Pierre appeared and clapping their hands they called for attention. Samia announced that they were serving the most popular Senegalese dish, "Yassah, for our sister from America." She waved her hand at me and said, "For Maya Angelou," adding, "Shall we sit?"

All the guests sank to the floor. My face and neck burned. Fortunately, because of my chocolate brown complexion, people could not know I was on fire with shame. Clever and so proper Maya Angelou, I had walked up and down over the tablecloth.

I sat, but found swallowing hard to do. The food had to force its way over that knot of embarrassment.

In an unfamiliar culture, it is wise to offer no innovations, no suggestions, or lessons.

	Statements	T	F	First four words
0	The author had met her friends regularly.	☐	☒	Years passed before I
1	There was a minority of European guests at the party.	☐	☐	
2	Maya Angelou found it hard to communicate with some of the other guests.	☐	☐	
3	She compared the host to an Egyptian woman she knew.	☐	☐	
4	The other guests approved of her walking on the carpet.	☐	☐	
5	A second, cheaper carpet was brought in.	☐	☐	
6	When the author realised her mistake, she was embarrassed.	☐	☐	
7	The author recommends behaving modestly in places you do not know well.	☐	☐	

SPEAKING 8 **What point was Maya Angelou trying to make to her hostess by walking on the rug? Do you think she reacted correctly when she realised her mistake? What would you have done? Talk in pairs.**

[5] **Samia plummeted in my estimation:** Ich verlor jeglichen Respekt für Samia

How they see us

SPEAKING 9 **Think about the questions below and make notes, then discuss them with a partner and share them in class:**

1 What do people from other countries know about Austria and the people who live here?
2 What do they consider 'typically Austrian'?
3 Where do they get their ideas about Austria from?

LISTENING 10 ◎ 26 p. 60

You are going to listen to five language assistants talking about what they found surprising in Austria. First you will have 45 seconds to study the task below, then you will hear the recording twice. While listening, match the speakers with their statements (A–L). There are two extra statements that you should not use. Write your answers in the boxes provided. The first one (0) has been done for you.

After the second listening, you will have 45 seconds to check your answers.

Speaker 1 – Felix	0	1
Speaker 2 – Rolle	2	3
Speaker 3 – Nathalie	4	5
Speaker 4 – Raoul	6	7
Speaker 5 – Lucy	8	9

A	I'm annoyed I can't use my phone as much as at home.	G	You can get punished for smoking on the street in my country.
B	It's too easy to get cigarettes in Austria.	H	I followed a friend's advice.
C	I got ill at the beginning of my stay here.	I	Some laws are stricter in my country.
D	We aren't afraid of the police where I come from.	J	I found a great shop nearby.
E	Austria is tidier than my country.	K	I think recycling is more difficult here.
F	I now have a different opinion on a topic.	L	It was difficult to get used to the opening hours of shops.

0	1	2	3	4	5	6	7	8	9
H									

WRITING 11 **You have decided to reply to one of the foreign language assistants from exercise 10. Listen to the recording again and take notes. Then write an email to the person you have picked about how you feel about their statement on Austria. Agree OR disagree with them and support your opinion with two or three good arguments.**

LISTENING 12 **a** **In pairs, write down what comes to mind when you read 'the sound of music'. Get together with another pair and compare your lists. Ask questions about words you find surprising.**

b **Listen to a British reporter talk about the film *The Sound of Music* while walking through Salzburg and answer the questions below.**

27

1 What do the *Sound of Music* tourists do in Salzburg?
2 What is *The Sound of Music* about?
3 When was the film first shown?
4 What does Mr Steiner say about the song *Edelweiss*?
5 What did the Austrian crew members of the film team think about the film?
6 What reasons are given for Austrians not liking the film?
7 What does a *Sound of Music* bicycle tour look like?

c **Do some research about the film on the internet. Do you agree with the statements made about the film? Why?/Why not?**

LANGUAGE 13 **Talking about a country's culture**

p. 58

Read the statements about *The Sound of Music* and circle the correct options.

"Climb every mountain, ford every stream[6], follow every rainbow, 'til you find your dream" is a beautiful (1) misunderstanding / statement / pitfall of philosophy. Critics may think that the film *The Sound of Music* isn't a (2) serious / offensive / ethnic one, but I think it's really deep. The message that we should not tolerate evil is just as (3) important / difficult / tolerant today. (*Jon Voight*)

It is a Hollywood production that has nothing to do with Austria other than being shot on location there. Austrians do not (4) identify / respect / offend one little bit with that film … Well, apart from Salzburg entrepreneurs drawing cash out of the pockets of American and Asian (5) friends / tourists / local people. (*Christian R. Vornberg*)

While the movie is usually not liked by most Austrians, it is at least accepted as an opportunity to show other people the actual (6) type / nature / culture of the country. (*Christoph Marshall*)

Sadly, the film is most likely where Americans get most of their (7) information / truth / thoughts about Austrian history, culture and traditions. It also helps keep up some unfortunate (8) customs / ideas / stereotypes that many Austrians would rather stay away from – lederhosen-clad men and dirndl-wearing women, for example. (*Kate Jackson*)

SPEAKING 14 **Discuss the questions below in small groups.**

1 Do you think a film can give a realistic picture of a culture? Why?/Why not?
2 Which films or TV series would you recommend to learn about Austrian culture?
3 What have you learned about other cultures from films or series?

[6] **to ford a stream:** einen Strom/Fluss überqueren

LANGUAGE IN USE 15 **Read the text about a *Sound of Music* tour. In most lines (1–15) there is a word that should not be there. Write these words in the spaces provided. 2–4 lines are correct. Make a ✓ in the space if the line is correct. There are two examples (0, 00) at the beginning.**

Tour *The Sound of Music*!

I think I'm the biggest *Sound of Music* fan ever! I love all the songs	✓	(0)
and must have seen the film some more than 30 times. It was a	some	(00)
dream come so true when I took a trip to Salzburg last summer. The	______	(1)
first thing I did was book a *Sound of Music* bus tour wanted to see	______	(2)
all the famous places from the film. Sadly, only it was raining very	______	(3)
heavily. The tour guide told to us that it's called 'string rain[7]' as	______	(4)
it comes straight down, but then the sun came on out and the	______	(5)
scenery was fantastic! I was embarrassed when some near local	______	(6)
people heard me singing one of the songs, *Edelweiss*, really loudly.	______	(7)
They didn't look very all that happy, but I suppose they get tired	______	(8)
of the buses full of tourists crowding into the city most all the time.	______	(9)
The best bit was that they played up the music from the film on	______	(10)
the bus as we were driving along and everyone was singing along	______	(11)
and laughing like crazy. We took down some great pictures in Mirabell	______	(12)
Gardens and danced around the fountain like being the kids in the	______	(13)
film. It was a really total unforgettable experience and I met a lot of	______	(14)
fun people from other countries. I'd have definitely recommend this tour!	______	(15)

SPEAKING + WRITING 16 **a** **What kind of tour would you recommend to tourists in your area? Work together in small groups to come up with a plan of what to do and see. Consider:**

- length of tour
- sights to see
- activities to do
- how to inform tourists about Austrian culture

b **When you have agreed on a plan, write a description of your tour, add some pictures and present it in class.**

[7] **string rain:** Schnürlregen

Living together – learning from each other

SPEAKING 17 **Complete the speech bubbles with the words below. Sometimes more than one answer is possible. Then discuss the questions with a partner.**

Austria ▪ conflicts ▪ countries ▪ culture ▪ difficulties ▪ ethnic ▪ immigrants ▪ language ▪ music ▪ roots

What do you know about the (1) __________ of your parents and grandparents?

What other (2) __________ do you speak apart from German?

What (3) __________ do your classmates with a migration background come from?

How should Austria deal with (4) __________?

If you had to leave (5) __________, what country would you like to go to?

What are the (6) __________ of learning German for a person from another country?

Do you think that (7) __________ plays an important role when talking about immigration? Give reasons.

Do you listen to (8) __________ in languages other than German or English?

What (9) __________ could arise between friends from different ethnic backgrounds?

What (10) __________ food do you like?

WRITING 18 **The school magazine of your English partner school is running a series of articles on intercultural understanding in school. You have decided to send them an article about your experience with classmates from another country.**

p. 59

In your article you should:

- outline challenges classmates from another country might face
- suggest how you can help them cope with these challenges
- point out what you can learn from classmates from another country

Write around 250 words. Give your article a title.

→ See *Writing coach, Article*, p. 180.

SPEAKING 19 a The pictures below show young people in distressing situations. Think about the following questions and discuss them with a partner.

1 Where are the scenes taking place?
2 How do the students feel in each of these pictures?
3 What is the atmosphere like?
4 What title would you suggest for each of these pictures?
5 What title would you suggest for both of them?
6 What could be the reason for the bullying shown in the pictures?

b Tell your partner a story that could go with the pictures. Partner A chooses the picture on the left, partner B the picture on the right.

c In pairs, brainstorm ideas about what young people can do to fight such bullying. Then present your ideas in class.

WRITING 20 a Use one of the pictures as a stimulus to write an inner monologue of about 200 words. Write it from the perspective of one of the people in the pictures or from your perspective looking at the pictures.

b Design an anti-racism poster or create an anti-racism meme and present it in class.

LANGUAGE 21 a Topic vocabulary: Intercultural issues
Find the word pairs. There is more than one possible match for most of the words.

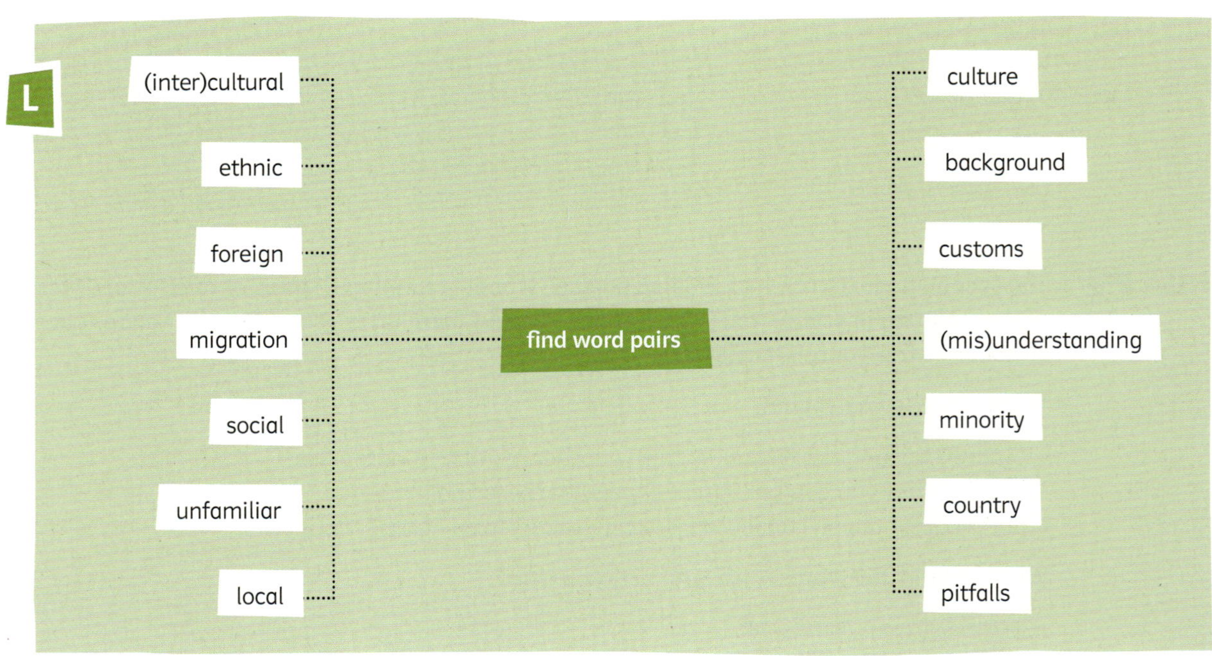

b **Complete the phrases and then make a sentence with each one.**

L

something

- to m__un___st___
- to be u___ to do__g
- to be a f__ of
- to a_r_e on
- to rec__me__

somebody

- to of___d
- to get u____ wi__
- to dis____e y__rs__f from
- to gr___
- to l___n fr_m

Looking back: Learning goals of Unit 11

			✓✓	✓	!!
READING	▸▸▸ B1+	I can scan a longer text on the topic of intercultural issues for relevant information. **(ex. 7)**			
LISTENING	▸▸▸ B1+	I can understand straightforward factual information in clear speech on the topic of intercultural issues. **(ex. 10, 12b)**			
WRITING	▸▸▸ B1+	I can write a straightforward connected email or inner monologue to describe feelings and reactions on the topic of intercultural issues. **(ex. 11, 20a)**			
	▸▸▸ B1+	I can write a range of texts to communicate information and ideas on the topic of intercultural issues. **(ex. 4, 5b, 16b, 18, 20b)**			
SPEAKING	▸▸▸ B1+	I can express and exchange ideas about more abstract cultural topics, such as intercultural issues. **(ex. 5a, 9, 14, 16a)**			
	▸▸▸ B1+	I can express and exchange ideas about my experiences, feelings and reactions. **(ex. 1b, 6, 8, 14, 17, 19a/b/c)**			
LANGUAGE	▸▸▸	I can use a sufficient range of vocabulary to express myself with reasonable precision on the topic of intercultural issues.			

An Austrian custom that a tourist might find strange is …

One custom from another country that people should know about is …

Unit 12
Going global

j64nm9

In this unit you will:
- look at the pros and cons of globalisation
- write about fresh strawberries in winter
- learn how Dan likes his coffee
- discuss the idea of fair trade

SPEAKING 1 **Discuss the pictures and quotes below with a partner.**

1 What do the pictures show about the world today? Can you tell where photos A to C were taken?
2 What are the quotes trying to say? Do you agree? Why?/Why not?

1

"No two countries that both had McDonald's had fought a war against each other since each got its McDonald's." (*Thomas L. Friedman, US author and journalist*)

A

B

C

D

2

"Globalisation means many things. At one level, it talks of trade, which since the 16th century has exchanged goods and now, increasingly, ideas and information across the globe. But globalisation is also a view of the world – it is an opinion about man and why men are on the world." (*John Berger, British critic, novelist and poet*)

What's globalisation (to you)?

READING 2 Read an explanation of 'globalisation' below.
What causes and consequences of globalisation does it mention?

p. 64

We now communicate and share each other's cultures through travel and trade, transporting products around the world in hours or days. We are in a huge global economy where something that happens in one area can have knock-on effects worldwide. This process is called 'globalisation'.

What is globalisation?

Globalisation is the process by which the world is becoming increasingly interconnected as a result of massively increased trade and cultural exchange. Globalisation has increased the production of goods and services. The biggest companies are no longer national firms but multinational corporations with subsidiaries[1] in many countries.

Globalisation has been taking place for hundreds of years but has speeded up enormously over the last half-century.

Globalisation has resulted in:
- increased international trade
- a company operating in more than one country
- greater dependence on the global economy
- freer movement of capital, goods and services
- recognition[2] of companies such as McDonald's and Starbucks in less developed countries

Although globalisation is probably helping to create more wealth in developing countries, it is not helping to close the gap between the world's poorest countries and the world's richest.

LANGUAGE 3 a Talking about globalisation

Think of examples of and/or explanations for these aspects of globalisation. Compare in class. Then sort the aspects into positive and negative ones. Some could be both.

p. 61

L

- variety of products available (e.g. food, clothes)
- increased damage to the environment
- worldwide communication
- hurts local economy
- no borders
- brings peoples of the world together
- dominance of Western ideas and values
- almost unlimited number of TV channels available
- individual freedom
- less cultural diversity

b Write sentences about causes and effects of globalisation using the linking words below.

as a result (of) ▪ because (of) ▪ consequently ▪ due to ▪ for this reason ▪ since ▪ therefore

Example: *The variety of products available has increased due to improved transportation.*

[1] **subsidiary:** Zweigstelle, Filiale
[2] **recognition:** Bekanntheit

LISTENING 4

28

p. 63

You are going to listen to five people talking about what globalisation means to them. First you will have 45 seconds to study the task below, then you will hear the recording twice. While listening, match the speakers with their statements (A–L). There are two extra statements that you should not use. Write your answers in the boxes provided. The first one (0) has been done for you.

After the second listening, you will have 45 seconds to check your answers.

Speaker 1 – Rashid	0	1
Speaker 2 – Olivia	2	3
Speaker 3 – Gillian	4	5
Speaker 4 – Henry	6	7
Speaker 5 – Bruno	8	9

A	Globalisation means freedom to travel.	G	I work for a British company in India.
B	The result of globalisation is that everyone is becoming more like Americans.	H	The company I worked for moved to another country.
C	Everyone wants to work for an international company here.	I	People in my country prefer American products to local ones.
D	It's difficult to find a job where I live.	J	We never had a free weekend due to work.
E	Globalisation brings advantages for the companies and the employees.	K	I can buy exotic food all year round.
F	International companies pay their workers badly here.	L	I feel better now that I don't work for a big company anymore.

0	1	2	3	4	5	6	7	8	9
G									

WRITING 5

p. 62

Browsing the internet you have come across the following blog post:

White_Sapphire

What's worse than globalisation?

To put my ideas on globalisation in a nutshell:
I really don't think we need to have fresh strawberries for dessert in winter. Can't we just eat the fruit that's in season?

reply

You have decided to comment on this blog post.
In your blog comment you should:

- explain how you feel about fresh strawberries in winter
- give examples of positive or negative aspects of globalisation
- say what globalisation means for your life

Write around 250 words.

→ See *Writing coach, Blog*, p. 182.

READING 6 a Look at these six events that helped make the world a smaller place. What do you know about them? How do you think they made the world 'smaller'?

1 The invention of the jet airplane
2 The fall of the Berlin Wall
3 The invention of the internet
4 The discoveries of Christopher Columbus
5 The spread of the Roman Empire
6 The launch of YouTube

b Now read the descriptions of the events. Match the headings above to the correct texts. There is one heading that doesn't fit any of the texts.

Shrinking the world

A ☐ Since it began in 2005, this has enabled people all over the world to connect and share their interests and experiences. It started with amateur videos, the very first one showing a visit to the zoo, but progressed to much wider content. Each day it has billions of views and seems to be gradually replacing TV.

B ☐ Lasting for nearly five centuries, this used to be one of the greatest civilisations in history. At its height in the third century AD, it had more than 70 million citizens. Stretching from Spain and Northern Africa, through France, into the UK, across Southern Europe and into Turkey and Arabia, it brought many technological inventions such as water heating systems.

C ☐ Scientists developed this in the 1930s, and the first commercial service flew from London to Johannesburg in 1952. This invention keeps on making the world smaller. Now so-called hypersonic aircraft are being designed to fly five times the speed of sound. This technology would make it possible to fly anywhere on Earth in under three hours.

D ☐ In 1492, a journey began to find a direct water route from Europe to Asia going west. When he found land, this famous explorer believed he had reached the East Indies and called the local people 'Indians', a name which stuck. Instead, the 'New World' was discovered, which began a period of exploration and helped the Spanish create a huge empire in the Americas.

E ☐ In November 1989, the whole world watched as one of its major symbols of segregation came crashing down. More than two million people from the eastern part of the city visited the West to participate in a celebration described as 'the greatest street party in the history of the world'. For 28 years, this had physically and symbolically kept East and West apart. With its fall, the Cold War was officially over.

SPEAKING 7 Now work in groups of three or four and do these tasks:

1 Share what you know about each of these events and discuss how they helped shape our modern world.
2 Put the events in order of influence (1 = most influential, 5 = least influential).

8 Form new groups and discuss your ranking from exercise 7. Try to come to an agreement on the most and least influential event. Then do some research on another important event or invention that has caused the world to become more connected. Present your findings in class.

remains of the Berlin Wall

SPEAKING + READING **9**

a What do you know about Cuba? Share your knowledge with a partner and in class.

b Read the following information about travel restrictions for Cubans. How did Cubans try to leave the country?

> For many decades, Cuban citizens were not allowed to travel abroad without special permission that was only rarely granted. Still, many of them tried to leave illegally. Over one million Cubans emigrated to the US alone, either going by boat or ship at night or using stolen or fake passports to take a plane out of Cuba. Since 2013, Cubans have been allowed to leave the island nation, but finding a country that will allow them to immigrate legally can still be problematic.

LISTENING **10**

29

p. 61

a In 10b you are going to listen to an FM4 feature with a man called Tony Lloyd, who considers himself a 'citizen of the world'. He is going to talk about what happened when he was trying to leave Cuba after travelling around the island for some time. What do you think he will say?

b Look at the events below. Listen to the first part of the story and put them in the correct order.

- ☐ a is asked questions in Spanish
- ☐ b is on holiday in Cuba
- ☐ c is asked to admit to something
- ☐ d goes to the airport
- ☐ e is asked questions in English
- ☐ f is asked to come for an interview

c Copy the events into your notebook in the correct order, leaving some space free under each one. Then listen again and add some details to the events.

WRITING **11**

How do you think the story will end? Write three to five sentences.

LISTENING **12**

30

Now listen to the second part of the story and answer the questions below.

1. Why are the immigration officers suspicious of Tony Lloyd?
2. How does the officer's explanation make Tony Lloyd feel? Why is he feeling that way?
3. How does the story end? What are Tony Lloyd's feelings now?

SPEAKING **13**

Do you know any other stories about problems at borders? They could come from books, films or your own experience. Prepare by taking some notes first, then tell your stories in small groups.

WRITING **14**

Imagine you are one of the immigration officers who interviewed Tony Lloyd at the border. Write a story about the event from his/her point of view.

For more fairness in global trade

SPEAKING + READING 15 **a** **Have you ever noticed Fairtrade labels on products you buy? Discuss what you think they mean with a partner.**

b **What is fair trade really about? Match the wrong ideas about fair trade on the left to the correct ideas on the right.**

> ***fair trade:*** a way of buying and selling which makes sure fair prices are paid to the producers
>
> ***Fairtrade:*** the trademark of an international organisation which certifies fair trade products

Myth

1 Fairtrade products are more expensive than other products.
2 Fair trade is a form of charity.
3 Fair trade has been around long enough and isn't needed any more.
4 Fair trade locks farmers into a fixed price.

Reality

a Fair trade is not about donating money. It encourages long-term change through trade. In addition, it works to improve the lives of small farmers and their communities.
b Only a small amount of global goods are sold on fair trade terms, and challenges like climate change or constantly changing market prices still create hard living conditions for farmers.
c The 'Fairtrade Minimum Price' is calculated to cover the costs of production, and only comes into play if the market price of coffee falls below the level set by the Fairtrade organisation.
d Fair trade cuts out the middlemen. Therefore the price of its products is roughly the same as that of conventional goods; however, more of the sales price goes to producers.

LISTENING 16 (31) **a** **You are going to listen to a conversation between Lizzie, Dan and Emily. First you will have 45 seconds to study the task below, then you will hear the recording twice. While listening, complete the sentences (1–6) using a maximum of four words. Write your answers in the spaces provided. The first one (0) has been done for you.**

After the second listening, you will have 45 seconds to check your answers.

0	Lizzie wants some coffee because ____ .	*she is tired*
1	Dan prefers the machine downstairs because its coffee ____ .	
2	The girls insist on ____ .	
3	Dan's older sister Kathy has just come back from ____ .	
4	On fair trade coffee plantations, pickers earn ____ .	
5	Coffee picking on fair trade plantations is ____ .	
6	Lizzie and Emily are also going to use ____ .	

b **Work in small groups. What do you think about Dan's changed attitude? Do you also know somebody who is in favour of fair trade?**

WRITING 17 **Write two paragraphs of about 50 words each. In one you try to *persuade* a friend to only drink fair trade coffee, in the other one you try to *convince* a friend that only drinking fair trade coffee is a good thing to do.**

→ See *Strategies box*, p. 101, for phrases you could use.

READING 18 a **Read the text about a coffee farmer in Costa Rica. Some parts are missing. Choose the correct part (A–L) for each gap (1–9). There are two extra parts that you should not use. Write your answers in the boxes provided. The first one (0) has been done for you.**

Why Fairtrade coffee?

Does buying Fairtrade products really make a difference to people's lives? We talked to Gerardo Arias Camacho,a coffee producer from Costa Rica, about how his community has been changed.

In the 1980s, the price of coffee fell so low that it didn't cover the cost of production. Many farmers left their land and (0) ______ to find work. I myself decided to go to America to make money and support my family. After eight years, I had earned enough to (1) ______ my father so that my parents could retire. But coffee prices were still so low that I was forced to go back to the States for another two years.

The coffee market is still unstable, but now that we have (2) ______, prices are stable and we receive a guaranteed premium[3] for the community. We spend this money on education, environmental protection, roads and bridges, and have (3) ______. We are sponsoring a scholarship programme so that our kids can stay in school.

My oldest son is in college, my ten-year-old has already had as much education as me, and my little princess is in her second year at school. With the help of fair trade, they might all (4) ______ and get a degree. They won't have to jump the border from Mexico to America, leaving their country for ten years, like me. They can decide what they want in life. I tell them, "You have two choices. You can be a coffee grower or you can (5) ______. But learn how to grow coffee first, like your father and your grandfather."

Since being Fairtrade-certified, our farms have become more environmentally friendly. Our coffee is now produced in a sustainable way. We have (6) ______ by 80% in 10 years. We used to cut a lot of trees down every year to fuel the ovens of our production plant. Now we have (7) ______ by waste products, including coffee skins and the skins of macadamia nuts.

I believe that my cooperative[4] would be out of business if it wasn't for fair trade. Free trade is not responsible trade. When prices go down, (8) ______ and prices drop further. Fair trade is the way trade should be: fair, responsible and sustainable.

When you are shopping, look for the Fairtrade label – you can be sure that the money is going (9) ______. It will help us, but it will also help people around the world because the benefits of protecting the environment are for everyone. It is a matter of helping each other.

As a Fairtrade farmer, I finally feel that I have a tool in my hand. It has given me knowledge so that I am more able to defend myself and my people. I feel there is a future in front of us, because we can stay in our own country and make a living growing coffee.

[3] **guaranteed premium:** garantierte Prämie zusätzlich zum Verkaufspreis
[4] **cooperative:** Genossenschaft (*eine Zusammenarbeit von Personen für wirtschaftliche Zwecke*)

A	installed a new oven which is fuelled	G	farmers produce more
B	straight to the producers	H	lowered coffee production
C	be something else	I	be able to go to university
D	went to the cities	J	pick coffee for a living
E	got a Fairtrade certification	K	improved our production plant
F	reduced the use of pesticides	L	buy the family farm from

0	1	2	3	4	5	6	7	8	9
D									

b What advantages of fair trade does the article mention? Make a list and compare with a partner.

LANGUAGE 19

p. 63

Talking about fair trade

Read the article again and find words and phrases that mean:

1 money you have to spend to grow or create something: ______

2 without a lot of changes: ______

3 money from the state or an organisation to pay for your education: ______

4 causing little damage to the environment, using few resources: ______

5 something you throw away: ______

6 a person or an organisation that creates things that can be sold: ______

7 a document that states officially that a certain standard is being kept:

______

8 things you do to save nature: ______

9 if somebody can be trusted to do things right, this person is: ______

10 another expression for 'good effects': ______

LISTENING 20

32

a You are going to listen to Dan's sister Kathy talking about picking coffee. Speculate what each picture in 20b is showing and compare your guesses with a partner.

b Now listen to Kathy and decide which picture she is talking about by writing the number of the recording into the correct box.

A

B

C

WRITING 21 Go to your local supermarket and find out what other Fairtrade products they sell. Use the internet to find out as much as you can about the production processes of one of these products and create a poster that advertises the product, also explaining how it is made.

SPEAKING 22 *Individual long turn:* Work with a partner. Choose task A or B, your partner does the other one. Give feedback to each other. Before you start, study the *Strategies box* on *Talking about advantages* below.

Task A

- Compare the pictures.
- Explain why exotic fruits and vegetables might be popular with some people.
- Point out the advantages of buying locally grown fruits and vegetables.

Task B

- Compare the pictures.
- Point out the advantages of finding the same fast food places everywhere.
- Explain why older people might prefer a traditional restaurant to a fast food place.

S

Strategies box

Talking about advantages

This means that you should focus on the advantages, but you could briefly mention any possible disadvantages as well. You might want to start by giving an example of a possible disadvantage, but then explain right away why this is not a valid point. Then you can focus on the advantages using the PEEL strategy. This way your argumentation will be more convincing.

Here are some ideas on how to start:
While some people may think that …, I firmly believe …; Many people say that …, but I am convinced they are wrong. I think …

LANGUAGE 23 **Topic vocabulary: Globalisation and fair trade**

Start by adding the causes and consequences of globalisation to the correct side of the arrow. Then add more phrases from the unit and your own ideas. Make a similar illustration for fair trade and its effects.

dominance of Western ideas and culture ▪ easier worldwide communication ▪ free trade between countries ▪ improved communications technology ▪ increased international trade ▪ problems for local economies

L

causes
- fast and cheap methods of transport
- …

globalisation

consequences
- greater variety of products available
- …

Looking back: Learning goals of Unit 12

			✓✓	✓	!!
READING	▸▸▸ B1+	I can compile information from several texts on the topic of globalisation. **(ex. 6b)**			
	▸▸▸ B1+	I can scan a longer text on the topic of globalisation for relevant information. **(ex. 18)**			
LISTENING	▸▸▸ B1+	I can understand straightforward factual information in clear speech on the topic of globalisation. **(ex. 4, 16a, 20b)**			
WRITING	▸▸▸ B1+	I can write a blog comment to explain a problem somewhat precisely. **(ex. 5)**			
	▸▸▸ B1+	I can write a paragraph to communicate information and ideas on the topic of globalisation. **(ex. 17)**			
SPEAKING	▸▸▸ B1+	I can enter unprepared into conversation on the topic of globalisation with some confidence. **(ex. 1, 7, 16b)**			
	▸▸▸ B1+	I can express and exchange ideas about more abstract cultural topics such as globalisation. **(ex. 1, 7, 8, 16b, 22)**			
	▸▸▸ B1+	I can express and exchange ideas about my experiences, feelings and reactions. **(ex. 7, 8, 9a, 13, 15a, 22)**			
LANGUAGE	▸▸▸	I can use a sufficient range of vocabulary to express myself with reasonable precision on the topic of globalisation.			

My personal feelings about globalisation are …

In the future the world will be made even smaller by …

Semester check 02

What's your progress with the learning goals of this semester? Make a mark on the line that shows where you see yourself, then do the tasks. Don't forget to check your answers with the key on p. 207 afterwards.

	✓✓	✓	!!
LESEN ▸▸▸ B1+ Ich kann in klar geschriebenen argumentativen Texten die wesentlichen Schlussfolgerungen erkennen.			

READING 1

Read the two texts expressing different views on artificial intelligence. Some parts are missing. Choose the correct part (A–J) for each gap (1–7). There are two extra parts that you should not use. Write your answers in the boxes provided. The first one (0) has been done for you.

(0) ______

Elon Musk is a South-African-born businessman who is the CEO of SpaceX and Tesla. SpaceX was the first private company to send a vehicle to the International Space Station with supplies.

(1) ______

Elon Musk has repeatedly said society needs to be more concerned about safety with the increased use of artificial intelligence. He says that AI is probably humanity's "biggest existential threat." His opinion is that "if you're not concerned about AI safety, you should be. AI is a fundamental risk to the existence of human civilisation. I keep sounding the alarm bells, but until people see robots going down the street killing people, they don't know how to react."

(2) ______

Musk continues, "AI is a risk in a way that car accidents, airplane crashes, faulty drugs or bad food were not – they were harmful to a set of individuals within society, of course, but they were not harmful to society as a whole." He has said that artificial intelligence will cause massive job disruption, that robots "will be able to do everything better than us," and that this will result in massive job losses.

(3) ______

The solution, says Musk, is regulation: "AI is a rare case where we need to be proactive about regulation instead of reactive." He thinks that governments step in only after "a whole bunch of bad things happen," and that this is too late. He is therefore calling on governments to start regulating AI now. Musk himself has invested in a range of AI companies in order to keep an eye on its development.

(4) ______

Mark Zuckerberg is the CEO of Facebook. He launched the company while studying at Harvard University – and became one of the youngest billionaires in the world.

(5) ______

Mark Zuckerberg has criticised Elon Musk, his fellow Silicon Valley billionaire, and others who sound alarm bells over artificial intelligence posing a threat to our safety and well-being. "AI is going to make our lives better in the future, and doomsday scenarios are pretty irresponsible," explains Zuckerberg. He disagrees with the spread of fear surrounding the potential of artificial intelligence.

(6) ______

"I have pretty strong opinions on this. I am optimistic," he says enthusiastically. "I think you can build things and the world gets better. But with AI especially, I am really optimistic. In the next five to ten years, AI is going to deliver so many improvements in the quality of our lives," he adds, pointing out that artificial intelligence is already helping diagnose diseases, for example.

(7) ______
Zuckerberg also points to self-driving cars as a way that AI will improve our lives. "One of the top causes of death for people is car accidents still, and if you can eliminate that with AI, that is going to be just a dramatic improvement. Whenever I hear people saying AI is going to hurt people in the future, I think, yeah, you know, technology can generally always be used for good and bad, and you need to be careful about how you build it, and you need to be careful about what you build and how it is going to be used."

A	Zuckerberg's serious doubts	F	A question of employment
B	AI – worry about nothing?	G	A healthy future
C	Musk, a fan of AI	H	A safer world for us all
D	Rocket man	I	A wealthy student
E	The need for control	J	The doubtful future of humankind

0	1	2	3	4	5	6	7
D							

HÖREN ▶▶▶ B1+ Ich kann in Filmen und Radiosendungen zu Themen von persönlichem Interesse einen großen Teil verstehen, wenn relativ langsam und deutlich gesprochen wird.

✓✓ ✓ !!

LISTENING 2

radio FM4

33

5ut25x

You are going to listen to an FM4 interview with an Austrian university professor about gender roles on TV. First you will have 45 seconds to study the task below, then you will hear the recording twice. While listening, complete the sentences (1–6) using a maximum of four words. Write your answers in the spaces provided. The first one (0) has been done for you.

After the second listening, you will have 45 seconds to check your answers.

0	In *VEEP* a woman plays _____ .	the first female president
1	Post-feminism means that women can _____ .	
2	The idea that women should do everything is problematic because it _____ .	
3	When looking at cult series, one can see that the progress our culture has made _____ .	
4	When a series is considered 'cult', it mainly shows the perspective of _____ .	
5	*Nurse Jackie* is a very different series because it focuses on _____ . (Give one answer.)	
6	Ambivalence is something that most women _____ .	

✓✓	✓	!!

SPRACH-VERWENDUNG IM KONTEXT ▸▸▸ Ich kann ein hinreichend breites Spektrum an sprachlichen Mitteln, die eher vorhersehbare Situationen beschreiben, korrekt erkennen und anwenden.

LANGUAGE IN USE 3

Read the text about the dangers faced by some journalists. Some words are missing. Choose the correct answer (A, B, C or D) for each gap (1–10). Put a cross (☒) in the correct box. The first one (0) has been done for you.

The most dangerous job in the world?

What comes to mind when we think about the most dangerous jobs in the world? We may think of firefighters, police officers, miners, or even bodyguards, but not (0) ______ of us would believe that there are some journalists who face greater dangers for reporting the news.

According to the United Nations, "Journalism is one of the (1) ______ dangerous professions in the world." Journalists go out to the streets in war zones or other dangerous areas to explore and report what is happening. (2) ______ , in this profession, the stories covered may result in the kidnapping, assault and even death of journalists and their staff. Many journalists are unable to (3) ______ to their home countries out of fear of being jailed or killed.

Navi Pillay, the former UN High Commissioner for Human Rights, said, "(4) ______ on human rights violations and giving a voice to the victims is what journalists do best. They contribute towards raising awareness of human rights issues, (5) ______ means this service deserves better protection than it has now."

Sadly, less protection (6) ______ to journalists than to individuals doing other risky jobs. People don't (7) ______ this until they see innocent journalists that have been arrested, kidnapped or even murdered. Photographer Tyler Hicks has said, "I have been (8) ______ by many people why I take the risks that I do to do this job. We do it because we want to validate what's happening (9) ______ the world. We hope that by being there to document it first-hand, we can bring the (10) ______ – and hopefully positive change."

0	A many	☒	B none	☐	C any	☐	D majority	☐
1	A extreme	☐	B ten	☐	C most	☐	D important	☐
2	A Badly	☐	B Always	☐	C Unfortunately	☐	D Unhappy	☐
3	A leave	☐	B live	☐	C renew	☐	D return	☐
4	A Reporting	☐	B Write	☐	C Report	☐	D Saying	☐
5	A what	☐	B although	☐	C while	☐	D which	☐
6	A was given	☐	B gives	☐	C is given	☐	D is giving	☐
7	A knowing	☐	B realise	☐	C hearing	☐	D mean	☐

8	A asked ☐	B asking ☐	C saying ☐	D told ☐
9	A between ☐	B around ☐	C within ☐	D upon ☐
10	A right ☐	B ending ☐	C truth ☐	D people ☐

✓✓	✓	!!

SCHREIBEN ▸▸▸ B1+ Ich kann Informationen und Gedanken zu konkreten wie abstrakten Themen, auch kulturellen (z. B. Musik, Filme, literarische Texte) mitteilen und einigermaßen präzise ein Problem erklären.

WRITING 4

Your English language assistant wants to read *Lord of the Flies* with your class. He/She has suggested different ways of reading the novel and wants to find out what students think about them. You have decided to do a survey among your classmates and hand in a report.

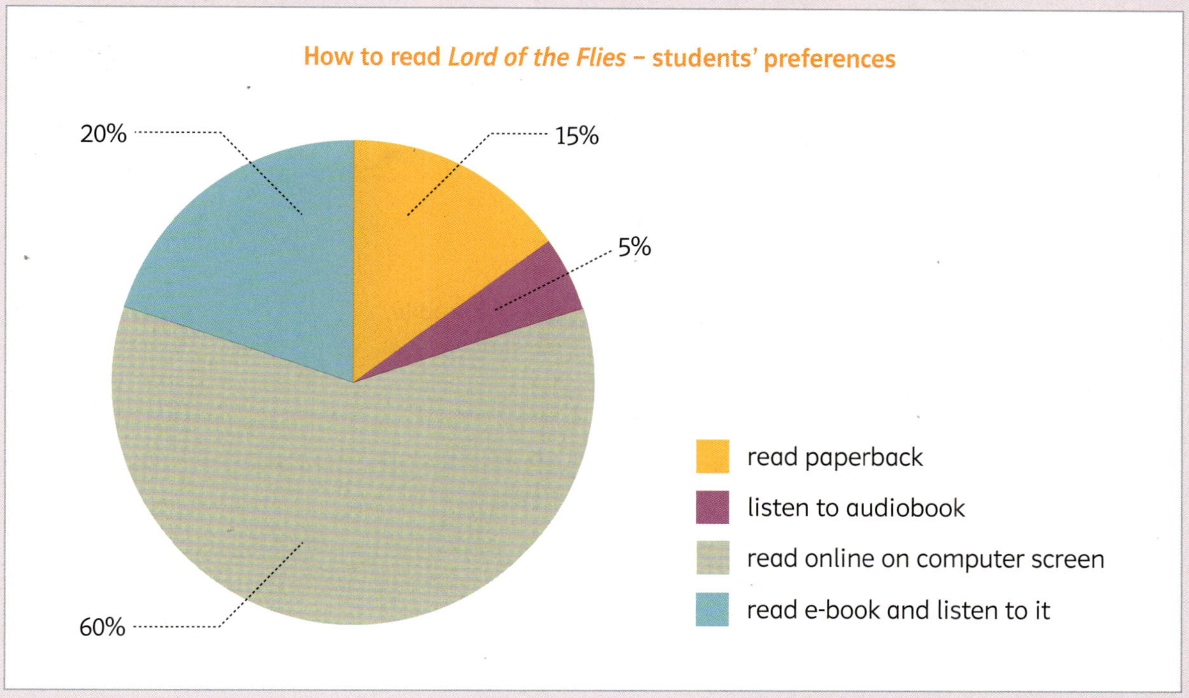

In your report you should:

- present the results of your survey
- give possible reasons for the results
- suggest what the language assistant should do

Write around 250 words. Divide your report into sections and give them headings.

		✓✓	✓	!!
SPRECHEN ▸▸▸ B1+	Ich kann Gedanken zu eher abstrakten, auch kulturellen Themen ausdrücken und mich darüber austauschen.			
▸▸▸ B1+	Ich kann ohne Vorbereitung mit einiger Sicherheit an Gesprächen über vertraute Themen teilnehmen.			

SPEAKING 5

a **Individual long turn (4 minutes)**

Study the task below and prepare for about 8 minutes. Your partner gives you feedback with the checklist in the key.

- Compare the pictures.
- Specify how you could help older people use a mobile.
- Explain if children should/should not use smartphones.

b **Paired activity (8 minutes)**

Do the task below in a group of three. Two of you talk, the third group member listens and gives you feedback with the checklist in the key.

Your class is doing a social project. Every student has to do volunteer work for a week. Your English language assistant wants to know which of the institutions listed below you and your partner would like to work for. Agree on two.

- kindergarten
- refugee camp
- animal shelter
- old people's home
- Red Cross

Grammar revisited

Relative clauses

You use relative clauses to add information or detail to nouns, noun phrases or even whole clauses. Relative clauses are usually connected to the main clause of a sentence by a relative pronoun.

You can use these relative pronouns:

who – for people
which – for things
whose – to say who or what something belongs to
where – for places
when – for time
why – for reasons

1 Clauses giving essential information (= defining relative clauses)	
In a defining relative clause, you add information that is essential for the sentence **to make sense.**	
▪ You want to describe **what somebody/something does** or **is**. (***Who***/***which*** is the **subject** of the **relative clause.**)	*I'm the kind of person* ***who*** *likes to joke around with others./An online presence* ***which*** *makes you look lazy is bad for you.* (= **the online presence** makes you look lazy)
▪ You want to describe **what somebody/something ELSE does** or **is**. (***Who***/***which*** is the **object** of the **relative clause.**)	*I saw the picture* ***which*** *Oliver uploaded to the school website.* (= Oliver uploaded **the picture**)
In this type of relative clause, you can leave out the relative pronoun (= **contact clause**).	*I saw the picture Oliver uploaded to the school website.*
Note: ▪ In both types of defining relative clauses above, you can **replace** ***who*** and ***which*** with ***that***, especially in informal contexts: *I'm the kind of person* ***that*** *likes to joke around with others.* *An online presence* ***that*** *makes you look lazy is bad for you.* ▪ You **cannot use** ***who*** or ***which*** after ***all***, ***everything***, ***nothing***, ***the only*** and **superlatives**: *I've told you all (that) I know./Is this the best (that) you can do?*	
▪ You want to describe **who** or **what something belongs to**.	*The man* ***whose*** *car has been stolen is over there.* *This is the car* ***whose*** *paint has been scratched.*
▪ You want to talk about **when** and **where** something takes place, and **why** something has happened.	*That was the moment (****when****) I knew I was wrong.* *He came back to the place (****where****) he had been born.* *Maybe this is the reason (****why****) he always looks grumpy.*
2 Clauses giving additional information (= non-defining relative clauses)	
In a non-defining relative clause, you add (interesting) **information** that is **not essential.** As it is not essential, you put this information **between commas**. Also, you **cannot use** ***that*** as a relative pronoun and you **cannot leave out** the **relative pronoun**.	
▪ You want to **add information about somebody/something**.	*Our English language assistant,* ***who*** *is from Newcastle, speaks with a really strong accent.* *I like our area best in September,* ***when*** *it's not so hot anymore and all the leaves are turning red.*
▪ You want to **add information about** an **action.**	*Tom eats his own pizza and any leftovers,* ***which*** *is really gross./Steve left the room,* ***which*** *didn't surprise me.*

Reported speech

You can use reported speech to tell somebody what other people say or said. As the meaning should stay the same, certain parts of the sentence have to change.

1 Tense changes

If the **reporting verb** is in the **past** (e.g. *said*), you generally have to **change the tense** of the reported sentence.

Present simple *Steve: "I want to buy a Mr Fox mug."*	**Past simple** *Steve **said** that he **wanted** to buy a Mr Fox mug.*
Present continuous *Steve: "I'm shopping for Lizzie's birthday."*	**Past continuous** *Steve **said** that he **was shopping** for Lizzie's birthday.*
Past simple *Steve: "I tried to get her a Mr Fox mug."*	**Past perfect** *Steve **said** that he **had tried** to get her a Mr Fox mug.*
Present perfect *Steve: "I've decided to go to Hebendam's."*	**Past perfect** *Steve **said** that he **had decided** to go to Hebendam's.*
***will* future** *Emily: "I'll help you with the shopping."*	**Conditional (*would*)** *Emily **said** that she **would help** me with the shopping.*
Modal verbs (*can*, *must*) *Steve: "I can never decide what to get for Lizzie."* *Steve: "I must start thinking about Lizzie's present earlier next year."*	**Modal verbs (*could*, *had to*)** *Steve **said** that he **could never decide** what to get for Lizzie.* *Steve **said** that he **would have to** start thinking about Lizzie's present earlier next year.*

Other modal verbs like ***could***, ***would***, ***might*** and ***should*** **stay the same** because they do not have different past forms.

"We could go to Hebendam's together."	*Emily suggested that they could go to Hebendam's together.*

Note: When the situation/feelings/opinions that you talk about is/are **still true**, you **do not have to change the tense** in reported speech. You can also keep other parts of the statement, if they are still true.

Mark: "My little sister always puts lucky charms into my sports bag."	*Mark said that his little sister always **puts** lucky charms into his sports bag.* (= she always does this, so it is still true)
Steve: "My sister has got black hair."	*Steve said that his sister **has got** black hair.* (= it's true that Steve's sister has got black hair)

2 Changes regarding time and place

References to **time and place might need to change** when you report a statement at a later time or in a different place.

now	then
today	that day
tonight	that night
tomorrow	the next/following day
next week/month/year	the next/following week/month/year

... ago	... before
yesterday	the day before/the previous day
last week/month	the week/month before/the previous week/month
here	there
this (place)	that (place)

3 Pronoun changes

Make sure all pronouns **refer to the correct people**:

Steve: "I need to do some shopping."	***He** said that **he** needed to do some shopping.*
Emily: "I'll help you with it."	***She** said that **she** would help **him** with it.*

Common reporting verbs for statements:

add, admit, announce, argue, comment, complain, confirm, doubt, explain, insist, mention, promise, realise, repeat, reply, report, say, suggest, think, warn

Questions

When you report what somebody asked, the **word order changes**. You report yes/no questions using ***if*** or ***whether***.

*Rose: "Steve, **did you buy** Lizzie's present?"*	*Rose wondered **if Steve had bought** Lizzie's present.*
*Emily: "Steve, **where are you going**?"*	*Emily asked Steve **where he was going**.*

Common reporting verbs: *ask, inquire, wonder, want to know*

Orders, requests and advice

When you report what somebody advised, requested or ordered/told you to do, you use this structure: **subject – reporting verb – person – *(not) to* – verb (infinitive)**.

Request

Rose: "Could you please get Lizzie's present?"	*Rose **asked Steve to get** Lizzie's present.*

Advice

Shop assistant: "Why don't you try Hebendam's?"	*The shop assistant **advised him to try** Hebendam's.*

Order

Police: "Don't steal from shops!"	*The police **told them not to steal** from shops.*

Common reporting verbs: *ask, forbid, order, request, tell, warn, want*

Gerund and infinitive

- **You can use a gerund (verb + *-ing*) as the subject of a sentence or as an object, just like nouns.**
  ***Gardening** is a great hobby. – Pat enjoys **gardening**.*
- **When you use two verbs together, the second verb is often a gerund.**
  *I **love swimming** in summer./Greg doesn't **like getting** up early./Steve **admitted not having bought** Lizzie's present.*
- **You always need a gerund when using a verb after a preposition (*by*, *from*, *without*, etc.).**
  *You can live **without eating**, but you can't live **without drinking**./He keeps **on making** the same jokes all the time, it's so annoying./Why don't you give **up smoking**?*

- **Whether you need to use an infinitive (*to invite*, *to take*) or a gerund often depends on the verb of the sentence.**

The following **verbs** are **always** followed by a **gerund**:	
▪ **likes and dislikes**	*can't stand, dislike, enjoy, feel like, hate, like, mind, prefer*
▪ **ideas and opinions**	*admit, consider, imagine, insist, recommend, suggest, understand*
▪ **starts and stops**	*begin, delay, finish, give up, practise, put off, spend, start*
▪ **others**	*avoid, can't help, deny, get used to, involve, mention, miss, risk*
These **verbs** are **always** followed by an **infinitive**:	
▪ **mental activity**	*agree, choose, decide, encourage, learn, tell, want, warn, wish*
▪ **future arrangements**	*arrange, expect, hope, manage, offer, plan, prepare, promise*
▪ **appearance**	*appear, pretend, seem, tend*
▪ **effort**	*attempt, fail, hurry, manage, refuse, try*

- **With some verbs the meaning can change depending on whether a gerund or an infinitive follows.**

Steve ***stopped talking*** *to the store detective.*	= He is no longer talking to the detective.
Steve ***stopped to tie*** *his shoelaces.*	= He stopped walking so he could tie his shoes.
Steve will always ***remember buying*** *Lizzie's present this year.*	= Steve will certainly remember this activity.
After this year, Steve will ***remember to buy*** *a present for Lizzie.*	= Steve will do what he has promised to do and not forget it.
Try putting *a reminder in your calendar, Steve!*	= Steve should do something new.
I'll ***try to think of*** *Lizzie's birthday next year.*	= Steve is trying something difficult.
Steve ***needs to repair*** *his computer.*	= He will do it himself.
Steve's keyboard ***needs repairing****.*	= He'll have to take it to the shop.
Emily ***went on talking*** *to the detective for ages.*	= She continued doing the same thing.
Emily then ***went on to talk*** *about her experience in Hebendam's.*	= She started to talk about something new.

Adverbs of degree

- **You can use adverbs of degree to describe the intensity or extent of something in more detail.**

weaker ←——————————→ **stronger**
not very – hardly – a bit/a little/slightly – fairly/quite/rather/pretty – very – really – extremely

- **You can use them to make adjectives or adverbs stronger or weaker.**

This haiku is nice. – This haiku is ***quite*** *nice. – This haiku is* ***really*** *nice.*
He can write poems well. – He can write poems ***fairly*** *well. – He can write poems* ***rather*** *well.*

- **You can use them to make verbs stronger or weaker.**

I love writing poetry ***very much****. I like haiku* ***a lot****. I* ***really*** *find them fascinating./*
I know Japanese ***a little****./This annoys me* ***a bit****.*

Word order

In English, sentences can change their focus and sometimes even their meanings depending on where the different sentence parts are. This is why you need to follow a specific order when you put the parts of a sentence together to make it correct and meaningful.

Subject	verb	object	extra information
Blind runners	*have*	*a running buddy*	*attached to their wrist.*

1 Direct and indirect objects

Some verbs can take more than one object. In **sentences with two objects** (direct: 'what?' and indirect: 'who?'), both objects come **right after the verb**. You can **choose which one** comes **first**. **If** you put the **direct object first**, the **indirect object** needs a **preposition**.

Subject	verb	direct object	indirect object
Emma	*sent*	*a postcard*	*to her friends.*
She	*bought*	*a present*	*for her mum.*

Subject	verb	indirect object	direct object
Emma	*sent*	*her friends*	*a postcard.*
She	*bought*	*her mum*	*a present.*

2 Extra information

You need to put extra information into the following sequence if there is more than one piece of extra information: **manner** (e.g. *happily*) – **place** (e.g. *in town*) – **time** (e.g. *last week*).

Subject	verb	object	manner	place	time
The goalball player	*threw*	*the ball*	*straight*	*into the net*	*during her first game.*

If you want to **stress time** or **place**, you can put it at the **beginning of** the **sentence**.

Time	subject	verb	object	manner	place
During her first game,	*the goalball player*	*threw*	*the ball*	*straight*	*into the net.*

Unlike German, you **cannot** place extra information **between** the **verb** and **object(s)** of a sentence.

Subject	verb	extra information	object
Er	*verlässt*	*leise*	*das Haus.*

Subject	verb	object	extra information
He	*leaves*	*the house*	*quietly.*

3 Adverbs of frequency

Adverbs of frequency (*always, sometimes, …*) go:

- **between** the **subject** and the **verb**. *Blind runners **always** have a running buddy.*
- **between** the **first** and **second verb**, **if** there is **more than one**. *Disabled people have **often** been treated unfairly on the job market.*
- **after** the verb ***to be***. *People's disabilities are **sometimes** invisible.*

4 Complex sentences

Unlike German, the **word order remains the same** even in more complex sentences with subordinate clauses (*Nebensätze*). You add the linking word to the beginning of the subordinate clause, but don't change the word order in either part of the sentence:

Weil	*er*	*ohne Hilfe*	*nicht gehen kann,*	*benutzt*	*er*	*einen Rollstuhl.*	
Because	*he*	*can't walk*	*without help,*	*he*	*uses*	*a wheelchair.*	

The passive

- **If you want to focus on actions and their effects, and not on who does them, you can use the passive. It is often used:**
  - in news reports: *The passengers* ***were evacuated*** *from the plane.*
  - in scientific writing: *The samples* ***were placed*** *under a microscope.*
  - when describing processes: *In bungee jumping, the rope* ***is attached*** *to the ankles of the jumper.*
  - when talking about customs and beliefs: *The custom* ***is believed*** *to date from the 19th century.*
  - when it doesn't matter, or when it's obvious or unknown who did something: *The school computer* ***has been stolen***.

- **You form the passive with the correct form of *to be* and the past participle (3rd verb form). You can make passive sentences in all tenses, as long as you follow the rules for the passive and the tense at the same time:**

Subject	modals if needed	form of *to be* in the correct tense	past participle (3rd form)	extra information
Lizzie		*was*	*bitten*	*by a hamster.*
The hamster		*has been*	*found.*	
This door	*must*	*be*	*closed*	*at 10 p.m.*
The door	*should*	*have been*	*closed*	*yesterday.*
The car		*is being*	*repaired.*	
I		*want to be*	*left*	*alone.*

- **In spoken English, you can also use *get* instead of *to be* with many tenses.**
  Lizzie ***got*** *bitten by a hamster.*

- **If it is important who/what did or created something, you add the information using the word *by*:**
  Thunderbolt Kid was written ***by*** *Bill Bryson.*

Articles (*the, a, an* – or no article)

You use articles to show whether you are talking about a specific example or an idea in general.

1 General ideas and things

If you talk/write about **general** ideas and **things**, you use:

- ***a/an*** with a **singular countable noun.**
  Is there ***a bookshop*** *around here?* (= any kind of bookshop)
  A cat *can be great fun to have as a pet.* (= any cat)
- **no article** with a **plural countable noun.**
  I'm interested in ***computers***. (= all computers)
  Cats *can be great fun to have as pets.* (= all cats)
- **no article** with an **uncountable noun.**
  I'm really into ***music***. (= any kind of music)
  Coffee *is not very healthy for you.* (= coffee in general)

countable nouns:
one cat, two cats, …
uncountable nouns:
music, money, fun, …

2 Particular, definite things

If you talk/write about **particular**, **definite things**, you use the definite article ***the***.

The bookshop *is in Broad Street.* (= there is only one bookshop in town)
The cat *has caught a mouse again and left it on* ***the doorstep****.*
(= we know which cat, and we know which doorstep)
This is ***the computer*** *I want.* (= a specific, definite computer)
The latest album *of the band isn't very good.* (= this particular album, all the others are great)
Hurry! ***The coffee*** *will get cold.* (= the cup of coffee that I've prepared for you)

You can **only use** the definite article ***the***:

- if your readers/listeners **already know** what you are talking/writing about.
  Once upon a time, there was a king. ***The king*** *spent most of his time alone.*
- if you **define** what you're talking/writing about **later** (in the sentence).
  The computer *I want to buy is really fast and very light.*
- if there is **only one example** of what you are talking/writing about.
  The sun *was already shining when I woke this morning.*

3 Rules and exceptions

You generally **do not use an article** with:

- names of **people**, **shops** or geographical **places** like countries, towns, roads or lakes.
  Ms Smith, on Wall Street, in Washington, at Lake Windermere
- nouns for **places** if you talk about the **purpose** these places are used for.
  She had to be taken to hospital. (= to be treated as a patient)
  In three years' time, I'll go to university. (= to study there as a student)
- **means of transportation.**
  I usually go to school by bike./You can go to England by plane, train or boat./Why don't you go on foot, it's healthier.

Note: Whether geographical features need an article or not often doesn't follow simple rules.

- **states and countries:** *in Great Britain*, but *in the United Kingdom, in the United States*
- **mountains/mountain ranges:** *on Mont Blanc*, but *on the Matterhorn, in the Alps*

Writing coach

Formal email

You write formal emails to give or ask for information, respond to a request, apologise, complain, make suggestions, or apply for a job. The recipient is usually someone that you do not know so well or do not know at all.

Your email should be polite and to the point. Use set phrases if appropriate and avoid colloquial language and contractions.

→ See also p. 40.

These are the main points to remember when writing a formal email:

- Start with:
  From: your name and email address
  To: the person you are writing to
  Subject: what the email is about
- Address the person you are writing to in a formal way and sign off at the end.
- Give your reason for writing in the introduction.
- Start a new paragraph for each content point (bullet point).
- Let the recipient know if you want to stay in contact before signing off.

Sample task

You are disappointed by a weekend trip to London as the trip did not meet your expectations. You have made some notes and decided to write an email of complaint to the travel agency.

In your email you should:

- explain why you chose *Easy & Excellent*
- describe what went wrong
- suggest what *Easy & Excellent* should do

Write around 250 words.

to Stansted, not Heathrow
arrived at hotel 2 a.m.

English?!?

15 minutes to underground station

Sample answer

From: Franziska Schindler <fran.schindler@email.com>
To: Paul Higgins <p.hig@easy-excellent.com>
Subject: Shortcomings[1] of travel arrangements to London

Dear Mr Higgins,

I am writing to complain about the travel arrangements to London as offered by *Easy & Excellent*.

I saw your advertisement on *popular_travels.com* and booked a weekend at the Golden Lion Hotel from 22nd April to 24th April this year. I was led to believe that the promises you made were a good choice for an inexpensive weekend trip. You stated that the flight connections were uncomplicated, that the hotel and breakfast would be excellent and that there would be easy transport from the hotel to the centre of London.

Unfortunately, this was not the case. To begin with, the flight to London was not to Heathrow but to Stansted. Thus, the transfer to the hotel took so long that I finally arrived at 2 a.m. Needless to say, the staff were unfriendly at that time of night. Moreover, the choice of breakfast was poor: tea, coffee, bread, butter and jam – not at all what I would consider an English breakfast. Worst of all was the fact that there were no quick connections from the hotel to the centre of London. In fact, taking the underground meant a 15 minutes' walk from the hotel.

I had been looking forward to this trip to London, but it was ruined by the problems mentioned above. Therefore, I feel that I deserve a refund of at least 50% of the price I paid. Unless I receive a satisfactory reply, I will inform *popular_travels.com* about the shortcomings of your travel company.

I look forward to hearing from you soon.

Best regards,

Franziska Schindler

Subject (Re): Write what the email is about.

Introduction: State your reason for writing.

Use all the information given in the prompt.

Formal linking devices

Support your complaints with details.

No contractions

Bullet point 3

Sign off with *Best regards*, *Yours*, *Yours sincerely*, *Yours faithfully*, etc.

Passives make it sound more formal

Bullet point 1

Use all the information given in the notes.

Bullet point 2

Use set phrases.

Express your wish to stay in contact.

[1] **shortcoming:** Mangel

Article

An article is written to be published in an (online) magazine and read by a specific audience who is interested in the topic you are writing about. It can be serious or amusing. Its purpose is to inform, entertain, convince, etc., or to simply captivate the reader.

To attract the readers' attention, your article needs to have a catchy title which gives them an idea of what it is about. This can be a question or a surprising/provocative statement.

These are the main points to remember when writing an article:

- Give your article a catchy title.
- Write an introduction that pulls the reader right in.
- Involve your readership.
- Start a new paragraph for each new aspect or idea given in the content points (bullet points).
- Link the paragraphs: The reader should never lose interest in what you are writing.
- Finish your article by giving the reader something to think about.

Your readership should be pulled in right from the beginning and never lose interest while reading the rest of the article. Include descriptions, anecdotes, examples and your opinion when appropriate. The ending should give your readers the feeling that they have not wasted their time reading it. It could be a question, an answer to a question or a summary. It could also give them something to think about or encourage them to take action.

To achieve all of the above, use lively, expressive language and involve your readers with direct and rhetorical questions, imperatives and exclamations. Depending on the topic and your readership, the language should be formal, neutral or personal.

→ See also p. 44.

Sample task

The school magazine of your English partner school has started a series of articles on creepy places around the world. You have decided to send them an article about a creepy place you have recently visited.

In your article you should:

- present the creepy place
- describe your visit
- specify why you think it is creepy

Write around 250 words.
Give your article a title.

Sample answer

Find a catchy title that gives the reader an idea of what the article is about.

A head start in Hallstatt – check it out!

This probably isn't for you if you are the nervous type. But if you're looking for a seriously creepy place to visit, go and see a room full of skulls in Hallstatt.

To begin with, we're not talking about one or two skulls here. Unbelievable, but true: There are over 1,200 skulls packed into the small bone house behind the church in Hallstatt. Are you wondering why? As there wasn't enough space for the dead in the cemetery, graves were reopened, and the skulls and bones were removed and stacked in the bone house to make space for the newly dead. What an idea!

I didn't know what to expect when I was told about the bone house. Like most visitors I started out visiting the church and the small cemetery, enjoying the gorgeous views of the village, the lake and the mountains. Then I continued my walk to the bone house and knew at once that this was the place for me to see. What a contrast! The innocent scenery outside and the gloomy atmosphere inside.

But what makes this sight really creepy is the fact that most of the skulls were decorated so people could remember who they were. They had their dates of birth and death written on them, and a few were painted with flowers or other symbols. Just spooky! The sight of them gave me the creeps and left me speechless.

So, if you want to visit a truly hair-raising place, check it out for yourself. You won't regret it.

Address the reader directly.

Use informal, personal language, write in a chatty tone.

Use direct or rhetorical questions.

Link the paragraphs to keep the reader interested.

Encourage the reader to take action.

A powerful introduction pulls the reader in right from the beginning.

Bullet point 1

Use exclamations.

Bullet point 2

Use descriptive and powerful adjectives.

Bullet point 3

Report

A report gives clear information on facts, projects, incidents or events and is based on evidence and research. It is written for a person in charge, an authority or an institution, using formal and polite language. It is clearly structured, making use of sections and headings so that the information is easy to follow.

→ See also pp. 109–111.

The ABC guideline for writing reports:

A – be **a**ccurate. The information has to be exact.
B – be **b**rief. Keep the report to the point.
C – be **c**lear. Make sure everybody understands it.

The (visual) layout:

From:
Subject:
Date:

Introduction

Heading
Bullet point 1

Heading
Bullet point 2

Heading
Bullet point 3

Sample task

Your class has been invited to visit Whitehall, your partner school in Cambridge. The school wants to offer attractive afternoon clubs to your class. It needs to know which clubs offered to the Austrian students they would like to attend. You have decided to do a survey among your classmates and send a report.

Austrian students' choice of afternoon clubs (n = 20)

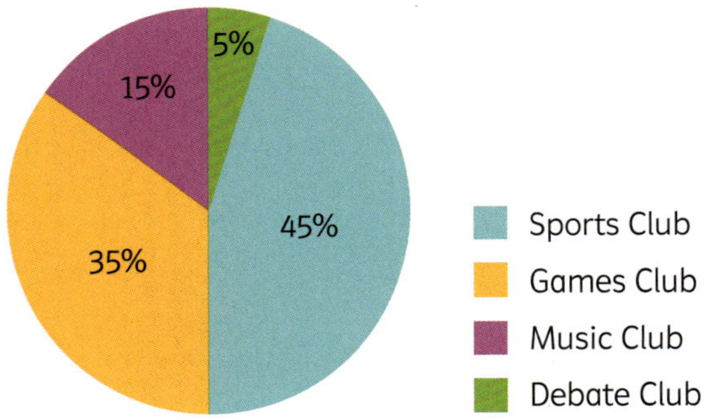

In your report you should:

- describe the results of your survey
- give possible reasons for the results
- suggest which clubs the school should offer

Write around 250 words. Divide your report into sections and give them headings.

Make sure you understand the situation:
Who is interested in the report? Why? What information do you have to give? Why is the information important?

Study the information in the graph carefully:
How many clubs are being offered? Which club is most popular among your classmates? Which club is least popular? Which information is important?

Study the instructions:
How can you describe the results without giving just the numbers as a percentage? What do you think about the results? Can you explain them? What suggestions can you make based on the results?

Sample answer

Ways to begin your report:
The aim of this report is to outline …; This report will consider …; As requested, I will explain/specify/suggest …

In your introduction you explain what the report is about.

Write clear headings for each section or paragraph.

Use formal linking words, such as *in fact, also, whereas, …*

Formal language: no contractions

From: Lukas Schauregger
Subject: Austrian students' club preferences
Date: 28th February 20..

Introduction

The following report outlines which of the suggested afternoon clubs the Austrian students would like to attend in Cambridge. The information is based on a survey done among 20 students in the class. My findings and recommendations are presented below.

Club preferences

A large majority of students wishes to go to the Sports Club. In fact, this club was chosen by almost half of the class. More than one third of students would like to attend the Games Club, whereas only a few students are interested in the Music Club. The Debate Club is the least popular, with only one person in twenty choosing to attend.

Sports are most popular

Sports are the most popular choice because our school has a strong extra-curricular sports programme. Our sports teams are usually successful in competitions. Also, many students enjoy playing online games and board games, such as chess, in their free time. As there is no focus on music at our school, students are probably not interested in it. The Debate Club is not popular because many students do not trust themselves to hold a formal debate in English yet.

Recommendations

I recommend that enough places are provided in the Sports Club for the majority of the class. The Austrian students certainly look forward to some competitive sports matches that could be organised by the school. Perhaps the person who is in charge of the Debate Club should be warned that only one student is interested in it.

Make sure it is clear who is writing the report and what it is about. Also, give the date.

Formal language: passive structures

Bp1:
Summarise the facts (results of the survey) given in the graph. Use phrases such as *almost half, more, less than half, a third, …*

Bp2:
Explain the facts by giving reasons. Why do you think the students have chosen a particular club? What do you think about the results?

Bp3:
Make useful suggestions for the school as a conclusion.

Blog

A blog (short for 'weblog') is an interactive webpage for publishing writing online. Anybody who has access to the internet can read the blogs there and comment on them. In a blog, you give your opinion on a topic, inform your readership, write about personal experiences using formal, semi-formal or informal language, depending on the topic and your readership. You may also address your readers directly and invite comments. If your blog is well-written and interesting, other bloggers will want to read and comment on it[1].

Blog post (blog entry)	Blog comment
You write a blog post to share your opinion on a particular subject with online readers. The topic could be of general interest, such as leisure, literature, politics or education. It could also be a diary-type travel journal. You could ask for information, advice or other bloggers' opinions as well. In your conclusion, you might want to let the readers know what you would like them to do: comment on your blog, read a certain book or article, try out some different food, or join a club, depending on your blog post.	You write a blog comment to express your opinion on a blog post or another blog comment. Make sure you have read the blog post (or comment) carefully and fully understand the writer's view before you comment on it. Start your blog comment by referring to the blog post or comment, agree or disagree with the writer, give or follow advice, make suggestions, or give your opinion on the topic that is under discussion.
These are the main points to remember when writing a blog post: **Layout** ▪ User name ▪ Title **Organisation** ▪ Introduction ▪ Main body (address and expand the bullet points making use of paragraphs) ▪ Conclusion	**These are the main points to remember when writing a blog comment:** **Layout** ▪ User name ▪ Email address **Organisation** ▪ Introduction (refer to the blog post/comment) ▪ Main body (address and expand the bullet points making use of paragraphs) ▪ Conclusion

[1] See the *Writing coach* in *way2go! 5* for sample tasks and answers.

Strategies overview

These strategies can help you make the most of what you know at exams.

Reading

Reading – Multiple matching (sentence parts or paragraphs) (MM)

Read the whole text first to get an idea of what it is about. Don't panic if you don't understand every word. Look at the sentence before and after each gap closely – what could fit? Leave out gaps you are not sure about, picking the wrong part could lead to another mistake elsewhere. Go over the text again near the end of the exam time and only then take your best guess for any gaps. In some multiple matching tasks, you read several shorter texts on a similar topic instead of a single long one and you match sentences to the texts.

Reading – Multiple choice (MC)

The questions are in the same order as the information in the text; this can help you find the right place in the text. Mark the sentences where you've found information on a question so you can check your answers quickly when you're done. If you are not sure about the answer to a question, eliminate the options you know are wrong and then take a guess. Always answer every question!

Reading – True/False/Justification (T/F/J)

A statement counts as 'false' if the text gives you different information on it. You have to justify your answer by showing where you found the information. Justify your answer for both true *and* false statements. You must use the first four words of the sentence that gives you the information. A new sentence starts after a full stop. A word is everything between two spaces. Short forms like *don't* count as one word.

Reading – Four-word sentence completion/Four-word answers (4W)

Carefully read the sentences/questions. Details like names or places can help you find the spot in the text where you have to look. Write your answer in four or fewer words. Longer answers are *always* considered wrong. Give one answer only, don't try to give two or more. Don't worry too much about grammar and spelling in short-answer tasks. Your answer is OK as long as your teacher can understand it.

Listening

Listening – Multiple matching (sentence parts or speakers) (MM)

Read all options before listening. While listening, fill in the letters. During the second listening, concentrate on the options you're not sure about. Cross out options used. At first, only write answers you're sure about, picking the wrong part could result in mistakes elsewhere. The task gets easier the more options you've matched correctly. If you're still not sure after having listened twice: guess! Note that some multiple matching tasks have several shorter recordings on a similar topic and you match sentences to the speakers.

Listening – Multiple choice (MC)

Underline keywords in the questions – they can help your brain listen for the right information. You may hear keywords from all four options, but only one answer is absolutely correct. Don't choose an option just because you hear a word from it – make sure that it means the same as your answer.

Listening – Four-word sentence completion/Four-word answers (4W)

While reading the task, think about what the answer could be: do you need a name, a number, a feeling? This helps your brain identify the correct information while listening. Don't write more than four words. Don't worry too much about grammar, your answer only has to be clear.

Language in use

Language in use – Banked gap fill (BGF)

This task type is similar to *Reading – Multiple matching (sentence parts)*, but you need to match single words or short phrases, so it tests your grammar and vocabulary skills more than your reading skills. While reading, think of a word that could fit, then check the words in the bank. Which one comes closest to your idea?

Language in use – Word formation (WF)

Read the sentences carefully to find out what kind of word (noun, verb, etc.) you need to complete the gaps. You *always* have to change the word in bold; it is never correct. Make sure that the new word fits the gap in terms of meaning and grammar – and that it is spelt correctly!

Language in use – Multiple choice (MC)

The options can test you on both vocabulary and grammar. The correct answer is the right word in the correct form. It can be helpful to think about what you could fill in before you look at the options.

Language in use – Editing (ED)

Read the instructions carefully because the number of correct lines can vary. Read the text slowly and word for word. Don't stop reading at the end of a line, read the whole sentence. Look for short words like prepositions, modal verbs or adverbs. Long content words like *bedroom* or *electronic* are usually correct. Reading a difficult line from right to left can help. The first and last word of a line are never wrong. A word that is in the line more than once is never wrong either.

Language in use – Open gap fill (OGF)

Every gap must be filled with exactly one word. Contractions such as *don't* or *I'm* count as one word. For many gaps, there is more than one possible answer. If you can't think of a word right away, the structure of the sentence can help you. For example, think about what kind of word (noun, verb, preposition, …) could fit. Make sure you use the right form of the word. A noun can be singular or plural, a verb might need a suffix for the third person singular or the past.

Writing

1 Study the task carefully and make sure you fully understand what you have to do before you start writing.

a What **type of text** (email, article, blog, …) do you have to write? This will affect your layout and your style. Check the *Writing coach* for text type conventions.
b What is your **reason for writing**? To give or get information, to give a report, to complain, to persuade somebody?
c **Who will read** your text? A friend, the manager of a hotel, a group of young people, bloggers you don't know? This will affect the style of your writing and the register (formal/informal).
d **What** do you have to write **about**? The content points (bullet points) tell you what to include and help you structure your text.

You have booked a reasonably priced all-inclusive hotel on the beach in Fort Lauderdale, Florida. Unfortunately, the hotel did not at all meet your expectations. You have decided to complain about it in an email to the manager.

In your email you should:

- give reasons why you booked the hotel
- describe what went wrong
- suggest what you expect the manager to do

Write around 250 words.

c reader?
d what about?
a text type?
b reason for writing?

2 Make notes of how and what to write before you start. Spend at least five to ten minutes planning your text. The better you have planned your text, the easier it will be to write it.

a **Brainstorm** ideas and draw mind maps. What will be your main ideas, examples, arguments? How can you support them? Can you write about cause and effect? Do you need to mention possible (dis)advantages? Will you have to write about a sequence of events? Are you required to offer a solution? Can you draw from your own experience? What grammatical structures and what tenses will you have to use? What will your introduction and conclusion be about?
b Will you be able to write around **80 words for each bullet point** in a 250-word text? Remember, **each bullet point** should deal with a **separate aspect**, so be careful not to repeat yourself. And don't forget to start a **new paragraph for each bullet point**.

3 Look at your text critically once you have finished it.

a Do a **rough word count** (the average number of words per line multiplied by the number of lines you have written). Think of how and where you can add or cut text if you have failed to meet the expected number of words by clearly more than 10%.
b Check if you have written an **appropriate** salutation, a closing, a title, headings, etc., **depending on the task type. Proofread** your text and try to spot personal mistakes that you might have made in earlier pieces of writing (spelling, grammar, punctuation, etc.).

Vocabulary

AE	*American English*	*opp.*	*opposite*	etw.	etwas
BE	*British English*	*abbr.*	*abbreviation*	jmdm.	jemandem
fml.	*formal*	*sb.*	*somebody*	jmdn.	jemanden
infml.	*informal*	*sth.*	*something*	jmds.	jemandes

Unit 01

	to **revise sth.**	etw. wiederholen *(den Lernstoff)*
	to **deal with sth.**	mit etw. umgehen
1	**identity** [aɪ'dentəti] *What defines your identity?*	Identität
	high frequency sound	Hochfrequenzton
	ankle	Fußknöchel
	worldwide	weltweit
	cell [sel]	Zelle
	to **stretch for ...** *The town's sandy beach stretches for over four miles.*	sich erstrecken über ..., ... weit reichen
	unique [juː'niːk]	einzigartig
	to **contain sth.** *Milk contains lots of proteins.*	etw. beinhalten
	particle ['pɑːtɪkəl]	Teilchen
2	to **make sth. up**	etw. erfinden
3	to **define a person's identity**	die Identität einer Person ausmachen
	gender	Geschlecht
4	to **define yourself in a certain way**	sich über etw. definieren
	surroundings *(pl. only)*	Umfeld, Lebensumstände
	to **distinguish sb./sth. from sb./sth.** *I find it difficult to distinguish Spanish from Portuguese.*	jmdn./etw. von jmdm./etw. unterscheiden
5	**accurate** ['ækjərət]	korrekt; genau, akkurat
6	**generally** *I generally wake up twice during the night.*	im Allgemeinen, generell
	cheerful soul	Frohnatur
	to **joke around**	herumblödeln
	witty	witzig, geistreich
	to **make sb. laugh**	jmdn. zum Lachen bringen
	easy-going	gelassen, locker
	to **get emotional about sth.**	*hier*: sich über etw. aufregen
	foodie *(infml.)*	Essensliebhaber/in
	to **be obsessed with sth.**	von etw. besessen sein
	content [kən'tent]	zufrieden
	to **be content to do sth.**	etw. gerne tun, zu etw. bereit sein
	tough [tʌf] *You need to be tough if you want to be a police officer.*	hart im Nehmen, zäh
	pretty *Tom is a pretty nice guy.*	ziemlich
	to **take delight in doing sth.**	Freude/Spaß daran haben, etw. zu tun
	mean	gemein
	annoying	nervig, ärgerlich
	to **make a fool of sb.** *My brother loves making a fool of me.*	sich über jmdn. lustig machen
	sympathetic [ˌsɪmpə'θetɪk] *Try to be sympathetic towards Caitlin. I think she has problems at home.*	mitfühlend, verständnisvoll
	sensitive ['sensɪtɪv] *He's not very sensitive. He always says what he thinks, even if it hurts people's feelings.*	sensibel, einfühlsam
	to **put up with sb./sth.** *I'm too tired to put up with your nonsense right now!*	jmdn./etw. aushalten/ ertragen
	greedy	gierig
	rare [reə] *We usually eat at home and rarely eat out.*	selten, nicht oft
	plain *That's plain rude.*	einfach, wirklich *(zur Verstärkung einer Aussage)*
	selfish	egoistisch, selbstsüchtig
	bossy	herrisch, rechthaberisch
	to **look down on sb.** *Teachers shouldn't look down on their students.*	auf jmdn. herabsehen, jmdn. geringschätzen
	He's a great laugh.	Er ist wirklich lustig.
	to **be sure of yourself**	selbstsicher sein
	lively ['laɪvli]	quirlig, lebhaft
	upbeat [ʌp'biːt]	optimistisch; fröhlich, beschwingt
	to **look up to sb.** *He looks up to his hero.*	zu jmdm aufsehen, jmdn. bewundern
	leftovers *Lunch is usually leftovers from the night before.*	(Essens-)Reste
	impolite	unhöflich
	jealous ['dʒeləs]	eifersüchtig, neidisch
	self-confident	selbstbewusst
8	to **have sth. in common**	etwas gemeinsam haben
	to **overlap** *The photos didn't fit, so they had to overlap at the sides.*	sich überschneiden, überlappen
	humorous	humorvoll, lustig
9	**outlook on life**	Lebenseinstellung
	to **display sth.** *She displayed her favourite photos on her bedroom wall.*	etw. ausstellen/ präsentieren
11	**virtual** ['vɜːtʃuəl]	virtuell
12	**terrifying**	erschreckend
	to **bother doing sth.** *Some students don't bother doing their homework properly.*	sich die Mühe machen, etw. zu tun

	worrying	besorgniserregend
	to **participate in sth.** *Who wants to participate in the quiz?*	an etw. teilnehmen
	at your best *I'm not at my best early in the morning!*	von seiner besten Seite, in bester Verfassung
	to **be affected by sth.**	von etw. betroffen sein
	to **get involved in sth.** *There are lots of reasons why you should get involved in extracurricular activities.*	bei etw. mitmachen, sich auf etw. einlassen
	(up) to the point where …	bis zu dem Punkt, an dem …
	to **lead** [li:d] **sth.** (led – led) *The study was led by doctor Williamson.*	etw. anführen/leiten
	constantly ['kɒnstəntli]	ständig, dauernd
	carefully edited	sorgfältig bearbeitet
	to **be bound to do sth.** *You're bound to make mistakes every now and then.*	etw. bestimmt tun; unvermeidbar sein, dass …
	to **have an impact on sth.**	etw. beeinflussen
	to **browse (through) sth.** *I browsed through the magazines.*	etw. durchsehen/ durchstöbern
	occasionally	gelegentlich
	lecturer	Vortragende/r an einer Universität
	to **figure sth. out** *I couldn't figure out how he did the card trick, so I asked him.*	etw. herausfinden
	to **be in control (of sth.)**	die Kontrolle (über etw.) haben
	to **get attention**	Aufmerksamkeit erregen
	vanity ['vænəti]	Eitelkeit
	social being	soziales Wesen
	to **engage** [ɪn'geɪdʒ] **with sb.** *She likes to talk and engage with people.*	sich auf jmdn. einlassen, mit jmdm. in Kontakt treten
	invisible [ɪn'vɪzəbəl]	unsichtbar
	poor judgement	schlechtes Urteilsvermögen
	nude [nju:d]	nackt
	to **regret sth.**	etw. bereuen
	to **be at a stage where …** *I'm at a stage in life where I don't care what people think.*	in einem Stadium sein, in dem …
	to **mess sth. up**	etw. vermasseln
	to **feel ashamed**	sich schämen
	embarrassment	Verlegenheit, Beschämtheit
	painful	schmerzhaft
	to **escape from sth.**	etw. entkommen
	depressing	deprimierend
	frustrating	frustrierend
	to **capture sth.** *She took a photograph to capture the moment.*	etw. festhalten/einfangen
14	**online presence**	Internetauftritt
	gig *(infml.)*	Konzert, Auftritt
	additional	zusätzlich
	gross [grəʊs] *(infml.)*	ekelhaft, widerlich
15	**brick**	Baustein, Ziegel
16	**snapshot**	Schnappschuss
17	**youth counsellor**	Jugendberater/in
	to **behave** *You'd better behave in class.*	sich benehmen

	to **come across as …** *It's easy to come across as arrogant if you always talk about yourself.*	… rüberkommen, … wirken
	good behaviour	gutes Benehmen
19	**The damage is done.**	Der Schaden ist angerichtet.
20	to **get to do sth.** *After you finish this project, you'll get to do a new one.*	etw. tun können/dürfen
	payphone	Münztelefon
	spare change	übriges Kleingeld
	to **tape sth.** *She taped herself giving the speech.*	etw. (auf Band) aufnehmen
	to **memorise sth.** *Some people are good at memorising difficult words.*	sich etw. merken/ einprägen
	spare [speə] *Do you have a spare key?*	Ersatz-…, Reserve-…
	to **formally introduce sb.**	jmdn. offiziell vorstellen
	potential [pə'tenʃəl] *John is a potential candidate for class representative.*	potentiell, möglich
	calculator	Taschenrechner
	to **ban sth.**	etw. verbieten
21	to **cope with sth.** *It must be hard to cope with school work if you have a part-time job too.*	mit etw. zurechtkommen
	bullying	Mobbing
	to **schedule** ['ʃedʒu:l] **time for sth.**	für etw. Zeit einplanen
	to **live up to sb.'s expectations**	jmds. Erwartungen gerecht werden
	role model	Vorbild
26	**brave**	tapfer
	charming	reizend, charmant
	curious	neugierig
	patient	geduldig
	clumsy	tollpatschig
	cruel ['kru:əl]	grausam
	to **take charge of sth.**	etw. in die Hand nehmen, für etw. die Verantwortung übernehmen
	to **get along with sb.**	mit jmdm. auskommen
	to **be considerate of sb.'s feelings**	auf jmds. Gefühle Rücksicht nehmen
	to **look out for sb./sth.**	auf jmdn./etw. achten
Looking back		
	factual information	Sachinformation

Unit 02

	art	Kunst
	to **express yourself** *Art can help you express yourself without words.*	sich ausdrücken
	exhibit [ɪg'zɪbɪt]	Ausstellungsstück
1	**piece of art**	Kunstwerk
	painting	Gemälde, Bild
	architecture ['a:kɪtektʃə]	Architektur
	ancient ['eɪnʃənt]	antik, (ur)alt
	concrete ['kɒŋkri:t] *I want concrete evidence before I believe that.*	konkret, greifbar

	abstract ['æbstrækt]	abstrakt
	inspiring	inspirierend
	dull	langweilig, geistlos
	unknown *This painting was created by an unknown artist.*	unbekannt
	disturbing *The film contains a number of disturbing scenes.*	verstörend
2	to **brighten sth. up** *Those flowers really brighten up the room.*	etw. aufhellen/aufheitern
4	**artistic**	künstlerisch, kunstvoll
	artwork	Kunstwerk(e); Bildmaterial
	composition	Komposition, Zusammenstellung
	contemporary arts	zeitgenössische Kunst
	the fine arts	die schönen Künste
	imagination *You can draw anything you like – just use your imagination.*	Fantasie, Vorstellungskraft
	masterpiece	Meisterwerk
	the performing arts	die darstellenden Künste
	poetry ['pəʊɪtri]	Dichtung, Dichtkunst
	sculpture ['skʌlptʃə] *Frida teaches sculpture at our school.*	Bildhauerei; Skulptur
	statue ['stætʃuː]	Statue
	talented	talentiert
	the visual arts	die bildenden Künste
5	**human** ['hjuːmən]	menschlich
	to **express sth.** *Artists often express strong emotions, like love or fear, in their work.*	etw. ausdrücken
	meaningful	bedeutungsvoll
	literature ['lɪtrətʃə]	Literatur
	to **be subdivided into ...** *The house was subdivided into apartments.*	unterteilt sein in ...
	to **merge** [mɜːdʒ] **sth. with sth.** *The two companies merged to form one large company.*	etw. mit etw. verschmelzen/vereinigen
	to **differ (from sth.)** *How do the pictures differ from each other?*	sich unterscheiden (von etw.)
	yet *He was never good at school, (and) yet he became a doctor.*	dennoch, trotzdem
	sb./sth. plays a key role	jmdm./etw. kommt eine Schlüsselrolle zu
	fiction	Romanliteratur
	non-fiction	Sachliteratur
	journalism ['dʒɜːnəlɪzəm]	Journalismus
	in some instances	in manchen Fällen
	to **provide sb. with sth.** *Our school provides children with free breakfast.*	jmdm. etw. bieten/zur Verfügung stellen
	to **give insight into sth.**	einen Einblick in etw. geben
	joy	Freude
	to **convey sth.** *The picture conveys the feeling of peace.*	etw. vermitteln
6	**classical** *He's a big fan of classical music.*	klassisch, traditionell
	classic *Did you spell 'whether' wrong? That's a classic mistake.*	klassisch, typisch
9	to **convince sb. (of sth.)**	jmdn. (von etw.) überzeugen
	to **interrupt sb.**	jmdn. unterbrechen
	to **observe sth.** *Visitors to the museum are advised to observe the rules.*	*hier:* etw. einhalten/befolgen
11	**shape** *What shape is the Earth?*	Form
	to **portray** [pɔː'treɪ] **sth.** *This photo portrays exactly the kind of person he is.*	etw. darstellen/abbilden
	impression *I got the impression that you're happy. Am I right?*	Eindruck
	to **draw from your own experience**	aus der eigenen Erfahrung schöpfen
14	**exhibition** (*short:* **exhibit**)	Ausstellung
	to **be on display**	ausgestellt sein
	entry is free	der Eintritt ist frei
	to **be likely** *They say boys are more likely to bully than girls.*	wahrscheinlich sein
	to **be devoted to sth.** *The gallery is devoted to the work of Van Gogh.*	etw. gewidmet sein
	collection	Sammlung
	venue ['venjuː]	(Veranstaltungs-)Ort
	to **give sb. an understanding of sth.**	jmdm. eine Vorstellung von etw. vermitteln
	display	Ausstellungsstück; Darstellung, Modell
	rotating	(sich) drehend
	to **promote understanding of sth.** *Her work helps to promote understanding of aboriginal culture.*	das Verständnis für etw. fördern
	to **maintain sth.**	etw. erhalten/pflegen
	to **feature** ['fiːtʃə] **sth.** *This museum features some of the most famous paintings in the world.*	etw. aufweisen/bieten
	outstanding	herausragend
	circular ['sɜːkjələ]	kreisförmig
	branch	Ast
	to **launch** [lɔːntʃ] **into sth.** *Carol launched into her world trip with enthusiasm.*	sich in etw. hineinstürzen
	to **surround yourself with sb./sth.** *When you feel sad, surround yourself with people you love.*	sich mit jmdm./etw. umgeben
	aircraft *Which airline has the most aircraft?*	Fluggerät/e, Flugzeug/e
	missile ['mɪsaɪl]	(Raketen-)Geschoss
	... -related *Eric is interested in everything that's science-related.*	auf ... bezogen, mit ... zu tun haben
	escape	Flucht
	story (*AE*), **storey** (*BE*)	Stockwerk
	to **be into sb./sth.** *The kids in my class are really into reading.*	auf jmdn./etw. stehen
	throughout three centuries	über drei Jahrhunderte

	to **house sb./sth.** *The stadium can house almost 70,000 sports fans.*	jmdn./etw. unterbringen/ beherbergen
	public building	öffentliches Gebäude
	to **construct sth.**	etw. errichten
	portrait ['pɔːtrət]	Porträt, Bildnis
	folk art ['fəʊk ˌɑːt]	Volkskunst
	impressionist	impressionistisch; Impressionist/in
	amongst others/other things	unter anderem
	to **reveal sth.**	etw. aufzeigen/zum Vorschein bringen
	ethnic group	Volksgruppe
	the only one of its kind	der/die/das einzige seiner/ ihrer Art
	settler	Siedler/in
	to **show sb. around**	jmdn. herumführen
21	to **set sth. up** *The company set up the exhibition.*	etw. aufbauen/einrichten
	light bulb	Glühbirne
	landscape	Landschaft
	to **be popular with sb.**	bei jmdm. beliebt sein
23	**curator** [kjʊ'reɪtə]	Leiter/in eines Museums, Kurator/in
25	**rhythm**	Rhythmus
	to **rhyme** *I think that the words in poems should always rhyme.*	sich reimen
	synthetic [sɪn'θetɪk]	künstlich
	beat	Takt
26	**recent**	neu; letze/r/s
	release	Veröffentlichung; *hier:* Lied
	lyrics	Liedtext
	to **relate to sth.** *I can't relate to that story.*	sich in etw. hineinversetzen, etw. nachempfinden
	to **remind sb. of sb./sth.** *He reminds me of somebody I went to school with.*	jmdn. an jmdn./etw. erinnern
	catchy tune	Melodie, die ins Ohr geht; Ohrwurm
	what's more, ... *The food is tasty, and what's more, it's healthy.*	außerdem, darüber hinaus
	performance	Darbietung
	music industry	Musikbranche
28	to **deserve sth.** *Your English is good. You deserve a high mark.*	etw. verdienen
30	to **determine** [dɪ'tɜːmɪn] **sth.**	etw. bestimmen/festlegen
	taste in music	Musikgeschmack
	bagpipes *I can't believe you play the bagpipes!*	Dudelsack
	response	Reaktion, Antwort
	preference ['prefərəns] **for sth.**	Vorliebe für etw.
	obvious	offensichtlich
	to **tend to do sth.**	dazu tendieren, etw. zu tun
	peer group	Altersgruppe, soziale Gruppe
	adolescence [ˌædə'lesəns]	Jugend(zeit)
	to **stick with sth.** *Let's stick with the plan.*	bei etw. bleiben

	(formal) musical training	Musikunterricht
	to **score highly on sth.**	bei etw. eine hohe Punktzahl erreichen
	the bottom line is ... *The bottom line is we need more money to finish the project.*	das Fazit ist ..., mit einem Wort, ...
	to **predict sth.**	etw. vorhersagen
31	**celebrity**	Prominente/r
	artefact	Artefakt (*ein von Menschenhand geschaffener Gegenstand*)

Unit 03

	advertiser	Werbetreibende/r
	faulty ['fɒlti]	fehlerhaft
1	to **panic**	in Panik geraten
	to **be forced (to do sth.)** *If you don't behave, I'll be forced to tell the headteacher.*	gezwungen werden (etw. zu tun)
	to **get dressed up**	sich schön anziehen
	to **head for sth.** *I waited for a moment and then headed for the door.*	etw. anpeilen, in Richtung etw. gehen
	ATM *(AE)*: *(abbr. for)* **automated teller machine; cash machine** *(BE)*	Bankomat
	detailed	detailliert
	necessity [nə'sesəti]	Notwendigkeit
	to **pay in cash/by credit card**	bar/mit Kreditkarte zahlen
	recreation	Erholung
	necessary evil	notwendiges Übel
	It's safe to say ... *It's safe to say I won't try bungee jumping again.*	Man kann mit Sicherheit sagen ...
	to **waste time**	Zeit verschwenden
	to **fear sth.**	etw. fürchten
2	**changing room**	Umkleidekabine
	cash desk	Kassa
	to **be served** *Are you being served or can I help you?*	bedient werden
	to **be on sale** *Hats are on sale today.*	im Angebot sein
	to **have sth. in stock**	etw. auf Lager/vorrätig haben
	customer	Kunde/Kundin
	exchange	Gespräch, Wortwechsel
4	to **give sb. a discount on sth.**	jmdm. auf etw. Rabatt geben
5	to **mend sth.**	etw. flicken/ausbessern
7	**mug**	Häferl, Tasse
	to **sell out** *I really wanted a concert ticket, but they'd already sold out.*	ausverkaufen
	to **come second** *Mark came second in the competition.*	den zweiten Platz belegen
	satisfied *(opp.* dissatisfied*)*	zufrieden
	silk	Seide
8	to **hand sth. in** *Please hand in your homework on Tuesday.*	etw. abgeben
9	**store detective**	Kaufhausdetektiv/in

	shoplifting	Ladendiebstahl
	incident	Vorfall, Ereignis
	to **insist on sth.** *He insisted on paying for my coffee, so I let him.*	auf etw. bestehen
	to **claim sth.**	etw. behaupten
	to **note sth.** *The man noted that the museum was closing, so we left.*	etw. erwähnen/anmerken
	to **complain about sth.**	sich über etw. beschweren
	to **suspect sth.** *The detective suspected that something wasn't right.*	etw. vermuten
	to **highlight sth.** *Teachers often highlight the fact that copying is wrong.*	etw. betonen/hervorheben
10	to **arrest sb. for sth.** *She was arrested for shoplifting.*	jmdn. wegen etw. verhaften
	receipt [rɪ'si:t]	Quittung, Beleg
11	**analyst** ['ænəlɪst]	Analytiker/in
	to **survey sb.** *250 people were surveyed about their shopping habits.*	jmdn. befragen
	to **take employment**	eine Anstellung annehmen
	footwear	Schuhwerk
	income	Einkommen
	male/female *The average teenage male prefers to shop online.*	Mann/Frau
	sum	Summe
	spending *Teenage spending has changed over the years.*	Ausgabe/n
	to **dine out**	auswärts essen
13	**police force**	Polizei(kräfte)
	skull	Schädel, Totenkopf
	suburban area	Vorstadt(gegend)
15	to **speculate about sth.**	Vermutungen über etw. anstellen
	to **point sth. out**	auf etw. hinweisen
	to **make out sb./sth.** *She could just make out her friend across the park.*	jmdn./etw. sehen/in der Ferne erkennen
17	**checkout**	Kassa
	grocery (store) *(AE)*	Lebensmittelgeschäft
	the public *If something goes wrong, the public has a right to know.*	die Öffentlichkeit
	to **track sth.** *Can you track the shipment on your computer?*	etw. (nach)verfolgen
	cash register	Registrierkassa
	to **have/keep sth. on file** *Thanks for applying for a job with us; we'll keep your details on file.*	etw. aufbewahren/ablegen
	to **simulate sth.**	etw. simulieren/nachstellen
	to **occur** *When did the accident occur?*	passieren, auftreten
	retail ['ri:teɪl] *Joanna works in retail.*	Handel, Einzelhandel
18	**complaint**	Beschwerde
	to **purchase** ['pɜ:tʃəs] **sth.** *(fml.)*	etw. erwerben/kaufen
	to **justify sth.** *He tried to justify why he hadn't done his homework.*	etw. rechtfertigen
	recipient [rɪ'sɪpiənt] *(fml.)*	Empfänger/in
	replacement	Ersatz
	refund	Rückerstattung
19	**set phrase**	Floskel, Standardformulierung
	determined *I was determined to work hard.*	entschlossen, bestimmt
	matter *This is a very personal matter.*	Angelegenheit
	promptly *Please make sure the problem is solved promptly.*	schnell, umgehend
	dissatisfaction	Unzufriedenheit
	disappointment	Enttäuschung
	to **take sth. into consideration**	etw. in Betracht ziehen
	to **draw sb.'s attention to sth.**	jmdn. auf etw. aufmerksam machen
	to **mislead** [,mɪs'li:d] **sb.**	jmdn. täuschen
	to **feel misled** [,mɪs'led]	sich getäuscht fühlen
20	**(mobile) phone case**	Handyhülle
	at a reasonable price	zu einem annehmbaren Preis
	advertised	beworben
	to **break** *I think my phone's broken.*	kaputtgehen
21	**advertising**	Werbebranche, Werbung
	advertisement/advert/ad	Werbung, Werbeanzeige, Inserat
	to **affect sb./sth.** *This bad test mark won't affect your final grade.*	auf jmdn./etw. Einfluss haben
	buying habit	Kaufgewohnheit
	special offer	Sonderangebot
22	**tray** [treɪ]	Tablett, Ablagekorb
	print ad	Printanzeige
	to **promote sth.**	für etw. werben
	as far as the eye can see	so weit das Auge reicht
	endangered *White tigers are endangered animals.*	vom Aussterben bedroht
	blank	leer, unbeschrieben
	to **catch sb.'s eye**	jmdm. ins Auge springen
	advertising executive	Werbemanager/in
	copy ['kɒpi] *Have you seen 'Mad Men'? Are you sure you want to become a copywriter?*	*hier:* Werbetext
	sufficient	ausreichend
	billboard *(AE)*, **hoarding** *(BE)*	Reklametafel, Plakatwand
	name-brand item	Artikel einer bekannten Marke
	to **convert sth. (into sth.)** *The old church was converted into a house.*	etw. (in etw.) umwandeln
	to **allow sth.** *Credit cards allow us to shop without cash.*	etw. ermöglichen
	remote	Fern-…; weit entfernt
	passer-by *(pl. passers-by)*	Passant/in
	to **trigger sth.** *Her weak performance triggered a lot of nasty comments.*	etw. auslösen
	motion sensor	Bewegungsmelder
	to **be aware of sth.**	sich etw. bewusst sein

	to be targeted *The new girl was targeted by bullies.*	anvisiert werden
	wise	klug, weise
	consumer	Konsument/in
24	**to advertise sth.** *The concert was advertised in several newspapers.*	etw. bewerben
26	**documentary** [ˌdɒkjəˈmentəri]	Dokumentarfilm, Doku
	sales technique	Verkaufstechnik
	to create anxiety	Angst schüren
	storytelling	Geschichtenerzählen
	to defeat sb.	jmdn. besiegen
	villain [ˈvɪlən]	Bösewicht
	ad campaign	Werbekampagne
29	**(much) anticipated**	mit Spannung erwartet
	to chase sb./sth.	jmdn./etw. verfolgen
	familiar	bekannt
	plump	rundlich, mollig
	scores of … *Pat received cards from scores of friendly people.*	zahlreiche …
	extra *In her teens, she worked as an extra in several films.*	Statist/in
	fame	Ruhm
	to soar [sɔː] *Temperatures will soar today.*	schlagartig ansteigen, in die Höhe schnellen
	phenomenon [fəˈnɒmɪnən]	Phänomen
	to air sth. *The speech will be aired live on CNN tonight.*	etw. ausstrahlen/senden
	appeal	Anziehungskraft, Reiz
	network	Sender, Fernsehgesellschaft
	to charge sb. *The hairdresser charged me 40 euros just for styling my hair!*	jmdm. Geld verrechnen
	investment	Investition
	to stand out *Dressing differently will help you stand out from the crowd.*	auffallen, hervorstechen
	to measure sth.	etw. messen
	either way *We can eat at home or go out; I'm happy either way.*	so oder so
	sheer *It was sheer luck that we found each other in such a large crowd of people.*	rein, schier
	awareness *We need to raise awareness of bullying in schools.*	Bewusstsein
31	**to persuade** [pəˈsweɪd] **sb.**	jmdn. überreden/überzeugen
	to entertain sb.	jmdn. unterhalten
	readership	Leserschaft
	to address sb. *In some schools pupils address teachers by their first name.*	jmdn. ansprechen
	descriptive	beschreibend, anschaulich
	to pull sb. in *Advertising campaigns are designed to pull you in.*	jmdn. anziehen/anlocken
	to publish sth.	etw. veröffentlichen
	involved	miteinbezogen, betroffen
	linking device	Bindewort
32	**to break up with sb.**	sich von jmdm. trennen
	to fast forward	vorspulen
	fast-paced	temporeich, flott, rasant
	compelling *I'm watching a really compelling TV series.*	fesselnd, überzeugend
	to aim [eɪm] **to do sth.** *Ads aim to make you buy stuff.*	etw. anstreben/zum Ziel haben
	roller coaster	Achterbahn
	memorable [ˈmemərəbəl] *Visiting Vienna was such a memorable experience.*	einprägsam, unvergesslich
33	**target group**	Zielgruppe
34	**endorsement** *Many celebrities give their endorsement of products.*	Unterstützung

Unit 04

	New Year's Eve	Silvester
	graveyard	Friedhof
	to become familiar with sth.	mit etw. vertraut werden
	to rediscover sth.	etw. wiederentdecken
1	**to celebrate sth.**	etw. feiern
	bull	Stier
	tin casting	Bleigießen
	bonfire *Bonfires were lit on the hills around the lake.*	(Freuden-/Lager-)Feuer
2	**Gosh!** *(infml.)* *Oh my gosh, I love this song!*	Du meine Güte! Mensch!
4	**fireworks** *What time did the fireworks start?*	Feuerwerk
6	**custom**	Brauch, Brauchtum
	customary [ˈkʌstəməri] *On Valentine's Day it's customary to give flowers to someone you love.*	üblich, gebräuchlich
	It's supposed to bring good luck.	Es soll (angeblich) Glück bringen.
7	**ski lodge**	Skihütte
8	**celebration**	Feier, Fest
	in advance *You need to pay in advance.*	im Voraus
	miraculous [mɪˈrækjələs]	wunderbar, außergewöhnlich
	the months ahead *Summer has ended, and the months ahead will be cold.*	die kommenden Monate
	to skip sth.	etw. auslassen
	stroke (of a bell)	(Glocken-)Schlag
	to guarantee sth.	etw. garantieren
	adrenaline rush	Adrenalinschub
	to gag	würgen; *hier:* ersticken
	to cram sth. in your mouth	sich etw. in den Mund stopfen
	to swallow sth.	etw. schlucken
	to bear consequences *Posting information online can bear serious consequences.*	Konsequenzen mit sich bringen
	prosperity	Wohlstand
	lingerie [ˈlɒnʒəri]	Damenunterwäsche

	undergarment(s)	Unterwäsche
	for … and … alike *The film is suitable for adults and children alike.*	sowohl für … als auch für …
	There's a catch.	Es gibt einen Haken.
	undies *(infml. for* underwear*)*	Unterwäsche
	inside-out	verkehrt herum (*mit der Innenseite nach außen*)
	passion	Leidenschaft
	slight	gering, leicht, fein
	to **settle your differences**	einen Streit beilegen
	to **host** [həʊst] **sth.** *Which country is hosting the next World Cup?*	etw. veranstalten/ausrichten
	gathering	Treffen
	fist fight	Faustkampf
	the elderly ['eldəli] *I was taught to respect the elderly.*	ältere Menschen
	to **resolve conflicts**	Konflikte lösen
	to **strengthen sth.**	etw. festigen/stärken
	to **result in sth.** *Playing with fireworks may result in someone getting hurt.*	zu etw. führen
	to **translate to …** *'Amuse bouche' translates to 'mouth amuser'.*	heißt übersetzt …, sich übersetzen lassen mit …
	to **boil** *When does water begin to boil?*	kochen
	to **get sth. out in the open**	etw. offen ansprechen
	side-by-side	Seite an Seite
	to **reflect sth.** *Mr Cooper's red face reflected how angry he was at us.*	etw. widerspiegeln
	intention	Absicht
	cemetery ['semətri]	Friedhof
	sleepover	Übernachtung(sparty)
	in the company of sb.	in jmds. Anwesenheit/Gesellschaft
	odd	eigenartig, komisch
	deceased [dɪ'si:st] *(fml.)*	verstorben
	grim	düster, makaber, grimmig
	the locals	die Einheimischen
	to **ensure** [ɪn'ʃɔ:] **sth.**	etw. sicherstellen
	to **light a fire**	ein Feuer anzünden
	to **remain open** *The graveyards remain open at New Year.*	offen bleiben
9	**main idea/point**	Hauptaussage
	supporting detail	Begründung, Zusatzinformation
11	**lecture**	Vortrag, Vorlesung
15	**otherwise**	sonst, ansonsten
	to **fancy doing sth.** *I don't fancy going out there in the frost and snow.*	etw. gerne tun, auf etw. Lust haben
	to **be keen on doing sth.** *You're really keen on going to the theatre, aren't you?*	etw. sehr gerne tun, auf etw. große Lust haben
16	to **admit sth. (to oneself)**	etw. zugeben; sich etw. eingestehen
	can't help (doing) sth.	etw. nicht lassen können
	to **delay (doing) sth.**	etw. verschieben/hinausschieben

	to **keep sth. up** *I started going to the gym every day, but I'm not sure I'll be able to keep that up.*	etw. fortführen/weiterhin tun
	to **go abroad**	ins Ausland gehen
17	**sinister** ['sɪnɪstə]	unheimlich, böse
	Christianity	Christentum
	to **rule over sth.**	über etw. herrschen
	to **misbehave**	sich schlecht benehmen, ungezogen sein
	pagan ['peɪgən]	heidnisch
	naughty ['nɔ:ti] *Have you kids been naughty?*	schlimm, unartig
	to **obey** [əʊ'beɪ] **sb./sth.** *We obeyed Tom because we were scared of him.*	jmdm./etw. gehorchen/folgen
	to **let off steam**	Dampf ablassen
	sophisticated	kultiviert, hoch entwickelt
	to **take hold** *Halloween has taken hold in Europe in recent years.*	sich durchsetzen
18	**Once upon a time …**	Es war einmal …
	traditional tale	Märchen, Sage
	tortoise ['tɔ:təs]	(Land-)Schildkröte
	hare [heə]	(Feld-)Hase
	sb. used to do sth. *I used to go to kindergarten with that girl over there.*	jmd. hat früher etw. getan, jmd. pflegte zu tun
	sb. would do sth. *My little sister would always cry when she saw a clown.*	jmnd. hat etw. früher getan
	for entertainment	zur Unterhaltung
	to **carry a message**	eine Botschaft/Moral haben
	oral ['ɔ:rəl]	mündlich
	to **perform sth.**	etw. aufführen/darstellen
	to **hand sth. down** *Traditional stories are handed down from parents to children.*	etw. überliefern/vererben
	character	(Roman-)Figur
	setting	Schauplatz, Hintergrund
	protagonist	Hauptfigur
	antagonist	Gegenspieler/in, Gegner/in
	evil ['i:vəl]	böse, schlecht
	plot	Handlung
	to **resolve a dilemma**	aus einem Dilemma herauskommen
	to **put a spell on sb.** *A witch had put a spell on the prince, turning him into a frog.*	jmdn. verwünschen/verzaubern
	curse *In order to break the curse, the princess had to kiss the frog.*	Fluch
	ending	Ende
	… and they lived happily ever after.	… und wenn sie nicht gestorben sind, dann leben sie noch heute.
21	**exposition**	Einführung (*in die Handlung*)
	tension	Spannung
	climax ['klaɪmæks]	Höhepunkt
	turning point	Wendepunkt
	resolution	Lösung (*des Konflikts*)
	justice ['dʒʌstɪs]	Gerechtigkeit

	to **endure** [ɪn'dʒʊə] **sth.** *He bit on his finger to endure the pain.*	etw. ertragen/aushalten
	to **tease** [ti:z] **sb.** *Good friends can tease each other without getting upset.*	jmdn. hänseln
	to **change your ways**	sich ändern/bessern
	to **wink at sb.**	jmdm. zuzwinkern
	to **set off** *Hansel and Gretel set off into the forest.*	aufbrechen, sich auf den Weg machen
	to **be about to do sth.** *I was about to call you when I got your text message.*	kurz davor sein, etw. zu tun
	to **catch up (with sb./sth.)** *I ran as fast as I could, but I couldn't catch up with Amy.*	aufholen, jmdn./etw. einholen
	to **boast about sth.** *He's always boasting about how well he can cook.*	mit etw. angeben/prahlen
	boastful	angeberisch
	to **challenge sb. to sth.** *The boys challenged the girls to a volleyball match.*	jmdn. zu etw. herausfordern
28	to **pretend to be sb./sth.**	vorgeben, jmd./etw. zu sein
	to **trap sb./sth.**	jmdn./etw. in eine Falle locken
29	to **advise sb. to do sth.** *I can only advise you to study after school.*	jmdm. etw. nahelegen/anraten
	to **persuade sb. to do sth.**	jmdn. zu etw. überreden
	to **talk sb. into (doing) sth.** *Could you talk your brother into coming to my party?*	jmdn. zu etw. überreden, jmdm. etw. einreden
	to **talk sb. out of (doing) sth.** *Luckily, we talked her out of getting a snake as a pet.*	jmdm. etw. ausreden
	Little Red Riding Hood	Rotkäppchen
30	to **stare** [steə] **(at sb./sth.)**	starren, jmdn./etw. anstarren
33	**mermaid** ['mɜ:meɪd]	Meerjungfrau
	shelter	Zufluchtsort, Schutz
	to **challenge sth.** *Why are you challenging my decision?*	etw. infrage stellen
35	**staring**	starrend
	to **beg sb. to do sth.**	jmdn. anflehen/anbetteln, etw. zu tun
	to **shiver**	zittern
	shivering	zitternd
36	**New Year's resolution**	guter Vorsatz fürs neue Jahr
37	**celebratory** [ˌselə'breɪtəri]	feierlich; Feier-…

Unit 05

	to **colour sth. (in)**	etw. anmalen/ausmalen
	Japanese [ˌdʒæpən'i:z]	japanisch
	orangutan [ɔ:ˌræŋu:'tæn]	Orang-Utan
	environment	Umwelt; Umgebung
1	to **imagine sth.**	sich etw. denken, sich etw. vorstellen
	calm	ruhig
	remote	abgelegen
	moist	feucht
3	**natural beauty**	natürliche Schönheit
	to **refer to sth.** *I am referring to the telephone conversation we had last week.*	sich auf etw. beziehen
	sunset/sunrise	Sonnenunter-/-aufgang
	breeze [bri:z]	Brise
	rainbow	Regenbogen
	thunder	Donner
	lightning	Blitz
	rainforest	Regenwald
	warmth	Wärme
	low tide/high tide *You can walk from the beach to the island at low tide.*	Ebbe/Flut
	heat [hi:t]	Hitze
	volcano [vɒl'keɪnəʊ] *How many volcanoes are erupting every day?*	Vulkan
	crashing waves	brechende Wellen; Meeresrauschen
	pollution	Verschmutzung
	bay	Bucht
	meadow ['medəʊ]	Wiese
	ocean *About two thirds of the world are covered by oceans.*	Ozean, Meer
	smog *Did you know that 'smog' comes from 'smoke' and 'fog'?*	Smog, Industriedunst
	wildlife	Pflanzen- und Tierwelt, Flora und Fauna
	drought [draʊt]	Dürre, Trockenheit
	steep slope	steiler Hang
	icy cold	eiskalt
	global warming	globale Erwärmung
	heavy rain	starker Regen
	rainfall	Niederschlag, Regen
	shade [ʃeɪd] *Let's sit over there in the shade.*	Schatten
	glacier ['glæsiə]	Gletscher
	stream	Strom, Fluss
	mountain peak	Berggipfel
	flood [flʌd]	Überschwemmung
	rain shower	Regenschauer
	fresh water	Süßwasser
	tropical	tropisch; Tropen-…
	pouring rain [ˌpɔ:rɪŋ 'reɪn]	strömender Regen
6	**enjoyable**	unterhaltsam, angenehm
	challenging	(heraus)fordernd
	tight	dicht, knapp
	a total of … *I worked at the cafeteria for a total of 20 hours.*	insgesamt …
	syllable ['sɪləbəl]	Silbe
	to **emphasise** ['emfəsaɪz] **sth.**	etw. betonen
	simplicity	Einfachheit
	expression	Ausdruck
	brief	kurz
	ideally	idealerweise, im Idealfall
	rather ['rɑ:ðə] *I'd rather have salad than soup.*	eher, lieber
	fairly *Entry tickets to some national parks are fairly expensive.*	ziemlich

7	**pattern**	Muster, Schema
	heaps of ...	haufenweise ..., jede Menge ...
	to **glitter**	glitzern
	faint [feɪnt] *She nodded and gave a faint smile.*	schwach, zart
	sweaty ['swetɪ]	verschwitzt
	dusty	angestaubt, staubig
	the woods	Wald, Wälder
9	**fascinating**	faszinierend
	to **fit together**	zusammenpassen
	immense *I am immensely grateful for all your help.*	immens, gewaltig
	to **find (the) time for sth.**	die Zeit für etw. finden
11	to **be keen on (doing) sth.**	von etw. begeistert sein
	to **get absorbed in sth.**	sich in etw. vertiefen
	to **be eager to do sth.**	etw. unbedingt tun wollen
	to **get a kick out of sth.**	(seine helle) Freude an etw. haben
	to **be hooked on sth.** *I am hooked on slacklining – I can't get enough of it!*	für etw. Feuer und Flamme sein
	enthusiastic [ɪn,θju:zi'æstɪk]	enthusiastisch, begeistert
13	**concerning** *I'd like to talk to you concerning the paper you turned in.*	bezüglich, in Bezug auf
15	**environmental issue**	Umweltproblem
	to **bother with sth.** *Why bother with recycling?*	sich um etw. kümmern/scheren
	to **separate your waste**	(seinen) Müll trennen
	to **end up somewhere**	(irgend)wo landen
	landfill	Müllhalde, Mülldeponie
	to **protect sb./sth.**	jmdn./etw. schützen
	greenhouse effect	Treibhauseffekt
	unless *People won't come unless we send them an invitation.*	außer, außer wenn
	to **pollute** [pə'lu:t] **sth.**	etw. verschmutzen
	species ['spi:ʃi:z]	Spezies, Pflanzenart/en, Tierart/en
	endangered species	vom Aussterben bedrohte Art/en
	polar bear [,pəʊlə 'beə]	Eisbär
	to **die out**	aussterben
	climate change	Klimawandel
	man-made *What's the difference between a natural and a man-made disaster?*	vom Menschen gemacht
	meat consumption	Fleischkonsum
	cause	Ursache
	extreme weather (conditions) *Extreme weather conditions will increase due to global warming.*	Unwetter, extreme Wetterverhältnisse
	natural disaster	Naturkatastrophe
18	**palm oil**	Palmöl
	farming	Anbau; Landwirtschaft
	to **carry on** *The destruction of our environment will carry on if no one does anything about it.*	weitergehen, weitermachen
	sustainable	nachhaltig
	primary forest	Urwald
	to **remain** *Only a few thousand of these birds remain today.*	verbleiben, übrig bleiben
	most widely used	meistverbreitet
	packaged	abgepackt
	significant	signifikant, wesentlich
	to **farm sth.** *The Harrinsons have farmed this land for years.*	etw. bebauen, ein Feld bestellen
	deforestation [di:,fɒrɪ'steɪʃən]	Abholzung
	loss *How will our planet cope with the loss of natural forests?*	Verlust
	to **endanger sth.** *Many animals are endangered by farming and pollution.*	etw. gefährden
	biodiversity [,baɪəʊdaɪ'vɜ:səti]	Artenvielfalt
	to **estimate** *She estimated it would take 10 minutes to walk to her hotel.*	(ab)schätzen
	extinct	ausgestorben
	to **make way for sth.** *Traditional farms often have to make way for big industries.*	für etw. Platz machen, etw. weichen
	to **live off sth.** *Some people can live off what they grow themselves.*	sich von etw. ernähren, von etw. leben
	resource [rɪ'zɔ:s]	Ressource, Hilfsmittel
	as a result	infolgedessen, als Ergebnis
	community	Gemeinde, Gemeinschaft
	developing country	Entwicklungsland
	stable *(opp.* unstable*)*	stabil, verlässlich
	source of income *It's hard to plan your future without a stable source of income.*	Einkommensquelle
	running water *Millions of people don't have running water in their home.*	fließendes Wasser
	supply	Angebot, Bestand
	to **act responsibly**	verantwortungsbewusst handeln
	to **depend on sth.** *Some farmers depend on help from the government.*	von etw. abhängen
	decade ['dekeɪd]	Jahrzehnt
	government	Regierung
	to **support sb./sth.**	jmdn./etw. unterstützen
	precious ['preʃəs]	kostbar
	to **chop down trees**	Bäume fällen
	standard of living	Lebensstandard
19	**demand (for sth.)**	Nachfrage (nach etw.)
	to **lead to sth.** *Palm oil production often leads to environmental problems.*	zu etw. führen
	habitat ['hæbɪtæt]	Lebensraum
	as a consequence of ...	als Folge von ...
	to **have a positive/negative effect on sb./sth.**	sich positiv/negativ auf jmdn./etw. auswirken
21	to **raise awareness of sth.** *We hope to raise awareness of plastic pollution.*	Bewusstsein für etw. schaffen
	rescue ['reskju:]	Rettung
	to **care for sb./sth.**	sich um jmdn./etw. kümmern

	extinction [ɪk'stɪŋʃən] *Orangutans are in danger of extinction.*	Ausrottung, Aussterben
	treetop	Baumkrone
	safety ['seɪfti]	Sicherheit
	to **set sth. on fire**	etw. in Brand setzen
	confused	verwirrt
	to **surround sb./sth.** *Animals are healthiest and happiest when they are surrounded by nature.*	jmdn./etw. umgeben/ umschließen
	to **survive** [sə'vaɪv] **sth.** *Sam was lucky to survive the car crash.*	etw. überleben
	in the wild	in der Wildnis
	permanent	dauerhaft
	release [rɪ'liːs]	Freilassung, Befreiung
	to **set sb./sth. free**	jmdn./etw. freilassen
22	**fact sheet**	Informationsblatt
	achievement	Leistung, Errungenschaft
23	to **emit** [i'mɪt] **sth.** *Cows emit methane gas.*	etw. ausstoßen/ verströmen
	methane ['miːθeɪn]	Methan(gas)
24	**emissions** *Many countries are trying to cut emissions from cars and factories.*	Emissionen, Abgase
	greenhouse gas emissions	Treibhausgasausstoß
	emblem ['embləm]	Symbol, Wahrzeichen
26	**animal agriculture**	Tierhaltung, Viehwirtschaft
	to **be responsible for sth.**	für etw. verantwortlich sein
28	to **direct sb.'s attention towards sth.**	jmds. Aufmerksamkeit auf etw. lenken
30	**humid air** [ˌhjuːmɪd 'eə]	feuchte Luft
	the seaside *Let's go to the seaside!*	(Meeres-)Küste
	rough climate [ˌrʌf 'klaɪmət]	raues Klima
	protection	Schutz

Unit 06

1	**outline**	Umriss
	capital (city)	Hauptstadt
2	**(language) variety** [və'raɪəti] *The book was about the different varieties of English spoken in the USA.*	Sprachvarietät, sprachliche Variante
	to **pronounce a word**	ein Wort aussprechen
3	**later in life**	im späteren Leben
4	**an awful lot of sth.** *Dan can eat an awful lot of food for lunch and still be hungry one hour later.*	schrecklich viel, eine Riesenmenge von …
	local language	Landessprache
	chances are (that) … *Chances are that if you drive fast, you will have an accident.*	wahrscheinlich …
	lingua franca [ˌlɪŋgwə 'fræŋkə]	Verkehrssprache, Lingua franca
	first language	Muttersprache
	to **colonise sth.**	etw. kolonialisieren
	to **reach one's peak**	seinen Höhepunkt erreichen
	a quarter of … *A quarter of all the people in the world speak English.*	ein Viertel …
	the sun sets in the west	die Sonne geht im Westen unter
	the British Empire ['empaɪə]	das Britische Weltreich
	literally *The pub is literally just around the corner from our place.*	buchstäblich, wörtlich
	daylight	Tageslicht
	official language	Amtssprache
	despite sth. *Skiing was fun despite the cold.*	trotz etw.
	to **spread** [spred] *Because of colonisation, the English language has spread all over the world.*	sich verbreiten/ausbreiten
	mass media	Massenmedien
	to **come across sth.** *I came across some childhood pictures of my dad.*	etw. begegnen, auf etw. stoßen
6	to **hold a conversation**	ein Gespräch führen
8	**settled**	besiedelt
	occupied	besetzt
	independent *India became an independent country in 1948.*	unabhängig
9	**Germanic** [dʒə'mænɪk] **language**	germanische Sprache
	equally *Maybe I have a different opinion, but it's equally important.*	gleichermaßen, ebenso
	Romance [rəʊ'mæns] **language**	romanische Sprache
	to **absorb sth.**	etw. aufnehmen
	loanword	Lehnwort
	fancy	schick, geschwollen
	Viking invasion [ɪn'veɪʒən]	Einfall/Überfall der Wikinger
	to **leave one's mark**	seine Spuren hinterlassen
	surprisingly, …	überraschenderweise …
	not surprisingly, …	erwartungsgemäß; kein Wunder, dass …
	Norse [nɔːs] *Thor was the Norse god of thunder.*	nordisch (*Sprache, Kultur*)
12	**initial** [ɪ'nɪʃəl] *My initial reaction to the film was shock.*	erste/r/s
	to **access sth.** *Only members can access the site.*	Zugang zu etw. haben, auf etw. zugreifen
	coast	Küste
	concern	Sorge, Bedenken
	lack of sth.	Mangel an etw.
	ethnic diversity [ˌeθnɪk daɪ'vɜːsəti]	ethnische Vielfalt
	to **be nominated for sth.**	für etw. nominiert sein
	acting award	Schauspielpreis
	sth. comes to mind *Say whatever comes to mind first.*	etw. fällt einem ein
	glamour ['glæmə]	Glanz, Glamour
	best-known place	bekanntester Ort
	to **progress** *You can see how far filmmaking technology has progressed when you watch old films.*	fortschreiten, sich weiterentwickeln
	to **boycott sth.**	etw. boykottieren
	director	Regisseur/in
	to **make a stand (against sb./sth.)**	sich (jmdm./etw.) widersetzen

	to **campaign for sb./sth.**	sich für jmdn./etw. einsetzen
	minority [maɪ'nɒrəti]	Minderheit
	judge	(Preis-)Richter/in
	nominee [ˌnɒmɪ'niː]	Nominierte/r
	to **speak out about sth.**	sich zu etw. äußern
	reputation	Ruf, Nachrede
	to **draw sb.** *She's such a good singer, always drawing a crowd.*	jmdn. anziehen/anlocken
	to **be recognised**	Anerkennung bekommen
14	to **award sb. a prize**	jmdm. einen Preis verleihen
	criticism of sth.	Kritik an etw.
	nomination	Nominierung
	demographic *This kind of music is popular with an older demographic.*	Bevölkerungsgruppe
	membership	Mitgliedschaft
	person of colour	Angehörige/r einer nichtweißen Bevölkerungsgruppe
	existing *The existing system is just not fair.*	bestehend
15	to **conduct sth.** *A survey was conducted among students and teachers.*	etw. durchführen
17	**film score**	Filmmusik
	aspiring *My sister's an aspiring artist. She spends every weekend painting.*	aufstrebend; ehrgeizig
	idiom ['ɪdiəm]	Redewendung
	detached from reality	realitätsfern
	romantic comedy	Liebeskomödie
	dance routine	Tanzchoreographie
	supporting actor/actress	Nebendarsteller/in
	box office	Kinokassa
	TV series ['sɪəriːz]	Fernsehserie
	pronunciation	Aussprache
	aristocratic	adelig
	staff [stɑːf]	Angestellte, Personal
	cast *Many of the film's cast came from an Austrian village.*	Besetzung
	episode	Folge
	leading actor/actress	Hauptdarsteller/in
	(film) script	Drehbuch
	prequel ['priːkwəl]	Vorläufer, Vorgeschichte
	due to *Due to the success of Hollywood films, the English language has spread even more.*	aufgrund, wegen
	merchandise ['mɜːtʃəndaɪs]	mit einem Film in Zusammenhang stehende Produkte
	sci-fi ['saɪfaɪ] *(abbr. for)* **science fiction**	Scifi, Science-Fiction
	legendary ['ledʒəndri]	legendär
	instantly recognisable	sofort (wieder)erkennbar
	to **vary** ['veəri]	variieren
	theme tune	Titelmelodie
18	**goods**	Güter
	fictional	erfunden, fiktiv
22	**film review** ['fɪlm rɪˌvjuː]	Filmrezension

	to **review sth.**	etw. rezensieren
	to **give yourself a treat**	sich etw. gönnen
	to **be based on sth.**	auf etw. beruhen/basieren
	remake	Neuverfilmung
	convincing	überzeugend
	pleasantly surprised	angenehm überrascht
	gripping	fesselnd
	breathtaking	atemberaubend
	(un)predictable	(un)vorhersehbar
	moving *The film was so moving, everybody cried.*	bewegend
	to **speak to sb.** *The film really spoke to me because the same thing happened to me last year.*	jmdn. ansprechen
	people of all ages	Menschen jeden Alters
	a must	ein Muss
	pacy (film/novel/story)	ereignisreich, actionreich
	to **expand sth.** *Reading is a great way to expand your vocabulary.*	etw. ausbauen/erweitern
	(well) worth seeing	sehenswert
	previous ['priːviəs]	vorhergehend, vorig
	top-notch *(infml.)*	prima; Spitzen-…
	to **lack sth.** *Our new boss was professional but lacked experience.*	etw. benötigen, an etw. mangeln
	suspense	Spannung
	backstory	Hintergrundgeschichte
24	**favour** *Could you do me a favour and walk my dog?*	Gefallen
	lead role	Hauptrolle
	starring sb. *I love films starring animals.*	mit jmdm. in der Hauptrolle
	to **be loosely based on sth.**	frei auf etw. basieren
	to **refuse to do sth.**	etw. ablehnen
	bad-tempered	übellaunig, launisch
	stubborn ['stʌbən]	stur
	genuinely ['dʒenjuɪnli] *The movie has some genuinely funny scenes.*	wirklich, echt

Unit 07

	disability	Behinderung
1	**handicapped**	beeinträchtigt, behindert
	permit ['pɜːmɪt]	Genehmigung
2	**offensive**	beleidigend
3	**guilty**	schuldig
	luxury ['lʌkʃəri]	Luxus
	elders *You should respect your elders.*	Ältere
	chatter	Geschwätz
	dyed hair	gefärbte Haare
5	**involvement** *Their involvement in the new project was welcome.*	Mitwirkung, Beteiligung
	to **follow the crowd**	mit der Masse gehen
	to **take responsibility**	Verantwortung übernehmen
	pressure	Druck

	peer pressure	Gruppenzwang
	to **protest (against) sth.**	gegen etw. protestieren
7	**acceptance**	Akzeptanz
	commitment *He showed a lot of commitment to his plan to help poor people.*	Hingabe, Engagement
	counter-culture *Counter-culture began with the hippies in the 1960s.*	Gegenbewegung, Gegenkultur
	participation	Teilnahme
	sense of belonging	Gefühl der Zugehörigkeit
12	to **stretch sth.**	etw. ausdehnen/ ausweiten
13	**sth. is coming up** *Christmas is coming up soon.*	etw. wird bald stattfinden, etw. steht vor der Tür
16	**disabled** [dɪs'eɪbəld]	behindert
17	**sensory disability**	Sinnesbeeinträchtigung
	physical ['fɪsɪkəl]	körperlich
	blindness	Blindheit
	hearing *You'll have to talk a little louder, my hearing isn't good.*	Gehör
	amputee [ˌæmpjə'tiː]	Amputierte/r
	paralysed ['pærəlaɪzd]	gelähmt
	mute [mjuːt]	stumm
	deafness ['defnəs]	Taubheit
	to **be hard of hearing**	schwerhörig sein
	vision	Sicht
	deaf [def]	taub
	amputated	amputiert
	muteness	Stummheit
18	**Supreme Court**	Oberster Gerichtshof
	election	Wahl
	innocence	Unschuld
	guilt [gɪlt] *He felt a sense of guilt after causing the accident.*	Schuld(gefühl)
	to **pick sth. up** *Dogs can pick up smells better than humans.*	etw. wahrnehmen
	discrimination	Diskriminierung
20	to **avoid sb./sth.**	jmdn./etw. meiden
21	**mental**	geistig
	condition [kən'dɪʃən] *The car was in a really bad condition.*	Zustand
	neurological condition	neurologische Erkrankung
	visibility [ˌvɪzə'bɪləti]	Sichtbarkeit
	to **overcome sth.** *Overcoming your fears can be a real challenge.*	etw. überwinden/ bewältigen
	wheelchair	Rollstuhl
	accessible facility	barrierefreie Einrichtung
	suitable ['sjuːtəbəl]	passend
	mobility	Beweglichkeit
	aid [eɪd]	Hilfe
	priority seat	reservierter Sitzplatz *(für Schwangere oder Menschen mit Behinderung)*
	able-bodied *Able-bodied people should not use parking meant for disabled people.*	nicht behindert, leistungsfähig
	respectful *(opp.* disrespectful*)*	respektvoll
	curiosity [ˌkjʊəri'ɒsəti]	Neugier
	valuable ['væljəbəl]	wertvoll
	empowered	bestärkt, ermächtigt
	validating *Jeff felt validated when Carol agreed with her.*	bestätigend
	bias ['baɪəs] *Sadly, some young people have a bias against older people.*	Vorurteil(e), Voreingenommenheit
	exceptional [ɪk'sepʃənəl]	außergewöhnlich
	inspirational	inspirierend
	careless *Jane is careless with her things, she can never find anything.*	achtlos
	condescending [ˌkɒndɪ'sendɪŋ]	herablassend
	remarkable	bemerkenswert
	to **be willing to do sth.** *I'd be willing to help you if you let me.*	gewillt/bereit sein, etw. zu tun
25	**paraplegic** [ˌpærə'pliːdʒɪk]	querschnittsgelähmt
	limbs [lɪmz]	Gliedmaßen
	assistance	Hilfe, Unterstützung
	sighted *In the famous novel 'Blindness', sighted people are a minority.*	sehend
27	**homelessness**	Obdachlosigkeit
	homeless	obdachlos
	unaccompanied minor	unbegleitete/r Minderjährige/r
	admission fee	Eintritt(spreis)
	to **dominate sth.**	etw. dominieren/ beherrschen
29	**rough childhood**	schwierige Kindheit
	drug addict ['drʌg ˌædɪkt]	Drogenabhängige/r
	to **befriend sb.** *Paula befriended the new girl.*	sich mit jmdm. anfreunden
	similarity	Ähnlichkeit
	to **live on the streets**	auf der Straße leben
	vast [vɑːst]	riesengroß, weitreichend
	predictably, ...	wie zu erwarten ...
	to **get into sth.** *Is it true you got into a fight?*	in etw. geraten
	to **sniff**	schnüffeln
	to **get addicted to sth.**	nach etw. süchtig werden
	dope *(infml.)*	„Stoff", Marihuana, Drogen
	one thing leads to another	eins führt zum anderen
	to **have a break** *He had a break when a teammate was injured and he got to play for the national team.*	*hier:* eine Chance bekommen
	to **announce sth.**	etw. ankündigen
	downward spiral [ˌdaʊnwəd 'spaɪərəl] *His singing career was on a downward spiral.*	Abwärtsspirale
	to **encounter sth.** *She first encountered these problems when she was five.*	etw. begegnen, auf etw. stoßen
	authority	Autorität(sperson)
	brother-in-law	Schwager
	rebellious	rebellisch
	to **contribute to sth.**	zu etw. beitragen

	to **work in IT**	im IT-Bereich arbeiten
	decent ['diːsənt] *Pete earns a decent amount of money in his job.*	anständig, ordentlich
	eventually *We had a long discussion and eventually I was happy with the decision.*	schlussendlich
	to **kick sb. out**	jmdn. rauswerfen
	to **lead a nomadic existence**	ein Nomadendasein führen
	sleeping bag	Schlafsack
	squat *(infml.)*	Absteige, Unterschlupf
	to **run out of sth.** *The company ran out of money and had to close down.*	etw. nicht mehr haben, etw. „geht aus"
	to **settle in(to) sth.** *Have you settled into your new flat yet?*	sich eingewöhnen/einleben in etw.
	to **disappear**	verschwinden
	northern hemisphere	Nordhalbkugel
	yet again *He's lost his job yet again.*	schon wieder, zum wiederholten Male
	rootless *He had moved so often that he felt rootless.*	wurzellos, heimatlos
	to **separate** *Angela's parents separated a year ago and are now getting divorced.*	sich trennen
	to **head downwards**	bergab gehen, sich verschlechtern
	dignity	Würde
	worst of all, …	und was am schlimmsten ist, …
	to **treat sb. (well/badly/…)**	jmdn. (gut/schlecht/…) behandeln
31	**ordinarily** *(adj.* ordinary*)*	gewöhnlich
	busker	Straßenmusikant/in
	to **shun sb./sth.**	sich von jmdm./etw. fernhalten
	understandable	verständlich
	ginger ['dʒɪndʒə]	rothaarig
	tomcat	Kater
	broad smile	breites Grinsen
	It wasn't long before …	Es dauerte nicht lange, bis …
	gorgeous ['gɔːdʒəs]	wunderschön, hinreißend
	to **stroke sb./sth.**	jmdn./etw. streicheln
	a one-off event	ein einmaliges Ereignis
	fellow	Kerl, Kamerad/in
33	**outsider**	Außenseiter/in
34	**misunderstanding**	Missverständnis
	paralysis [pə'ræləsɪs]	Lähmung
	condescension [ˌkɒndɪ'senʃən]	herablassende Haltung
	greater understanding	besseres Verständnis
	empowerment	Ermächtigung, Stärkung
35	**summer term**	Sommersemester
Looking back		
	to **scan a text**	einen Text nach gewünschten Informationen durchsuchen
	delivery	Präsentation, Vortragsweise
	somewhat precisely	einigermaßen präzise/genau
	with some confidence	mit einiger Sicherheit
	with reasonable precision	mit hinreichender Genauigkeit

Unit 08

4	**word of mouth**	mündliche Überlieferung, Mundpropaganda
	trader	Händler/in
	invention	Erfindung
	printing press	Druckerpresse
	print media	Print-/Druckmedien
	broadcast media *Broadcast media, such as radio and television, are still powerful nowadays.*	Übertragungsmedien; Rundfunk, Sendeanstalten
	media outlets *Media outlets like newpapers and television make information available to the public.*	Medienunternehmen
	to **struggle**	kämpfen, sich abmühen
	We have come full circle.	Hier schließt sich der Kreis.
6	**delivery man/woman**	Lieferant/in
8	to **skid**	(aus)rutschen
	miraculously	auf wundersame Weise
	injury ['ɪndʒəri]	Verletzung
	(the) authorities	Behörden
	to **work sth. out** *Finally, I could work out a solution.*	etw. herausfinden/lösen
	to **explode**	explodieren
	fuel ['fjuːəl]	Treibstoff, Benzin
	thankfully *Thankfully, nobody was hurt.*	zum Glück
	to **scream** [skriːm]	schreien, kreischen
	to **be in tears**	in Tränen aufgelöst sein
	miracle ['mɪrəkəl]	Wunder
	to **burgle a house**	ein Haus ausrauben
	to **be lucky** *The police say you were lucky to survive.*	Glück haben
	to **free sb./sth.**	jmdn./etw. befreien
	fire brigade ['faɪə brɪˌgeɪd]	Feuerwehr
	prison sentence	Haftstrafe
	court hearing [ˌkɔːt 'hɪərɪŋ]	Gerichtsverhandlung
	burglar	Einbrecher/in
	burglary	Einbruch
	ladder	Leiter
	head first *Jumping head first into a lake can be dangerous.*	mit dem Kopf voran
	to **sue** [suː] **sb.** *She sued the radio station for the false story they had reported about her.*	jmdn. verklagen
	carelessness	Achtlosigkeit, Fahrlässigkeit
	to **drown**	ertrinken
	to **commit a crime**	eine Straftat begehen
11	to **call sth. off** *The meeting was called off.*	etw. absagen
16	**chart**	Graphik, Diagramm
	slightly more than half	etwas mehr als die Hälfte

	a third	ein Drittel
	three quarters	drei Viertel
	approximately	in etwa, ungefähr
17	**report**	Bericht
	recommendation	Empfehlung
	research [rɪ'sɜːtʃ]	Recherche, Forschung
	evidence	Beweis, Nachweis
	concise [kən'saɪs]	kurz und prägnant
	to **engage sb.** *Maths doesn't really engage me, but I like chemistry.*	jmdn. fesseln/begeistern
	superior [suː'pɪəriə] *Alice is my superior.*	Vorgesetzte/r
	contraction *'Don't' is a contraction of 'do not'.*	Abkürzung, Kurzform
	factual ['fæktʃuəl]	sachlich
18	**aim** [eɪm]	Ziel, Absicht
20	**bookworm** ['bʊkwɜːm]	Bücherwurm, Leseratte
	page-turner	fesselndes Buch
	audiobook	Hörbuch
	dust jacket	Schutzumschlag
	font	Schriftart
	cover	Umschlag, Cover
	to **come in …** *This T-shirt only comes in small sizes.*	in/als … erhältlich sein
	paperback	Taschenbuch
	hardcover	gebundenes Buch
21	**satisfying**	zufriedenstellend
	believable	glaubwürdig
	cliché ['kliːʃeɪ]	Klischee
23	**accessible**	zugänglich
	convenience [kən'viːniəns]	Annehmlichkeit, Komfort
	publisher	Verlag; Verleger/in
	advent ['ædvent] *Sharing information became much easier with the advent of the internet.*	Beginn, Anbruch
	sequel ['siːkwəl] *Are they making a sequel to this film?*	Fortsetzung (*eines Films/ Buches …*)
	to **be years apart**	Jahre auseinanderliegen
26	**coming-of-age novel**	Entwicklungsroman, Roman über das Erwachsenwerden
	romance	Liebesroman
29	**court of law** *Problems between neighbours should be solved outside a court of law.*	Gericht, Gerichtssaal
	criminal	kriminell; Kriminelle/r
	prisoner	Häftling
	to **rob sb.**	jmdn. ausrauben

Looking back

	to **compile information**	Informationen zusammentragen

Unit 09

	volunteering [ˌvɒlən'tɪərɪŋ]	ehrenamtliche Tätigkeit(en)
	politics ['pɒlətɪks] *Politics is a rough game.*	Politik
1	**turkey**	Truthahn
	debate [dɪ'beɪt]	Debatte, Diskussion
	flag	Flagge
	neighbouring *Austria and Germany are neighbouring countries.*	benachbart; Nachbar-…
	population	Bevölkerung
	long-standing tradition	langjährige Tradition
	mock … *We'll have our mock exams on Friday.*	Pseudo-…, Schein-…, Probe-…
	candidate ['kændɪdət]	Kandidat/in
	election	Wahl
	city council [ˌsɪti 'kaʊnsəl]	Stadtrat
2	**class representative**	Klassensprecher/in
	head student	Schulsprecher/in
	to **make a difference** *You can really make a difference in this world with social work.*	etw. bewegen/ändern
	to **vote (for/against sb./sth.)**	wählen, stimmen (für/gegen jmdn./etw.)
	party	Partei
	mayor [meə]	Bürgermeister/in
	politician [ˌpɒlɪ'tɪʃən]	Politiker/in
3	to **hold an election** *The elections were held in August.*	eine Wahl abhalten
	to **elect sb.** *We elected him as our class representative.*	jmdn. wählen
	to **come to power**	an die Macht gelangen
	to **register to vote**	sich ins Wählerverzeichnis eintragen lassen
	to **be in power**	an der Macht sein
	to **be in office** *How long was Obama in office?*	im Amt sein
	leader ['liːdə]	Anführer/in
	council meeting	Ratssitzung
	majority [mə'dʒɒrəti]	Mehrheit
5	to **make up your mind (about sth.)**	sich entscheiden, sich über etw. schlüssig werden
	to **feel excluded**	sich ausgeschlossen fühlen
	to **cast your vote**	seine Stimme abgeben
	fate	Schicksal
	That gets me going.	Das regt mich auf.
	electoral system	Wahlsystem
	to **stress sth.** *Our teacher stressed the importance of teamwork.*	etw. betonen
	democracy [dɪ'mɒkrəsi]	Demokratie
	in Parliament	im Parlament
	MP: (*abbr. for*) **Member of Parliament**	Parlamentsabgeordnete/r
	head of state	Staatsoberhaupt
	wealth [welθ]	Reichtum
	just *Teachers are supposed to be just.*	gerecht
	communism ['kɒmjənɪzəm]	Kommunismus
	on paper *Your plan sounds good on paper, but I don't know if it'll actually work.*	auf dem Papier, in der Theorie

	citizenship	Staatsbürgerschaft
	to **be on edge** *I was on edge during the whole conversation with the headmaster.*	nervös sein
	to **push sth. through**	etw. durchboxen/-setzen
	poll [pəʊl]	Abstimmung, Umfrage
	polling station	Wahllokal
	policy ['pɒləsi] *Our school has a strict anti-bullying policy.*	Regeln, Strategie, Vorgehen
	mature [mə'tʃʊə]	reif, erwachsen
10	**terrorism**	Terrorismus
	to **argue sth.**	etw. behaupten/ argumentieren
	to **succeed** [sək'si:d] *I would argue that good English is important if you want to succeed in certain jobs.*	erfolgreich sein
	to **propose sth.** *I'd like to propose a certain date for the meeting.*	etw. vorschlagen
15	**caring**	fürsorglich
	decisive [dɪ'saɪsɪv] *(opp.* indecisive*)* *A strong leader knows what he/ she wants and is decisive.*	entschlussfreudig
	open-minded *(opp.* close-minded*)*	aufgeschlossen, offen für Neues
	trustworthy	vertrauenswürdig
16	**deserted** [dɪ'zɜ:tɪd]	verlassen
	deserted island	einsame Insel
	grown-up *What's it really like being a grown-up?*	Erwachsene/r
	to **look after sb.** *Will you look after my dog while I'm on holiday, please?*	sich um jmdn. kümmern
	obedience [ə'bi:diəns]	Gehorsam
	blush [blʌʃ]	Schamesröte
	hunter	Jäger/in
	to **count** *Taking action is what really counts.*	zählen, wichtig sein
21	**charitable organisation**	Wohltätigkeitsorganisation
24	**firefighter**	Feuerwehrmann/-frau
	to **put out a fire**	einen Brand löschen
	to **hand sth. out**	etw. austeilen
28	**voter**	Wähler/in
	leadership	Führung
29	**self-conscious**	verlegen, unsicher
Looking back		
	to **identify sth.**	etw. erkennen
	main conclusion	wesentliche Schlussfolgerung
	clearly signalled argumentative text	klar geschriebener, argumentativer Text

Unit 10

	AI: *(abbr. for)* **artificial intelligence**	KI, künstliche Intelligenz
1	**discovery**	Entdeckung
2	**human being**	menschliches Wesen
	robot ['rəʊbɒt]	Roboter
	helpful	hilfreich, hilfsbereit
3	**ankle**	Fußknöchel
	cheek	Wange, Backe
	chest [tʃest]	Brust
	chin [tʃɪn]	Kinn
	elbow	Ellenbogen
	eyebrow	Augenbraue
	forehead ['fɒrɪd]	Stirn
	heel	Ferse
	hip	Hüfte
	jaw [dʒɔ:]	Kiefer
	knee [ni:]	Knie
	shin [ʃɪn]	Schienbein
	shoulder	Schulter
	stomach ['stʌmək]	Bauch
	thigh [θaɪ]	Oberschenkel
	thumb [θʌm]	Daumen
	waist	Taille
	wrist	Handgelenk
4	**disease** [dɪ'zi:z]	Krankheit
	from ... onward *From now onward you will need to look after yourself better.*	von ... an
	brain cell	Gehirnzelle
	stroke	Schlaganfall
	condition	Zustand
	medical treatment	medizinische Behandlung
	dehydrated [ˌdi:haɪ'dreɪtɪd]	dehydriert, ausgetrocknet
	headache ['hedeɪk]	Kopfweh
	to **rest**	sich ausruhen
	to **be asleep**	schlafen
	to **beat** *The human heart beats between 50 and 100 times per minute.*	schlagen
	heartbeat	Herzschlag
	to **pump**	pumpen
	heart disease	Herzerkrankung
	cause of death	Todesursache
	overweight *Being overweight is really unhealthy for you.*	übergewichtig
	heart attack	Herzinfarkt
	to **recover (from sth.)** *It took me a long time to recover from my accident.*	sich (von etw.) erholen
	to **take a deep breath**	tief einatmen
	whilst *He got interested in football whilst taking P.E. at school.*	während
	the lungs	die Lunge
	oxygen ['ɒksɪdʒən]	Sauerstoff
	to **breathe (in/out)**	(ein-/aus-)atmen
	bloodstream	Blutkreislauf
	carbon dioxide [ˌkɑ:bən daɪ'ɒksaɪd]	Kohlendioxid
	cancer	Krebs
	to **narrow** *Look out, the road narrows after the bridge.*	sich verengen
	liver	Leber
	organ ['ɔ:gən]	Organ
	antibodies	Antikörper
	hormone ['hɔ:məʊn]	Hormon

	vital ['vaɪtəl] *Doctors check a patient's vital organs after an accident.*	wichtig, lebenswichtig
	to **process** ['prəʊses] **sth.** *I'm lactose intolerant, which means I can't process milk.*	etw. verarbeiten/abbauen
	drugs	Drogen; Medikamente
	kidney	Niere
	to **injure sth.** *Chris injured his leg in a skiing accident.*	(sich) etw. verletzen
	appetite ['æpətaɪt]	Appetit
6	**sprained** *She couldn't walk well with her sprained ankle.*	verstaucht
	to **have a sore throat** [ˌsɔː 'θrəʊt]	Halsschmerzen haben
	medication	Medikamente
	scar	Narbe
	ligament ['lɪgəmənt]	Band, Sehne
	swollen	geschwollen
	prescription *You can't get these pills without a prescription.*	Rezept (*für Medikamente*)
	X-ray *My son had to have an X-ray on his arm.*	Röntgen
	runny nose	rinnende Nase, Rotznase
	open wound [ˌəʊpən 'wuːnd]	offene Wunde
	to **have a fever**	Fieber haben
	to **be allergic to sth.**	gegen etw. allergisch sein
	painkiller	Schmerzmittel
	plaster cast	Gipsverband
	bandage ['bændɪdʒ]	Verband
	unconscious [ʌn'kɒnʃəs]	bewusstlos
	to **get stitches**	genäht werden
	GP: *(abbr. for)* **general practitioner**	Allgemeinarzt/-ärztin
7	**(doctor's) surgery**	Ordination
	pharmacy ['fɑːməsi]	Apotheke
8	**medical facility**	medizinische Einrichtung
9	**a torn ligament**	ein Bänderriss
	pollen ['pɒlən] *My sister is allergic to pollen.*	Pollen, Blütenstaub
	infection	Infektion, Entzündung
	to **cover sth.**	etw. bedecken/abdecken
	cigarette smoke	Zigarettenrauch
	to **flower** *I take medication every spring when the trees begin to flower.*	blühen
	to **tackle sb.** *You're allowed to tackle other players in rugby and ice hockey.*	jmdn. angreifen
	dairy ['deəri]	Milchprodukte
11	**collision**	Kollision, Zusammenstoß
	to **be in shock**	einen Schock haben
	appointment *I have a doctor's appointment tomorrow morning.*	Termin
	to **call an ambulance** ['æmbjələns]	die Rettung rufen
	to **upset sb.** *You shouldn't upset young kids by telling them horror stories.*	jmdn. aufregen
	to **be injured**	verletzt sein
12	**heart monitor**	Herzüberwachungsgerät
	CT scan *Suzie had a CT scan last week and it showed she was healthy.*	CT, Computertomographie
	MRI scan	MRT, Magnetresonanz-tomographie
	power steering	Lenkhilfe, Servolenkung
	engine ['endʒɪn]	Motor
	self-driving	selbstfahrend
	vaccination [ˌvæksi'neɪʃən]	Impfung
	X-ray machine	Röntgengerät
	to **get by with/without sth.** *How did people get by without the internet in the past?*	mit/ohne etw. auskommen
14	**vehicle** ['vɪəkəl]	Fahrzeug
	drive-through *I can't believe they have drive-through pharmacies in the States!*	Drive-in (*Lokal/Betrieb zum Durchfahren*)
15	**can't get enough of**	von etw. nicht genug kriegen können
	laundry ['lɔːndri] *I hate having to do the laundry myself.*	Wäsche
	parking lot	Parkplatz
16	to **sit up front**	vorne sitzen
	(race) track	(Renn-)Strecke
18	**traffic accident**	Verkehrsunfall
	partial automation	Teilautomatisierung
	warning	Warnung
	to **alert sb. to sth.** *Traffic signs alert drivers to possible dangers.*	jmdn. auf etw. hinweisen, jmdn. vor etw. warnen
	to **brake** *The car had to brake sharply but was able to stop in time to avoid a collision.*	bremsen
	optimum route	optimale Route/Strecke
	to **spread sth.**	etw. verteilen
	scarce [skeəs]	knapp
	as a unit	als Einheit
	to **accelerate** [ək'seləreɪt]	beschleunigen
	traffic congestion	Verkehrsstau
	to **drink and drive**	betrunken Auto fahren
	at the wheel	am Steuer
	to **navigate sth.**	etw. navigieren
	human failings	menschliche Schwächen
	unforeseen	unvorhergesehen
	to **swerve** [swɜːv]	ausscheren
	lane *Young drivers often don't like driving in the fast lane.*	Fahrspur
	traffic jam	Verkehrsstau
	to **have the capability to do sth.**	in der Lage sein, etw. zu tun
	to **eliminate sth.**	etw. eliminieren/beseitigen
	to **allow space**	Platz lassen
	to **change lanes**	die Spur wechseln
	selfishness	Egoismus, Selbstsucht
	autonomous [ɔː'tɒnəməs]	autonom, selbständig
	to **adopt sth.** *Once we adopt the idea of the self-driving car, there will be far fewer accidents.*	etw. übernehmen/annehmen

	to **be in high gear** *The party was already in high gear when we got there.*	in vollem Gange sein
	at the forefront	an vorderster Front
	emergency [ɪ'mɜːdʒənsi]	Notfall
	to **be concerned** *The president is concerned about the political situation.*	besorgt/beunruhigt sein
	mass unemployment	Massenarbeitslosigkeit
	egotistical	egoistisch
20	**upright**	aufrecht
	to **gain sth.** *I gained a lot of driving experience over the holidays.*	etw. gewinnen/erlangen
21	**solar-powered**	mit Sonnenenergie betrieben
	floating car	schwebendes Auto
22	to **diagnose sth.**	etw. diagnostizieren/ feststellen
	therapy ['θerəpi]	Behandlung, Therapie
	decision-making	Entscheidungsfindung
	first aid	Erste Hilfe
23	to **imprison sb.**	jmdn. einsperren
	mild-mannered	sanftmütig
	to **question sth.**	etw. infrage stellen
	to **be beyond sb.'s imagination**	jmds. Vorstellungskraft sprengen
	wasteland	Ödland
	body heat	Körperwärme
	to **be convinced (of sth.)**	(von etw.) überzeugt sein
25	**technical achievement**	technische Errungenschaft
26	to **chew sth.**	etw. kauen

Unit 11

	key *The key argument is that discrimination is wrong.*	*hier:* entscheidend, wichtig
	rug	Teppich
	national anthem [ˌnæʃənəl 'ænθəm]	Nationalhymne
1	**pitfall**	Falle, Tücke
	sole of your foot	Fußsohle
	to **offend sb.**	jmdn. beleidigen
	to **bump sth. (together)**	etw. zusammenstoßen
	to **slap sb.**	jmdn. ohrfeigen
	to **tip sb.** *Don't forget to tip the waiter!*	jmdm. Trinkgeld geben
	earnings	Verdienst, Einkommen
2	**front door**	Eingangs-/Haustür
	fox	Fuchs
	inhabitant [ɪn'hæbɪtənt]	Einwohner/in
3	to **remember sth. vividly**	sich lebhaft an etw. erinnern können
	sth. feels foreign	etw. fühlt sich fremd/ ungewohnt an
	to **assume** [ə'sjuːm] **sth.** *You should never assume someone speaks English.*	etw. annehmen, von etw. ausgehen
	to **gather sth.** *Let's gather all the information we need.*	etw. sammeln
	bare feet *I love having bare feet.*	nackte Füße, barfuß
	to **make a mess**	Dreck/Unordnung machen
	to **be nuts** *(infml.)* *Are you nuts? You can't smoke here!*	plemplem/verrückt sein
4	**loo** [luː] *(infml.)*	Klo, Toilette
6	to **applaud**	applaudieren, klatschen
	to **sneeze** [sniːz]	nießen
7	**civil rights**	Bürgerrechte
	server *(AE)*	Kellner/in, Servierer/in
	to **comprehend sth.**	etw. begreifen/verstehen
	favourable *Most of our customers have reacted favourably to the changes.*	wohlwollend, positiv
	maid [meɪd]	Hausmädchen
	shame	Scham
	innovation	Innovation, Neuheit
	host [həʊst]	Gastgeber/in
	to **approve of sth.** *My parents don't approve of my boyfriend because they think he's too old for me.*	etw. gutheißen
	modest ['mɒdɪst]	zurückhaltend, bescheiden
	hostess ['həʊstes]	Gastgeberin
10	**nearby** *Is there a café nearby?*	in der Nähe
	opening hours	Öffnungszeiten
12	**film crew** ['fɪlm ˌkruː]	Filmteam
13	**deep** *She's a great friend; you can have really deep conversations with her.*	*hier:* tiefgründig
	to **tolerate sth.**	etw. tolerieren
	to **shoot a film**	einen Film drehen
	location	Schauplatz
	entrepreneur [ˌɒntrəprə'nɜː]	Unternehmer/in
	opportunity	Gelegenheit
	unfortunate [ʌn'fɔːtʃənət] *Going to India during the rainy season was an unfortunate decision.*	ungünstig, unglücklich
	stereotype ['steriətaɪp]	Stereotyp, Klischee
14	**realistic**	realistisch, wirklichkeitsnah
15	**a dream come true**	ein Traum, der in Erfüllung geht
	to **crowd into sth.**	sich in etw. hineindrängen
	fountain ['faʊntɪn]	Springbrunnen, Brunnen
17	**difficulty**	Schwierigkeit
	root	Wurzel
	to **arise** *You need to speak to an expert should problems arise.*	auftreten, sich ergeben
19	**distressing**	Besorgnis erregend, belastend
20	**stimulus** ['stɪmjələs]	Anregung, Impuls
	racism ['reɪsɪzəm]	Rassismus
21	to **distance yourself from sb./sth.**	sich von jmdm./etw. distanzieren

Unit 12

	globalisation	Globalisierung
	How do you like your coffee?	Wie trinkst du deinen Kaffee?
	fair trade	fairer Handel
1	to **exchange sth.**	etw. austauschen

	across the globe	rund um die Welt
2	**economy** [i'kɒnəmi]	Wirtschaft
	to **have a knock-on effect on sth.**	sich unmittelbar auf etw. auswirken
	interconnected	verbunden, vernetzt
	exchange	Austausch
	firm	Firma
	multinational corporation	Weltkonzern, Multi
	to **speed up**	beschleunigen
	to **operate** ['ɒpəreɪt] *We have people operating in 50 countries around the world.*	tätig sein, Geschäfte betreiben
	dependence	Abhängigkeit
	to **close a gap**	eine Lücke schließen
3	**variety of products**	Produktvielfalt
	border	(Landes-)Grenze
	dominance	Dominanz, Vorherrschaft
	Western values	westliche Werte
	individual freedom	Freiheit des/der Einzelnen
	peoples	Völker
4	**exotic**	exotisch
	all year round	das ganze Jahr über
5	**in a nutshell, ...**	kurz gesagt, ...; um es auf den Punkt zu bringen, ...
	to **be in season** *Strawberries are in season from May to August.*	Saison haben, saisonal verfügbar sein
6	**spread**	Ausbreitung, Verbreitung
	empire ['empaɪə]	Reich
	launch [lɔːntʃ]	Start
	to **shrink** (shrank – shrunk)	schrumpfen
	to **enable sth.** *Buying a weekend ticket enables you to use the buses from Friday to Sunday.*	etw. ermöglichen
	civilisation [ˌsɪvəlaɪ'seɪʃən]	Zivilisation
	commercial	kommerziell, gewerblich
	technology [tek'nɒlədʒi]	Technologie
	explorer	Entdecker/in, Forscher/in
	exploration	Erforschung, Erkundung
	the Americas	Nord-, Mittel- und Südamerika
	segregation	Teilung, Trennung
7	to **shape sth.**	etw. prägen/formen
	influential	einflussreich
9	**restriction**	Beschränkung
	to **grant permission**	eine Genehmigung erteilen
	to **emigrate**	auswandern
	passport	Reisepass
	to **immigrate**	einwandern
10	to **admit to sth.** *Francis admitted to the mean posting about his boss.*	etw. zugeben, etw. gestehen
12	**immigration officer**	Beamte/r der Einwanderungsbehörde
	to **be suspicious** [sə'spɪʃəs] **of sb.**	jmdm. gegenüber misstrauisch sein
15	**Fairtrade**	Fairtrade (*Markenname*)
	trademark	Handelsmarke, Markenzeichen
	myth [mɪθ]	Mythos, Irrglaube
	reality [ri'æləti]	Realität, Wirklichkeit
	charity	Almosen
	to **donate money**	Geld spenden
	to **encourage sth.** *Some say that violent computer games encourage bad behaviour in children.*	etw. fördern/begünstigen
	long-term	langfristig
	terms *They finally agreed to do the project on my terms.*	Bedingungen
	living conditions	Lebensumstände
	to **calculate (sth.)**	rechnen, (etw.) berechnen
	to **cover the costs of production**	die Produktionskosten abdecken
	to **come into play** *Once money comes into play, things often get complicated.*	ins Spiel kommen
	to **cut out the middleman**	den Mittelsmann (Zwischenhändler) ausschalten
	conventional	konventionell, herkömmlich
16	**plantation**	Plantage
	picker	Pflücker/in
	to **be in favour (of sth.)** *Everybody who is in favour of this plan, please raise your hand now.*	dafür sein, für etw. sein
18	to **retire** [rɪ'taɪə] *In many countries, people can retire at the age of 65.*	in Pension gehen
	scholarship ['skɒləʃɪp]	Stipendium
	(school/university) degree	(Schul-/Uni-)Abschluss
	coffee grower	Kaffeebauer/-bäurin
	certified ['sɜːtɪfaɪd]	zertifiziert, bescheinigt
	to **fuel sth.**	etw. anheizen/mit Brennstoff versorgen
	oven ['ʌvən]	Ofen
	production plant	Produktionsanlage
	to **be out of business**	nicht mehr im Geschäft sein, Konkurs machen
	if it wasn't for ... *If it hadn't been for my parents' support, I never would have got this far.*	wenn ... nicht wäre/n, ...
	to **drop** *Prices for skiing equipment drop quickly after the skiing season.*	fallen
	straight *I came home and went straight to my room.*	direkt, geradewegs
	certification	Zertifizierung, Bescheinigung
	pesticide ['pestɪsaɪd]	Pestizid, Schädlingsbekämpfungsmittel
	to **lower** ['ləʊə] **sth.**	etw. verringern
	to **pick sth.**	etw. pflücken
	to **do sth. for a living** *My cousin drives a truck for a living.*	etw. beruflich machen, mit etw. seinen Lebensunterhalt verdienen
19	to **cause damage (to sth.)**	Schaden (an etw.) verursachen
	to **keep a certain standard**	sich an gewisse Anforderungen halten
22	**locally grown food**	Lebensmittel aus der Region, heimische Lebensmittel

valid point	stichhaltiges Argument
I firmly believe that …	Ich bin fest davon überzeugt, dass …
23 **arrow** ['ærəʊ]	Pfeil

Writing coach

to **make a suggestion**	einen Vorschlag machen
colloquial language	Umgangssprache
contraction	Abkürzung, Kurzform
recipient	Empfänger/in
to **sign off**	ein Schreiben beenden
email of complaint	Beschwerde per E-Mail
travel agency	Reisebüro
to **state sth.**	etw. anführen/angeben
prompt	Aufgabenstellung
I was led to believe that …	Man hat mich glauben lassen, dass …
needless to say, … *Needless to say, I expect a full refund.*	natürlich …
satisfactory	zufriedenstellend
reply	Antwort
to **captivate sb.**	jmdn. fesseln/faszinieren
provocative [prə'vɒkətɪv]	provokant, herausfordernd
anecdote	Anekdote
appropriate [ə'prəʊpriət] (*opp.* inappropriate)	angemessen, passend
depending on … *Prices vary depending on the region you choose.*	je nach(dem) …
in a chatty tone/style	im Plauderton
to **take action**	etw. unternehmen, eingreifen
exclamation	Ausrufesatz
creepy	gruselig
grave [greɪv]	Grab
to **reopen sth.**	etw. nochmals öffnen
to **remove sth.**	etw. entfernen
to **stack sth.**	etw. stapeln
newly *The song is from her newly released album.*	kürzlich, neu
innocent	unschuldig
gloomy ['glu:mi]	düster, trostlos
speechless	sprachlos
finding	Ergebnis

Semester checks – answer key

Semester check 01, pp. 86–89

READING 1 **Lifestyle centre or shopping centre? (MC)**

Key: **1** D, **2** C, **3** C, **4** A, **5** D

LESEN ►►► B1+ Ich kann unkomplizierte Texte über vertraute Themen mit befriedigendem Verständnis lesen und wichtige Information auffinden.

5: ✓✓ **4–3:** ✓ **2–0:** !!

What next? Discuss your wrong answers with a partner. Try to find out why the option you picked was wrong. Did you misunderstand the text or options in the task? Underline the sentence in the text that points to the correct answer.

LISTENING 2 **A history of the world in 100 objects (4W)**

Key: **1** the British Museum/all over the world, **2** a website/on the internet, **3** years ago/as a small child/to see mummies, **4** has changed/is different now/is that they're fascinating, **5** died of/suffered from/worked as, **6** Humphry Davy/a Brit/a British man

HÖREN ►►► B1+ Ich kann unkomplizierte Sachinformationen über gewöhnliche alltags-, berufs- oder ausbildungsbezogene Themen verstehen und dabei Hauptaussagen und Einzelinformationen erkennen, sofern klar artikuliert und mit vertrautem Akzent gesprochen wird.

6–5: ✓✓ **4–3:** ✓ **2–0:** !!

What next? Check with your teacher if you have an answer not given above – it might still be correct. You could also read the transcript of this podcast online and see if you can find the correct answers if you take time to read the text carefully. Then listen to the podcast again in a few weeks and do the task again. Is it easier now?

LANGUAGE IN USE 3 **Music, dancing, and a whole lot of green! (OGF)**

Key: **1** putting, **2** which/that, **3** was, **4** spent, **5** their/an, **6** streets/roads (NOT shops), **7** on/along, **8** to, **9** dish/soup, **10** in, **11** as/because/and

SPRACHVERWENDUNG IM KONTEXT ►►► Ich kann ein hinreichend breites Spektrum an sprachlichen Mitteln, die eher vorhersehbare Situationen beschreiben, korrekt erkennen und anwenden.

10–9: ✓✓ **8–6:** ✓ **5–0:** !!

What next? Make sure you know why you have to use the words given above. For all mistakes, copy the whole phrase into your notebook and study it (e.g. *1: it involves putting on clothes*).

WRITING 4 **Article**

SCHREIBEN ►►► B1+ Ich kann unkomplizierte, detaillierte Beschreibungen zu einer Reihe verschiedener vertrauter Themen verfassen.

Look at the article you have written and tick the questions.

Did you ...	Yes	No
1 write around **250 words**?		
2 give your article a **catchy title**?		
3 write a short introduction that gets the **reader interested**?		
4 write three **paragraphs** (one for each bullet point) of about **equal length**?		

Did you ...	Yes	No
5 observe the **function words** (*explain, give examples, point out*)?		
6 engage the reader with **questions** or **imperatives**?		
7 finish your article by giving the reader **something to think about**?		
8 use a variety of **linking devices**?		
9 use **powerful adjectives** to make reading your article interesting?		
10 **proofread** your article for mistakes you might have made?		

SPEAKING 5 a Individual long turn

SPRECHEN ▸▸▸ B1 Ich kann relativ flüssig eine unkomplizierte, aber zusammenhängende Beschreibung zu vertrauten Themen geben.

Study the list below before your partner starts with his/her long turn. Tick the questions while your partner is speaking. Give honest feedback by telling your partner what went really well and what needs improving.

Did your partner ...	Yes	No
1 speak for about **3 minutes**? This means for about 1 minute for each bullet point?		
2 speak **fluently without** reading from **notes** he/she has made?		
3 give **clear descriptions** of the pictures?		
4 say what the pictures have **in common** and what is **different** about them?		
5 use the **present continuous** to describe what the people in the pictures are doing?		
6 provide some **explanation** when giving examples in bullet point 2?		
7 talk about what **young people in general** (not only him/her) like buying?		
8 really **recommend** a shop so that you became interested in this shop?		

b Paired activity

SPRECHEN ▸▸▸ B1 Ich kann ohne Vorbereitung an Gesprächen über vertraute Themen teilnehmen und Informationen austauschen.

Ask a friend to give you and your partner honest feedback based on the list below.

Student A ...	Yes	No
considers the **situational context**.		
listens to what B says.		
invites B to give his/her **opinion**.		
reacts to B's arguments **politely** and competently.		
gives **good examples** for all bullet points.		
speaks **fluently**.		
doesn't dominate the discussion.		

Student B ...	Yes	No
considers the **situational context**.		
listens to what A says.		
invites A to give his/her **opinion**.		
reacts to A's arguments **politely** and competently.		
gives **good examples** for all bullet points.		
speaks **fluently**.		
doesn't dominate the discussion.		

Semester check 02, pp. 164–168

READING **1** **Artificial intelligence (MM)**

Key: **1** J, **2** F, **3** E, **4** I, **5** B, **6** G, **7** H

LESEN ▸▸▸ B1+ Ich kann in klar geschriebenen argumentativen Texten die wesentlichen Schlussfolgerungen erkennen.

7–6: ✓✓ **5–4:** ✓ **3–0:** !!

What next? Discuss your wrong answers with a partner. Try to find out why the option you picked was wrong. Did you misunderstand the text or options in the task? Underline the sentence in the text that points to the correct answer.

LISTENING **2** **Gender roles on TV (4W)**

Key: **1** do everything on TV, **2** puts pressure on them, **3** is limited, **4** men, **5** nurses/stressful job/underpayment/long hours/pressure on families, **6** deal with every day/have to deal with

HÖREN ▸▸▸ B1+ Ich kann in Filmen und Radiosendungen zu Themen von persönlichem Interesse einen großen Teil verstehen, wenn relativ langsam und deutlich gesprochen wird.

6: ✓✓ **5–4:** ✓ **3–0:** !!

What next? Now that you have got the answers you maybe couldn't hear before, listen again. Can you identify the correct answers in the recording now? Feel free to stop the recording or listen again as often as you need to.

LANGUAGE IN USE **3** **The most dangerous job in the world? (MC)**

Key: **1** C, **2** C, **3** D, **4** A, **5** D, **6** C, **7** B, **8** A, **9** B, **10** C

SPRACHVERWENDUNG IM KONTEXT ▸▸▸ Ich kann ein hinreichend breites Spektrum an sprachlichen Mitteln, die eher vorhersehbare Situationen beschreiben, korrekt erkennen und anwenden.

10–9: ✓✓ **8–6:** ✓ **5–0:** !!

What next? Make sure you can explain why only the answers given above are correct. For example:

- Gap (1) is between an article and an adjective – only an adverb can go here.
- Gap (2): only C can be used as a linking word at the start of a sentence.
- Consider the preposition after gap (3): only one of the four words works with it.

Do you know how/where you could use the three wrong options correctly? Make sentences with them and look at how the sentences are different from one another.

WRITING **4** **Report**

SCHREIBEN ▸▸▸ B1+ Ich kann Informationen und Gedanken zu konkreten wie abstrakten Themen, auch kulturellen (z. B. Musik, Filme, literarische Texte), mitteilen und einigermaßen präzise ein Problem erklären.

Look at the report you have written and tick the questions.

Did you …	Yes	No
1 read the **prompt** carefully? Who wants the report and what should it contain?		
2 **interpret** the **graph correctly**?		
3 **start** your report **with** *From*, *Subject*, *Date*?		
4 divide your report into **sections** with **headings**?		
5 write an **introduction** and **three paragraphs** (one for each bullet point)?		
6 use **quantifiers** (*half*, *a third*, *more than*, etc.) describing the graph?		

Did you ...	Yes	No
7 use **modals** (*might*, *should*, *could*, etc.) when writing about bullet points 2 and 3?		
8 use **formal language** including passive structures and formal linking words?		
9 write **around 250 words** in total?		
10 **proofread** your report for mistakes you might have made?		

SPEAKING 5 a Individual long turn

SPRECHEN ▸▸▸ B1+ Ich kann Gedanken zu eher abstrakten, auch kulturellen Themen ausdrücken und mich darüber austauschen.

Study the list below before your partner starts with his/her long turn. Tick the questions while your partner is speaking. Give honest feedback by telling your partner what went really well and what needs improving.

Did your partner ...	Yes	No
1 speak for about **4 minutes**? This means a bit more than 1 minute for each bullet point?		
2 speak **fluently without** reading from **notes** he/she has made?		
3 **compare** the **different situations** in the pictures?		
4 use the **present continuous** to describe what the people in the pictures are doing?		
5 use the **PEEL strategy** (evidence, examples, reasons) in bullet point 2?		
6 use **modals** (*could*, *might*, *should*, etc.) when talking about bullet point 2?		
7 use **appropriate vocabulary** (related to the topics of communication, media, etc.)?		
8 give **good reasons** for the advantages in bullet point 3?		
9 **finish** by **giving** his/her **opinion** on the advantages of mobiles for children?		

b Paired activity

SPRECHEN ▸▸▸ B1+ Ich kann ohne Vorbereitung mit einiger Sicherheit an Gesprächen über vertraute Themen teilnehmen.

Ask a friend to give you and your partner honest feedback based on the list below.

Student A ...	Yes	No
considers the **situational context**.		
listens to what B says.		
invites B to give his/her **opinion**.		
reacts to B's arguments **politely** and competently.		
gives **good examples** for all bullet points.		
speaks **fluently**.		
doesn't dominate the discussion.		

Student B ...	Yes	No
considers the **situational context**.		
listens to what A says.		
invites A to give his/her **opinion**.		
reacts to A's arguments **politely** and competently.		
gives **good examples** for all bullet points.		
speaks **fluently**.		
doesn't dominate the discussion.		